CHOMSKY'S UNIVERSAL GRAMMAR

Applied Language Studies
Edited by David Crystal and Keith Johnson

This new series aims to deal with key topics within the main branches of applied language studies – initially in the fields of foreign language teaching and learning, child language acquisition and clinical or remedial language studies. The series will provide students with a research perspective in a particular topic, at the same time containing an original slant which will make each volume a genuine contribution to the development of ideas in the subject.

Series List

Chomsky's Universal Grammar
An Introduction
V. J. Cook

The ELT Curriculum
Design, Innovation and Management
Ronald V. White

CHOMSKY'S UNIVERSAL GRAMMAR

An Introduction

V. J. Cook

Basil Blackwell

Copyright © V. J. Cook 1988

First published 1988
Reprinted 1989

Basil Blackwell Ltd
108 Cowley Road, Oxford, OX4 1JF, UK

Basil Blackwell Inc.
432 Park Avenue South, Suite 1503
New York, NY 10016, USA

British Library Cataloguing in Publication Data
Cook, Vivian
Chomsky's universal grammar: an
introduction.—(Applied language studies).
1. Chomsky, Noam—Contributions in
linguistics 2. Linguistics
I. Title II. Series
410'.92'4 P85.C47
ISBN 0–631–15301–2
ISBN 0–631–15302–0 Pbk

Library of Congress Cataloging in Publication Data
Cook, V. J. (Vivian James), 1940–
Chomsky's universal grammar: an introduction / V. J. Cook.
p. cm.
Bibliography: p.
Includes index.
ISBN 0–631–15301–2.
ISBN 0–631–15302–0 (pbk.)
1. Chomsky, Noam,. 2. Grammar, Comparative and general.
3. Government-binding theory (Linguistics) 4. Language acquisition.
I. Title.
P85.C47C66 1988
415—dc19 87–30265

Typeset in 10 on 12pt Ehrhardt
by Columns of Reading
Printed in Great Britain by Billing & Son Ltd., Worcester

Contents

Acknowledgements   vii

1 **The Nature of Universal Grammar**   1
   Structure-dependency   2
   The Head Parameter   7
   The Projection Principle   9
   I and E Approaches to Language   12
   Types of Universals   17
   The Language Faculty   20
   Principles and Rules   23

2 **Concepts of Government/Binding Theory**   28
   The Framework of Government/Binding Theory   28
   Government   35
   The Pro-drop Parameter   37
   Binding Theory   43
   Core and Periphery   50

3 **First Language Acquisition**   55
   Plato's Problem   55
   The Evidence Available to the Learner   59
   Some Insufficient Ways of Acquiring Language   62
      Imitation   62
      Explanation   63
      Correction and approval   63
      Social interaction   67
      Dependence on other faculties   69
   The Physical Basis for Universal Grammar   72
   Parameter-setting   74
   Markedness and Language Development   79

4 **X-bar Theory and θ-Theory**   86
   Phrase Structure   86
   X-bar Theory   94
   C-selection and the Projection Principle   102
   Grammatical Functions   107
   S-selection and θ-Theory   110
   Extensions to X-bar Syntax   117

5 Movement and Case Theory   121
  NP-movement   121
  Wh-movement   125
  V-movement   129
  Bounding Theory   133
  Case Theory   136
  Chains and LF Movement   143

6 Government   148
  C-command and Government   148
  Binding Theory Revised   157
  Infinitival Clauses and Control Theory   159
  Types of Noun Phrases   162

7 Uses of the Theory: Second Language Learning   170
  Uses of the Theory   170
  The Relationship between First and Second Language
    Learning   174
  L2 Learning and the Poverty of the Stimulus Argument   176
    Imitation   177
    Grammatical explanation   177
    Correction and approval   178
    Social interaction   178
    Dependence on other faculties   179
  The Universality of UG   179
  The Availability of UG   182
    Direct access to UG   182
    Indirect access to UG   182
    No access to UG   183
  Acquisition and Development in L2 Learning   186

  References   190

  Index   196

Acknowledgements

This book would never have happened without the inspiration of the work of the person whose name appears on every page, Noam Chomsky. Nor would it have been conceived if David Reibel had not first introduced me to this field. Essential ingredients to the book itself were the colleagues and friends who patiently went through the successive drafts, namely Gordon Brown, Paul van Buren, David Crystal, Fritz Newmeyer, Andrew Radford, Iggy Roca, and Anjum Saleemi. Keith Brown deserves a special mention for the innumerable times he put me on the right track. People who helped me with the non-English examples include Don Moybin, Suzanne Saddekni, and Shi Baohui. The book would never have been finished but for the stabilizing influence of Abdullah Ibrahim, Sidney Bechet, and Ronald Shannon Jackson.

1 The Nature of Universal Grammar

The aim of this book is to convey why Chomsky's theory of language is stimulating and adventurous and why it has important consequences for all those working with language. The goals of the theory are to describe language as a property of the human mind and to explain its source. To achieve these goals it establishes an apparatus of considerable complexity. Though the specific proposals put forward are not necessarily correct, the theory provides the unified framework within which they may be tested. This book is intended chiefly for those who wish to know enough of the overall framework and details of the theory to evaluate its usefulness for their own purposes, such as applied linguists or psychologists, rather than for specialist students of syntax for whom technical introductions are more appropriate, such as van Riemsdijk and Williams (1986), Horrocks (1987) or Radford (1988).

The central concept is **Universal Grammar (UG)**; 'the system of principles, conditions, and rules that are elements or properties of all human languages . . . the essence of human language' (Chomsky, 1976, p. 29). All human beings share part of their knowledge of language; regardless of which language they speak, UG is their common inheritance. While within the tradition of Chomsky's thinking over the past three decades, the current theory couches UG in terms of the specific proposals advanced in the model usually known as the **Government/Binding (GB) Theory**, first synthesized in *Lectures on Government and Binding* (Chomsky, 1981a) and developed further in *Knowledge of Language* (Chomsky, 1986a) and *Barriers* (Chomsky, 1986b). (Since the first two of these will be referred to frequently, they will be abbreviated to LGB and KOL respectively.) The combination of Universal Grammar with Government/Binding inevitably leads to a complex overall theory involving abstract and difficult sub-theories, but at the same time it creates a new simplicity; knowledge of language comes down to variations in a small number of properties.

UG is a theory of knowledge, not of behaviour; its concern is with the internal structure of the human mind. The nature of this knowledge is inseparable from the problem of how it is acquired; a proposal for language knowledge necessitates an explanation of how it came into being. UG theory holds that the speaker knows a set of principles that apply to all languages, and parameters that vary within clearly defined limits from one language to another. Acquiring language means learning how these principles apply to a particular language and which value is appropriate for each parameter. Each principle of language that is proposed is a substantive claim about the mind of the speaker and the nature of acquisition. UG is not making vague or unsubstantiable suggestions about properties of the mind but precise statements based on specific evidence. The general concepts of the theory are inextricably connected with the specific details; the importance of UG is its attempt to integrate grammar, mind, and acquisition at every moment.

Structure-dependency

To give an immediate idea of UG let us look at a specific principle. One of the first to be proposed was the principle of **structure-dependency**, which asserts that knowledge of language relies on the structural relationships in the sentence rather than on the sequence of items. Let us start with a typical English question such as:

   Will the letter arrive tomorrow?

A common way of describing questions is to see them as inverting the subject and auxiliary; *will* has moved to the beginning of the sentence:

   ⬆ The letter will arrive tomorrow.

What has actually moved? One possibility is that questions are formed by moving the word that occurs in a particular place in the sentence, say the third word.

   ⬆ 1   2   3   4   5
     the letter will arrive tomorrow

But moving only the third word does not work for other questions; for example if the third word were moved in:

   ⬆ 1 2 3 4   5 6 7   8   9
     this is a dagger which I see before me

the result would be:

   *A this is dagger which I see before me?

(From now on an asterisk will be placed before ungrammatical sentences.)
   Questions do not depend on moving the third word, the fourth word, or any word in a particular place in the sequence; the crucial factor is the type of

word involved: it must be an auxiliary such as *will*, or *can*. Indeed the English auxiliaries are partly defined by the fact that they can occur at the beginning of questions. What happens is then:

the letter   will   arrive tomorrow
                auxiliary

The form of English questions does not depend on the linear order of words in the sentence so much as on the syntactic category of the words involved. An English speaker's knowledge of yes/no questions depends on knowing which word belongs to the syntactic category of auxiliary.

The analysis can be extended to questions with relative clauses. Take the sentence:

The man who is tall is John.

A related question can be formed by moving the auxiliary to the beginning. But the problem is which of the two auxiliaries is the one to move.

the man who   is   tall   is   John
                auxiliary   auxiliary

Moving the first yields:

*Is the man who tall is John?

Moving the second gives:

Is the man who is tall John?

A hasty conclusion would be that questions involve moving the second auxiliary. However this does not work if the relative clause comes later in the sentence. Starting from:

John   is   the man who   is   tall
          auxiliary 1   auxiliary 2

and moving the first auxiliary, we get the question;

Is John the man who is tall?

not:

*Is John is the man who tall?

where the second auxiliary moves rather than the first. Simple counting of the first, second, or nth auxiliary again does not suffice to explain what is happening. English questions involve movement of the auxiliary from the *main* sentence rather than from the relative clause, regardless of whether it comes first or second. It is the position of the auxiliary within the syntactic structure of the sentence that is crucial – whether it is in the main sentence or the relative clause. This generalization about English covers many additional questions such as:

Was the woman who fell in love with Bogart in *Casablanca* played by Ingrid Bergman or Lauren Bacall?

To form questions it is necessary to know not only the syntactic categories of the words but also their structural relationships within the sentence, not only which word is an auxiliary but also whether it is in a main sentence or a subordinate clause.

The importance of the example, however, lies in the general principle of structure-dependency; all sentences in English depend upon the speaker's knowledge of structure, not just questions. The formation of passive sentences such as:

The President was assassinated.

has often been taken to be movement of *the President* to the front of the sentence from a later position; it is the complete Noun Phrase *the President* that is moved, not the fourth or nth word, and only an appropriate Noun Phrase can be moved; knowledge of syntactic category and of structural relationships is again required. Questions with question-words such as *who* or *what* also move the question-word from an original position. To move *where* to the beginning of:

Where did you go?

it is necessary to identify the question-word and to know its role in the structure of the sentence. UG theory prefers general statements that cover many instances rather than particular statements that cover only one. These separate pieces of information about yes/no questions, question-word questions, and passives can be summed up in the single overall statement: English is structure-dependent. All movement in English requires a knowledge of syntactic categories and of the structure of the sentence.

But the same applies to the grammar of other languages. French is also structure-dependent: the question:

Où sont les neiges d'antan?
(Where are the snows of yesteryear?)

reflects the movement of the question-word *où* to the beginning. The same is true of questions in Urdu, such as:

Kis ne Hameed ko kitab di?
(Who did Hameed give a book to?)

where the question-word *kis* has moved to the beginning of the sentence. (It should be pointed out that sentences from languages other than English are used in this book as examples and are not necessarily based on complete analyses of the languages involved.) When stating questions in French or in Urdu or in English, it is not necessary to specify that each and every instance is structure-dependent. Instead the generalization can be made that each of these languages has structure-dependent rules.

But is it necessary to repeat this statement for each language? Whenever elements of the sentence are moved, such movement takes account of the syntactic categories of words and the structural relationships of the sentence rather than the linear order of words; 'all known formal operations in the grammar of English, or of any other language, are structure-dependent' (Chomsky, 1972c, p. 30). An important insight will be missed if structure-dependency is treated as a feature of a particular language. Instead it seems the principle of structure-dependency is used in all human languages.

Why should this be the case? As human beings it seems perfectly obvious to us that this is what language is like; how could it be any other way? But there is no logical necessity for a language to be structure-dependent. Computers find no particular problems in dealing with structure-independent movement, for instance, by reversing the order of the sentence to get a question. The sentence:

John is tall.

could become:

*Tall is John?

Yet no language works like this; it is never the linear order alone that is changed but the order of structural elements. Structure-dependency is a discovery about the nature of human language; it is a property of human language in general, a principle of Universal Grammar.

The important aspects of language knowledge are not those that are true of one individual language but those that are true of all languages; to show the internal structure of the mind, the grammar must reflect properties of all minds, rather than just those that happen to know English or French. Chomsky has always seen linguistics as developing by making deeper accounts of human language in general rather than accounts of particular languages; 'Real progress in linguistics consists in the discovery that certain features of given languages can be reduced to universal properties of language, and explained in terms of these deeper aspects of linguistic form' (Chomsky, 1965, p. 35). Diverse phenomena in English can be reduced to a single principle of structure-dependency; similar phenomena in other languages can be linked to the same principle. Many other principles, and hence aspects of mind, can be discovered by the same process.

Why should this principle occur in all languages and why should we find it so obvious? It is unlikely that people ever encounter sentences that contravene structure-dependency outside the pages of linguistics books; how do they instantly know that:

*Is John is the man who tall?

is wrong? Children learning English probably never hear any sentences of this type; how do they learn structure-dependency? A theory of language acquisition has to explain how 'children unerringly use computationally complex structure-dependent rules rather than computationally simple rules that involve only the predicate "leftmost" in a linear sequence of words' (KOL, pp. 7–8). The UG theory claims that such principles are inherently impossible to learn; if they are not learnt, they must be part of the human mind.

STRUCTURE-DEPENDENCY

Nature: a principle common to the syntax of all languages

Definition: operations on sentences such as movement require a knowledge of the structural relationships of the words rather than their linear sequence

Example:
(1)   *Is the man who is tall John?*
(2)   **Is the man who tall is John?*

Gloss: question formation in English involves moving the auxiliary from the main clause to the front; thus making (1) grammatical and (2) ungrammatical

Extension: Chapter 5 deals with movement in detail

Source: Used by Chomsky in many places, e.g. Chomsky (1980a), KOL and Chomsky (1988)

The Head Parameter

Structure-dependency seems common to all languages. Yet languages obviously differ in many ways; if knowledge of language consisted simply of unvarying principles, all human languages would be identical. To see how the theory captures variation between languages let us take the example of the head parameter, which specifies the order of elements in a language. The preliminary assumption is that sentences may be broken up into constituent phrases, structural groupings of words; thus the sentence:

The London train arrived at platform five.

contains a **Verb Phrase (VP)**, *arrived at platform five*, a **Prepositional Phrase (PP)** *at platform five* and two **Noun Phrases (NP)** *the London train* and *platform five*. Each phrase contains one element that is most essential, its **head**; all phrases are 'endocentric'. So the VP *arrived at platform five* has a head Verb *arrived*, the NP *the London train* has a head Noun *train*; the PP *at platform five* has a head Preposition *at*, and so on.

The Government Binding (GB) theory incorporates a particular theory of the structure of phrases, called **X-bar syntax**, which is developed in chapter 4. Its aim is to express generalizations about the phrase structure of all human languages rather than features that are idiosyncratic to one part of language or to a single language. An important way in which languages vary is in the order of the elements within the phrase. The head of a phrase can occur on the left of the other elements in the phrase or on the right. So in the NP:

the man with the bow tie

the head Noun *man* appears on the left of *with the bow tie*. In the VP:

liked him very much

the head Verb *liked* appears on the left of *him very much*. Japanese is very different; in the sentence:

E   wa kabe ni kakatte imasu.
picture wall on is hanging

the Verb *kakatte imasu* occurs on the right of the Verb Phrase and *ni* (*on*) is a postposition that comes on the right of the Preposition Phrase rather than a preposition. There are two possibilities for phrases: **head-left** or **head-right**.

Chomsky (1970) suggested that the position of heads could be specified once for all the phrases in a given language. Rather than a long list of individual rules specifying the position of the head in each phrase type, a single generalization suffices: 'heads are last in the phrase' or 'heads are first in the phrase'. If English has heads first in the phrase, it is unnecessary to specify that Verbs come on the left in Verb Phrases, as in:

liked him

or Adjectives on the left in Adjective Phrases, as in:

nice to see

or Prepositions on the left in Prepositional Phrases, as in:

to the bank

Instead, a single head-first generalization captures the order of elements in English phrases.

Japanese can be treated in the same way; specifying that Japanese is a 'head-last' language means that the Verb is on the right:

Watashi wa nihonjin desu. (I Japanese am)

and that it has postpositions:

Nihon ni. (Japan in)

And the same for other languages. Human beings know that phrases can be either head-first or head-last; an English speaker has learnt that English is head-first; a speaker of Japanese that Japanese is head-last, and so on. The variation between languages can now be expressed in terms of whether heads occur first or last in the phrase. This is the **head parameter**; the variation in order of elements between languages amounts to a single choice between head-first or head-last. Universal Grammar captures the variations between language in terms of a limited choice between two or so possibilities, known as a parameter. The effects of the parameter yield languages as different as English and Japanese. 'Ideally, we hope to find that complexes of properties differentiating otherwise similar languages are reducible to a single parameter, fixed in one or another way' (LGB, p. 6).

The discussion has first shown that the speaker of a language knows a single principle that applies to different parts of the syntax – the phrases of the language have heads to the left. Then it postulated a parameter that all languages have heads either to left or right. Unlike the universal necessity for structure-dependency, the head parameter admits a limited range of alternatives: 'head-first' or 'head-last'. Alongside the unvarying principles that apply to all languages UG incorporates 'parameters' of variation; a language 'sets' or 'fixes' the parameters according to the limited choice available. While both English and Japanese reflect structure-dependency in one way or another, English sets the head parameter in a particular way, Japanese in another. To acquire English, children need sufficient evidence to discover that the heads of phrases come on the left; to acquire Japanese, evidence that they come on the right.

THE HEAD PARAMETER

Nature: a principle of syntax concerning the position of heads within phrases, e.g. Nouns in NPs, Verbs in VPs, etc.

Definition: a language has the heads on the same side in all its phrases

Examples:
English is head-first
in the bank (Preposition head to the left of NP in a Prepositional phrase)
liked the man (verb to the left of NP in a Verb phrase)
Japanese is head-last
Watashi wa nihonjin desu. (I Japanese am)
Nihon ni. (Japan in)

Extension: X-bar syntax in chapter 4

The Projection Principle

As well as the syntactic principles discussed so far, the theory emphasizes the lexicon; speakers know what each word in the language means, and how it is said; they also know how it behaves syntactically. The theory integrates the syntactic description of the sentence with the properties of lexical items via the **Projection Principle** which requires the syntax to accommodate the characteristics of each lexical item. It has always been recognized that there are restrictions on what words can occur in what constructions; some Verbs are followed by Noun Phrases:

Helen likes Scotch whisky.

and some are not:

Peter fainted.

The linguistic description expresses this through the 'lexical entry' that each word has in the dictionary. The lexical entry for each Verb has to show *inter alia* whether or not it is followed by an NP, i.e. is transitive or intransitive.

The context for the Verb is given here in square brackets, with an underlined gap for the location of the item itself as in:

like [__ NP]

A particular verb has an idiosyncratic combination of possibilities – *believe* can have an object Noun Phrase:

I believe you.

or a sentence with *that*:

I believe that you are right.

but not a sentence with *to* and no subject:

*I believe to be right.

None of these can follow *go*; and so on. Each lexical item in the language has idiosyncratic properties of its own recorded in its lexical entry. Such entries reflect the speaker's knowledge of the occurrence restrictions for large numbers of words.

The grammar of English contains what appears to be the rather similar information that some sentences have a Verb Phrase consisting of a Verb and a Noun Phrase:

Jim likes strong beer.

while others have a V without an NP, i.e. are intransitive:

Sarah fainted.

This can be put as the syntactic rule:

A Verb Phrase consists of a Verb and an optional Noun Phrase.

The rewrite rule convention introduced in Chomsky (1957) expressed the same insight in a more formal way as:

VP → V (NP)

→ means 'consists of', V stands for Verb, VP for Verb Phrase, and NP for Noun Phrase; round brackets enclose elements that do not necessarily always occur. This rule seems to repeat the same information encountered in the lexical entries. On the one hand there are lexical entries indicating that Verbs are transitive [__ NP] or intransitive; on the other a rule of syntax VP → V (NP) that indicates that VPs may have optional NPs.

The distinctive claim of the theory is that such duplication is unnecessary. If there are verbs with entries such as:

like [__ NP]

there is no need for a rule that some VPs include NPs because this is taken care of by the lexical entry; it automatically follows from the entry for *like* that it must be followed by NP and that sentences in which it has no following NP are excluded, as in:

*Sam likes.

The information need not to be stated again in the syntax. The lexical entry is said to 'project' onto the syntax; the lexical specifications of the word ensure that the syntax has a particular form. This is summed up in a central principle of GB, the **Projection Principle**:

The properties of lexical entries project onto the syntax of the sentence.

Much of the information that could be expressed as rules is handled as projections from lexical entries. Rules such as:

VP → V (NP)

give redundant information since the element NP is no longer optional but predictable from the behaviour of particular lexical items: *like* can have an NP, *go* cannot. In other words, there is no need to say that sentences may be transitive or intransitive if the information available for every Verb specifies whether it can have a following NP or not. The lexicon is not a separate issue, a list of words and meanings; it plays a dynamic and necessary part in the syntax. The knowledge of how the Verb *like* behaves is inseparable from the knowledge of syntax. Rather than syntax and lexis being distinct entities, GB does not segregate syntactic and lexical phenomena. Consequently many aspects of language that earlier models dealt with as 'syntax' are now handled as idiosyncracies of lexical items; the syntax itself is considerably simplified by the omission of many rules, at the cost of greatly increased lexical information.

The Projection Principle is a further universal of human language; all languages integrate their syntactic rules with their lexical entries in this fashion. Since, again, there is no logical necessity for language to be this way and no obvious means by which a child could acquire it, the Projection Principle also seems a built-in feature of the mind.

THE PROJECTION PRINCIPLE

Definition: the properties of lexical entries project onto the syntax of the sentence

'lexical structure must be represented categorially at every syntactic level' (KOL, p. 84)

Gloss: syntax and the lexicon are integrated by seeing the characteristics of the specification of lexical items as projecting onto the syntax rather than having to be specified in rules

Example: *Sue likes whisky.*

The properties of the lexical entry *like* [__ NP] ensure that the Verb is followed by an NP in the sentence.

Extension: chapter 4

So far a fragment of Universal Grammar theory has been presented to represent the type of material with which it deals. The principle of structure dependency reflected the overall syntactic orientation of the theory and the abstract level at which such principles operate. The central area of language knowledge is syntax, which takes the form of principles that are utilized in all languages; structure-dependency applies equally to French, English or Urdu, in combination with all the other principles of UG. The head parameter showed how a single abstract property of syntax accounts for a wide variation between languages. Languages only differ within circumscribed limits; several surface differences between them may be reduced to a single parameter of variation. Finally the Projection Principle demonstrated the integration of syntax and the lexicon. Language knowledge on the one hand consists of a few powerful principles and parameters; on the other of information about the idiosyncratic properties of numerous words.

I and E Approaches to Language

Let us now put this within the context of different approaches to linguistics. Chomsky's recent work distinguishes **Externalized (E-) language** from **Internalized (I-) language** (KOL, ch.2; Chomsky, 1987). E-language linguistics, chiefly familiar from the American structuralist tradition, aims to collect samples of language and then to describe their properties. E-language is a collection of sentences 'understood independently of the properties of the mind' (KOL, p. 20); E-language research constructs a grammar to describe the regularities found in such a sample; 'a grammar is a collection of descriptive statements concerning the E-language' (p. 20). The linguist's task is to bring order to the set of external facts that make up the language. The resulting grammar is described in terms of properties of such data through 'structures' or 'patterns'. I-language linguistics however is concerned with what a speaker knows about language and where this knowledge comes from; it treats language as an internal property of the human mind rather than something external. The grammar consists of principles and parameters.

Chomsky claims that the recent history of linguistics shows a move from an E-language to an I-language approach, which sees language as 'a system represented in the mind/brain of a particular individual' (Chomsky, 1988, p. 36); I-language research aims to represent this mental state; a grammar describes the speaker's knowledge of the language, not the sentences that have been produced. Success is measured by how well the grammar captures and explains language knowledge in terms of properties of the human mind. Chomsky's theories fall within the I-language tradition; they aim at exploring the mind rather than the environment. 'Linguistics is the study of I-languages, knowledge of I-languages, and the basis for attaining this knowledge' (Chomsky, 1987).

The E-language approach includes not only theories that emphasize the physical manifestations of language but also those that treat language as a social phenomenon, 'as a collection (or system) of actions or behaviors of some sort' (KOL, p. 20). The study of E-language relates a sentence to the language that preceded it, to the situation at the moment of speaking, and to the social relationship between the speaker and the listener. It concentrates on social behaviour between people rather than the inner psychological world. Much work within the fields of sociolinguistics, or discourse analysis, comes within an E-language approach in that it concerns social rather than mental phenomena.

The opposition between these two approaches in linguistics has been long and acrimonious; neither side concedes the other's reality. It has also affected the other disciplines related to linguistics. The study of language acquisition is divided between those who look at interaction and communicative function and those who look for rules and principles; language teachers can be divided into those who advocate E-language methods that stress communication and behaviour and I-language methods that stress language knowledge, though the former are more in fashion at present; computational linguists roughly divide into those who analyse large stretches of text and those who write rules. An E-linguist collects samples of actual speech or actual behaviour; evidence is concrete physical manifestation. An I-linguist invents possible and impossible sentences; evidence is whether speakers know if they are grammatical. The E-linguist despises the I-linguist for not looking at 'real' facts; the I-linguist derides the E-linguist for looking at trivia. The I-language versus E-language distinction is as much a difference of research methods and of admissible evidence as it is of long-term goals.

The distinction between **competence** and **performance**, first drawn in Chomsky (1965), partly corresponds to the I- versus E-language split.

Competence is 'the speaker/hearer's knowledge of his language', performance 'the actual use of language in concrete situations' (Chomsky, 1965, p. 4). Let us start with a current definition of competence: 'By "grammatical competence" I mean the cognitive state that encompasses all those aspects of form and meaning and their relation, including underlying structures that enter into that relation, which are properly assigned to the specific subsystem of the human mind that relates representations of form and meaning' (Chomsky, 1980a, p. 59). The grammar of competence describes I-language in the mind, distinct from the use of language, which depends upon the situation, the intentions of the participants, and other factors. Competence is independent of situation.

Chomsky's notion of competence has sometimes been attacked for failing to handle knowledge of the appropriate use of language; and the concept of communicative competence has been proposed to remedy this lack (Hymes, 1972). The current theory does not deny that a theory of use complements a theory of knowledge; I-language linguistics happens to be more interested in the theory of knowledge. Chomsky accepts that language is used purposefully; in his later writings he has introduced the term **pragmatic competence** – knowledge of how language is related to the situation in which it is used. Pragmatic competence 'places language in the institutional setting of its use, relating intentions and purposes to the linguistic means at hand' (Chomsky, 1980a, p. 225). It may be possible to have linguistic without pragmatic competence. A schoolboy in a Tom Sharpe novel *Vintage Stuff* (Sharpe, 1982) takes everything that is said literally; when asked to turn over a new leaf, he digs up the headmaster's camellias. But knowledge of language use is different from knowledge of language itself, pragmatic competence differs from linguistic competence. The description of grammatical competence explains how the speaker knows that:

Why are you making such a noise?

is a possible sentence of English and that:

*Why you are making such a noise?

is not. It is the province of pragmatic competence to explain whether the speaker who says:

Why are you making such a noise?

is telling someone to stop, or is asking a genuine question, or is just muttering a *sotto voce* comment. The sentence has a structure and a form that is known by the native speaker, independently of the various ways in which the sentence can be used: this is the province of grammatical competence.

Chomsky does however insist that the discussion of language function cannot be limited to the sole purpose of communication:

> Language can be used to transmit information, but it also serves many other purposes: to establish relations among people, to express or clarify thought, for play, for creative mental activity, to gain understanding, and so on. In my opinion, there is no reason to accord privileged status to one or the other of these modes. Forced to choose, I would say something quite classical and rather empty: language serves essentially for the expression of thought.
>
> *(Chomsky, 1979b, p. 88)*

The claim that the sole use of language is communication devalues the importance of other uses; 'Either we must deprive the notion "communication" of all significance, or else we must reject the view that the purpose of language is communication' (Chomsky, 1980a, p. 230).

In all Chomskyan models a characteristic of competence is its creative aspect; the speaker's knowledge of language must be able to cope with sentences that it has never heard or produced before. E-language depends on history – pieces of language that happen to have been said in the past. I-language competence must deal with the speaker's ability to utter or comprehend sentences that have never been said before – to understand:

Ornette Coleman's playing was quite sensational.

even if they are quite unaware who Ornette Coleman is or what is being talked about. It must also reflect the native speakers' ability to judge that:

*Is John is the man who tall?

is an impossible sentence, even if they are aware who is being referred to, and are able to understand what the question is about; 'having mastered a language, one is able to understand an indefinite number of expressions that are new to one's experience, that bear no simple physical resemblance to the expressions that constitute one's linguistic experience' (Chomsky, 1972a, p. 100). Creativity in the Chomskyan sense is the mundane everyday ability to create and understand novel sentences according to the established knowledge in the mind – novelty within the constraints of the grammar. 'Creativity is predicated on a system of rules and forms, in part determined by intrinsic human capacities. Without such constraints, we have arbitrary and random behavior, not creative acts' (Chomsky, 1976, p. 133). It is not creativity in an artistic sense, which might well break the rules or create new rules, even if ultimately there may be some connection between them. The sentence:

There's a book on the table.

is as creative as:

There is grey in your hair.

in this sense, regardless of whether one comes from a poem and one does not.

Let us now come back to performance, the other side of the coin from competence. One sense of performance corresponds to the E-language collection of sentences; in this sense performance means any data collected from speakers of the language – today's newspaper, yesterday's diary, the improvisations of a rap singer, the works of William Shakespeare, everything anybody said in England yesterday. Whether it is W. B. Yeats writing:

There is grey in your hair.

or a radio disc jockey saying:

If you have been, thank you for listening.

it is all performance. An E-language grammar would have to be faithful to a large sample of such language. But an I-language grammar does not rely on the regularities in a collection of data; it reflects the knowledge in the speaker's mind rather than performance.

However a second use of the term performance should be noted, namely that which contrasts language knowledge with the psychological processes through which the speaker understands or produces language. Knowing the Highway Code is not the same as being able to drive along a street; while the Code in a sense informs everything the driver does, driving involves a particular set of processes and skills that are indirectly related to knowledge of the Code. Language performance has a similar relationship to competence. Speakers have to use a variety of psychological and physical processes in actually speaking or understanding that are not part of grammatical competence, even if they have some link to it; memory capacity and lung capacity affect the length of sentence that can be uttered but are nothing to do with knowledge of language itself. Samples of language may include many phenomena caused by these performance processes; speakers produce accidental spoonerisms – *you have hissed my mystery lectures* – and hesitations and fillers such as *er* and *you know*; they get distracted and produce ungrammatical sentences; they lose track and start the sentence all over again. One reason for the I-linguist's doubts about using samples of language as evidence is that they reflect many other psychological processes that obscure the speaker's actual knowledge of the language.

The differences between I and E language approaches are summarized in the following diagram. An I-language theory is not concerned with analyses based on large amounts of observed data, nor with the social exchanges used in conversation, nor with variations of social class or purpose in speaking, whatever their interest in their own right. Instead it holds up a mirror to mind.

E-LANGUAGE	*vs*	I-LANGUAGE

E-LANGUAGE *vs* I-LANGUAGE

E-LANGUAGE   *vs*   I-LANGUAGE

Samples of language (performance)
  – describes features of
  the sample via 'structures',
  etc.

Single invented sentence
  – describes aspects of the mind via
  'principles'.

Social convention   Mental reality

'Behaviour'   'Knowledge'

The external situation   The internal representation

Pragmatic or communicative   Grammatical competence
  competence

Main source: Chomsky, KOL; Chomsky, 1987

Types of Universals

Can a principle that is *not* found in all languages still be called a universal and related to UG? The concept of **movement** plays an important role and is employed to describe a number of constructions ranging from passives to questions, as we have already seen. But some languages do not appear to move elements of the syntactic structure. In Japanese for example the statement:

Niwa wa soko desu.
(garden there is) The garden is there.

differs from the question:

Niwa wa doko desu ka?
(Garden where is?) Where is the garden?

by having the element *ka* at the end and by having the question-word *doko* in the place of *soko*. The question-word *doko* is not moved to the start, as must happen in English (except for 'echo' questions such as *You said what?*). Japanese does not use syntactic movement for questions, though it may need another type of movement called LF movement, as we shall see in chapter 5. Other languages also share this property; questions in Bahasa Malaysia for example can be formed by adding the question element *kah* to the word that is being asked about (King, 1980):

Dia nak pergi ke Kuala Lumpurkah?
(He is going to Kuala Lumpur?) Is he going to Kuala Lumpur?

without moving it to the front. Some languages do not then require movement. The presence or absence of syntactic movement is a parameter of variation between languages; English requires movement, Malay and Japanese do not. The setting of this parameter has a chain of consequences in the grammar. A language with movement requires a complex theory to relate the moved and unmoved forms; it assumes an original level at which the elements are unmoved. Languages like Japanese can dispense with this. In particular, though structure-dependency has widespread effects on the language, it has been presented here primarily as a restriction on syntactic movement; questions in English are structure-dependent in that they involve structural constituents, not the linear order of words. The question:

Which video shall we watch?

is based on movement of the constituent *which video*, not on moving the second or fourth or nth word. Since Japanese does not move syntactic elements, it does not need structure-dependency for movement (apart from LF movement to be described later). In what sense can a universal that does not occur in a particular language be a universal? Japanese does not, however, *break* any of the requirements of syntactic movement; it does not need structure-dependency for movement because it does not use movement. Its absence does not prove it is not universal. The disproof would be a language that had syntactic movement that was *not* structure-dependent. Provided that the universal is found in some human language, it does not have to be present in all languages. UG does not insist all languages are the same; the variation introduced through parameters allows universals to be absent in particular languages. It does not however allow them to be broken.

This can be contrasted with a longstanding approach to universals in which the linguist attempts to discover a typology of the languages of the world by seeing what they have in common; this leads to what are variously called 'implicational', 'statistical', or 'Greenbergian' universals. An example is the **Accessibility Hierarchy** (Keenan and Comrie, 1977). All languages have relative clauses in which the subject of the relative clause is related to the Noun as in the English:

Alexander Fleming was the man who discovered penicillin.

A few languages do not permit relative clauses in which the object in the relative clause relates to the Noun. For example the English:

This is the house that Jack built.

would not be permitted in Malagasy. Still more languages do not allow the indirect object from the relative clause to relate to the Noun. The English sentence:

John was the man they gave the prize to.

would be impossible in Welsh, for instance. Further languages cannot have relative clauses that relate to the Noun via a preposition, as in:

They stopped the car from which the number plate was missing.

or via a possessive; the English sentence:

He's the man whose picture was in the papers.

would not be possible in Basque.

The Accessibility Hierarchy is represented in terms of a series of positions for relativization:

Subject > Object > Indirect Object > Object of Preposition > Genitive > Object of Comparison

All languages start at the left and have subject relative clauses; some go one point along and have object clauses as well; others go further along and have indirect objects; some go all the way along and have every type, including objects of comparison. It is claimed that no language can avoid this sequence; a language may not have, say, subject relative clauses and object of Preposition relative clauses but miss out the intervening object and indirect object clauses. The Accessibility Hierarchy was established by observations based on many languages; it is an implicational universal. There is no compelling reason within UG why this should be the case, no particular principle or parameter involved; it is simply the way languages turn out to be. Implicational universals such as the Accessibility Hierarchy are data-driven; they arise out of observations; a single language that was an exception could be their downfall, say one that had object of Preposition relative clauses but no object relative clauses. Universals within UG are theory-driven; they may not be breached but they need not be present. There may indeed be a UG explanation for a particular data-driven universal such as the Accessibility Hierarchy, even if it has not yet been proposed; this would still not vitiate the distinction between the theory-driven UG type of universal and the data-driven implicational universal.

Nor is it necessary to show that a universal occurs in dozens of languages. UG research often starts from a property of a single language, such as structure-dependency in English. If the principle can be ascribed to the language faculty itself rather than to experience of learning a particular language, it can be claimed to be universal on evidence from one language alone; 'I have not hesitated to propose a general principle of linguistic structure on the basis of observations of a single language' (Chomsky, 1980b, p. 48). Newton's theory of gravity may have been triggered by an apple but it did not require examination of all the other apples in the world to prove it. Aspects of the theory of UG are disprovable; a principle may be attributed to UG that further research will show is peculiar to Chinese or to English; tomorrow someone may discover a language that breaches structure-dependency. The purpose of any scientific theory is that it can be shown to be wrong; 'in science you can accumulate evidence that makes certain hypotheses seem reasonable, and that is all you can do – otherwise you are doing mathematics' (Chomsky, 1980b, p. 80). Structure-dependency is a current hypothesis, like gravity or quarks; any piece of relevant evidence from one language or many languages may disconfirm it.

The Language Faculty

Already lurking in the argument has been the assumption that language knowledge is independent of other aspects of the mind. Chomsky has often debated the necessity for this separation, which he regards as 'an empirical question, though one of a rather vague and unclear sort' (Chomsky, 1981b, p. 33). Support for the independence of language from the rest of the mind comes from the unique nature of language knowledge. The principle of structure-dependency does not necessarily apply to all aspects of human thinking; it is not at all clear that such UG principles could operate in areas of the mind other than language. Speakers can entertain mathematical or logical possibilities that are not structure-dependent; they can even invent sentences that are not structure-dependent by means of their logical faculties, as the asterisked sentences of linguists bear witness. Nor do the principles of UG seem to be a prerequisite for using language as communication; it might be as easy to communicate by means of questions that reverse the linear order of items as by questions that are based on structure-dependent movement; a language without restrictions on the types and positions of heads in phrases might be easier to use. Structure-dependency and the head parameter are facts unique to language; the language faculty has particular properties that do not belong to other faculties. Further arguments for independence come from language acquisition; principles such as structure-dependency do not appear to be learnable by the same means that, say, children learn to walk or to do arithmetic; language acquisition uses special forms of learning rather than those common to other areas.

Chomsky does not, however, claim that the proposal to integrate language with other faculties is inconceivable, but that the proposals to date have been inadequate; 'since only the vaguest of suggestions have been offered, it is impossible, at present, to evaluate these proposals' (Chomsky, 1972c, p. 26). In the absence of more definite evidence, the uniqueness of language principles such as structure-dependency points to an autonomous area of the mind devoted to language knowledge, a 'language faculty', separate from other mental faculties such as mathematics, vision, logic, and so on. Language knowledge is separate from other forms of representation in the mind; it is not the same as knowing mathematical concepts, for example.

Thus the theory divides the mind into separate compartments, separate modules, each responsible for some aspect of mental life; UG is a theory only of the language module, which has its own set of principles distinct from other modules and does not inter-relate with them. This contrasts with cognitive theories that assume the mind is a single unitary system, for example John Anderson's ACT* model which sees the mind as a single elaborate network (Anderson, 1983), and which therefore traces structure-dependency back to a general cognitive property. The separation from other faculties is also reflected in its attitude to language acquisition; it does not see language acquisition as dependent on either 'general' learning or specific conceptual development but *sui generis*. Thus it conflicts with those theories that see language development as dependent upon general cognitive growth; Piaget for instance argues for a continuity in which advances in language development arise from earlier acquired cognitive processes (Piaget, 1980).

In some ways its insistence on modularity resembles a nineteenth-century tradition of 'faculty' psychology, which also divided the mind into autonomous areas (Fodor, 1983). The resemblance is increased by a further step in the argument. We speak of the body in terms of organs – the heart, the lungs, the liver, etc. Why not talk about the mind in terms of mental organs – the logic organ, the mathematics organ, the commonsense organ, the language organ? 'We may usefully think of the language faculty, the number faculty, and others as "mental organs", analogous to the heart or the visual system or the system of motor coordination and planning' (Chomsky, 1980a, p. 39). The mistake that faculty psychology made may have been its premature location of these organs in definite physical sites, or 'bumps', rather than its postulation of their existence. On the one hand 'The theory of language is simply that part of human psychology that is concerned with one particular "mental organ", human language' (Chomsky, 1976, p. 36); on the other 'The study of language falls naturally within human biology' (Chomsky, 1976, p. 123). For this reason the theory is sometimes known as the biological theory of language (Lightfoot, 1982); the language organ is physically present among other mental organs and should be described in biological, as well as psychological, terms, even if its precise physical location and form are as yet unknown. 'The statements of a grammar are statements of the theory of mind about the I-language, hence statements about the structures of the brain formulated at a certain level of abstraction from mechanisms' (KOL, p. 23). The principles of UG should be relatable to physical aspects of the brain; the brain sciences need to search for physical counterparts for the mental abstractions of UG – 'the abstract study of states of the language faculty should formulate properties to be explained by the theory of the brain' (KOL, p. 39); if there are competing accounts of the nature of UG, a decision between them may be made on the basis of which fits best with the structure of brain mechanisms.

The language faculty is concerned with an attribute that all people possess.

All human beings have hearts, all human beings have noses; the heart may be damaged in an accident, the nose may be affected by disease; similarly a brain injury may prevent someone from speaking, or a psychological condition may cause someone to lose some aspect of language knowledge. But in all these cases a normal human being has these properties by definition. Ultimately the linguist is not interested in a knowledge of French or of Arabic or of English but in the language faculty of the human species. It is irrelevant that some noses are big, some small, some Roman, some hooked, some freckled, some pink, some spotty; the essential fact is that normal human beings have noses. All the minds of human beings include the principles that movement is structure-dependent and that heads are on a certain side of phrases; they are part of the common UG. It is not relevant to UG theory that English has a particular set of properties, French another, German another; what matters is what they have in common.

The words 'human' or 'human being' have frequently been used in the discussion so far. The language faculty is indeed held to be specific to the human species; no other creature apart from human beings possesses a language organ. The evidence for this consists partly of the obvious truth that no species of animal has spontaneously come to use anything like human language; apes and dolphins, whatever they do in captivity, appear not to use anything like language in the wild. Some controversial studies in recent years have claimed that apes in particular are capable of being taught languages. Without anticipating later chapters, it might be questioned whether the languages used in these experiments are fully human-like in utilizing principles such as structure-dependency; they may be communication systems that use none of the distinctive features of human language. It may on the other hand be possible that they are learnt via other faculties than language at the animal's disposal; in a human being some aspects of language may be learnable by some other means than the language faculty; I know that Japanese has Verbs on the right as academic knowledge without having any knowledge of Japanese in the language faculty; similarly patterns of learning used by the animal for other purposes may be adapted to learning certain aspects of language. The danger in this argument is that it could evade the issue; how is it possible to tell 'proper' language knowledge gained via the language faculty from 'improper' language knowledge gained in some other way? Presumably only by returning to the first argument: if it embodies principles of UG and has been acquired from 'natural' evidence, then it is proper; none of the systems learnt by animals seem proper in this sense either because they fail to reflect abstract features of language or because they are artificially 'taught'.

The species-specificness of UG nevertheless raises difficult questions about how it could have arisen during evolution; Piaget, for instance, claims 'this mutation particular to the human species would be biologically inexplicable' (Piaget, 1980, p. 31). While the possession of language itself clearly confers an immense advantage on its users over other species, why should structure-dependency or the head parameter confer any biological advantage on their possessor? Indeed one puzzle is why human languages are actually different: it would seem advantageous if the whole species spoke the same language. Presumably our lack of distance from human languages makes them seem so different; the differences between Japanese and English may be no more than those between an Alsatian dog and a Labrador.

Principles and Rules

So far it has been suggested that the theory relies heavily on the notion of the individual's knowledge of principles as they apply to the language, partly through variable parameters, interconnected with a knowledge of how the lexical items of the language are used in the syntax. Knowledge of language does not consist of rules as such but of underlying principles from which individual rules are derived; the concept of the rule, once the dominant way of thinking about linguistic knowledge, has now been minimized. 'What we know is not a rule system in the conventional sense. In fact, it might be that the notion of rule in this sense ... has no status in linguistic theory' (KOL, p. 151).

Let us apply this reasoning to the Verb Phrase rule that has already been introduced, namely;

VP → V (NP)

This states that a Verb Phrase always has a Verb and optionally has a Noun Phrase. Firstly, the part of the rule is redundant that reflects how the head parameter is set in English. The speaker knows the general fact about English, that the head is on a particular side of the phrase; thus there is no need for the rule to specify that V is on the left of (NP) because this follows from the general principle. Secondly, the lexical items of the language are specified in terms of their possibilities of syntactic occurrence, according to the Projection Principle. So the optional element NP need not be mentioned in the rule as the lexical entry for each verb shows whether it can be followed by an NP – the entry for *sleep* specifies that it cannot be followed by NP, and so on; this aspect of the rule is also redundant. Finally, as suggested earlier, all phrases of a particular type always have a head of that type; it is not necessary to state that VPs have head Verbs because this is a general fact about language. The information in the VP rule is reduced either to general principles or to the properties of lexical entries; the rule itself is no longer needed. Rules are idiosyncratic phenomena that account for specific aspects of one language, such as the Verb Phrase in English. Principles account for properties of all rules and all languages; UG is concerned with establishing a single principle that applies to all rules in English, such as the head parameter, rather than with devising large numbers of rules repeating the same piece of information. This is the major conceptual shift of the theory: rules are to be explained as the interaction of principles and lexical properties rather than existing in their own right. 'One can formulate algorithms that project rule systems from a choice of values for the parameters of UG, but it is not obvious that this is a significant move or that it matters how it is done' (KOL, p. 151). Rules can still be used as labels for the combination of principles involved in a particular point; the VP rule is a convenient summary of a particular interaction between the head parameter, the principle of head type, and the Projection Principle; but it is nothing more.

So rules are artefacts of the interaction between the principles and the lexicon. The information stated in rules should be reinterpreted as general principles that affect all rules rather than as a property of individual rules. 'There has been a gradual shift of focus from the study of rule systems, which have increasingly been regarded as impoverished, ... to the study of systems of principles, which appear to occupy a much more central position in determining the character and variety of possible human languages' (Chomsky, 1982a, pp. 7–8). The theory is not concerned with specific syntactic points such as 'passive', or 'relative clause', or 'question', which are simply shorthand labels for particular interactions of principles and parameters. The passive is not looked at as an independent issue but as a complex of many principles, each of which will also have effects elsewhere in the syntax.

The reliance on principles rather than rules has consequences also for the interpretation of the term **generative grammar** that has been associated with the Chomskyan approach since it first appeared. 'Generative' means that the description is rigorous and explicit; 'when we speak of the linguist's grammar as a "generative grammar" we mean only that it is sufficiently explicit to determine how sentences of the language are in fact characterized by the grammar' (Chomsky, 1980a, p. 220). The chief contrast between traditional grammar statements and the rules of generative grammar lay not in their content so much as their expression; generative rules were precise and testable without making implicit demands on the reader's knowledge of the language. The justification for rewrite rule systems was that they formalized grammar into a rigorous enclosed set of definitions; a rule such as:

$$S \rightarrow NP\ VP$$

essentially defined a sentence (S) as consisting of a NP and a VP. The reader then hunted for the definition of NP:

$$NP \rightarrow (det)\ N$$

namely that a Noun Phrase consists of a determiner (*det*) and a Noun (N). And so on, until this process of hunting for definitions concluded in the dictionary where the meaning of the eventual lexical items themselves were defined. Principles do not lend themselves to the same formal treatment. The theory of **Generalized Phrase Structure Grammar (GPSG)** claims firmly to be part of generative grammar on the grounds that it uses formal explicit forms of statement, but challenges the right of the current Chomskyan theory to be called 'generative'; generative grammar 'includes little of the research done under the rubric of the "Government Binding" framework, since there are few signs of any commitment to the explicit specification of grammars or theoretical principles in this genre of linguistics' (Gazdar et al, 1985, p. 6); it is noteworthy for instance that one introduction to 'generative grammar' (Horrocks, 1987) devotes about half its pages to Chomskyan theories, including GB, while another survey chapter on 'generative grammar' (Gazdar, 1987) dismisses Chomsky in the first two pages. Thus, though the theory still insists that grammar has to be stated explicitly, this is no longer embodied in the formulation of actual rules; the rigour comes in the principles and in the links to evidence.

Although Chomsky later claimed 'true formalization is rarely a useful device in linguistics' (Chomsky, 1987), the theory nevertheless insists on its scientific status as a generative theory to be tested by concrete evidence about language. It sees the weakness of much linguistic research as its dependence on a single source of data – observations of actual speech – when many other sources can be found. A scientific theory cannot exclude certain things in advance; the case should not be prejudged by admitting only certain kinds of evidence. 'In principle, evidence ... could come from many different sources apart from judgments concerning the form and meaning of expressions: perceptual experiments, the study of acquisition and deficit or of partially invented languages such as Creoles, or of literary usage or language change, neurology, biochemistry, and so on' (KOL, pp. 36–7). Some of these disciplines may not as yet be in a position to give hard evidence; neurology may not be able to show how language is stored physically in the brain: in principle it has relevant evidence to contribute and may indeed do so one day. Fodor (1981) contrasts what he calls the 'Wrong View' that linguistics should confine itself to a certain set of facts with the 'Right View' that 'any facts about the use of language, and about how it is learnt ... could in principle be relevant to the choice between competing theories.' When UG theory is attacked for relying on intuitions and isolated sentences rather than concrete examples of language use or psycholinguistic experiments, its answer is to go on the offensive by saying that in principle a scientific theory should not predetermine what facts it deals with; E-language approaches are deficient in the range of evidence they account for compared to I-language theories.

The question of evidence is sometimes expressed in terms of 'psychological reality'. Language knowledge is part of the speaker's mind; hence the discipline that studies it is part of psychology. Chomsky has indeed referred to 'that branch of human psychology known as linguistics' (Chomsky, 1972a, p. 88). Again it is necessary to forestall too literal interpretations of such remarks. A rewrite rule such as:

$S \rightarrow NP\ VP$

did not have any necessary relationship to the performance processes by which people produce and comprehend sentences. To borrow a distinction from computing, the description of knowledge is 'declarative' in that it consists of static relationships, not 'procedural' in that it does not consist of procedures for actually producing or comprehending speech. The description of language in rules such as these may perhaps bear some resemblance to speech processes. With knowledge expressed as principles and parameters, the resemblance seems even more far-fetched; it is doubtful whether every time speakers want to produce a VP they consider in some way the interaction of the head parameter, the head requirement, and the lexical entries of verbs. Conventional psychological experiments with syntax tell us about how people perform language tasks but nothing directly about knowledge. They can provide useful indirect confirmation of something the linguist already suspects and so give extra plausibility perhaps. But they have no priority of status; the theory will not be accepted or rejected as a model of knowledge because of such evidence alone. Chomsky insists that the relevant question is not 'Is this psychologically real?' but 'Is this true?' He sees no point in dividing evidence up into arbitrary categories; 'some is labelled "evidence for psychological reality", and some merely counts as evidence for a good theory. Surely this position makes absolutely no sense ...?' (Chomsky, 1980a, p. 108). The linguist searches for evidence of structure-dependency and finds that questions such as:

Is John the man who is tall?

are possible and questions such as:

*Is John is the man who tall?

are impossible. The linguist may then look for other types of evidence – how speakers form questions in an experiment, the sequence in which children acquire types of question, the kinds of mistake people make in forming questions. All such evidence is grist to the mill in establishing whether the theory is correct; 'it is always necessary to evaluate the import of experimental data on theoretical constructions, and in particular, to determine how such data bear on hypotheses that in nontrivial cases involve various idealizations and abstractions' (Chomsky, 1980b, p. 51). Psychological experiments provide one kind of data, which is no more important than any other. A speaker's claim that:

Is John the man who is tall?

is a sentence of English and:

*Is John is the man who tall?

is not provides a concrete piece of evidence about language knowledge. What matters is not whether the sentence has ever been said but whether a sentence of that form could be said and how it would be treated if it were. It may well be that such evidence is incomplete and biased; in due course it will have to be supplemented with other evidence. But we have to start somewhere. The analysis of this easily available evidence is rich enough to occupy generations of linguists. It is simplest to start from the bird in the hand, our own introspections into the knowledge of language we possess; when that has been dealt with, other sources can be tapped.

To sum up, the distinctive feature of Chomsky's I-language approach is that its claims are not unverifiable assertions but are checkable statements. The theory can easily be misconceived as making abstract statements unconnected to evidence, which can be countered by sheer assertion and argument. Much criticism of Chomskyan concepts attempts to refute them by logic and argument rather than by attacking their basis in precise data and evidence. A case in point is Chomsky's well-known argument that children are born equipped with certain aspects of language. This is based on the fact that children know things about language that they could not have learnt from the language they have heard, as we see in chapter 3; it can be refuted by showing that the alleged fact is incorrect: either children could learn everything about language from what they hear or adults do not have the knowledge ascribed to them. 'An innatist hypothesis is a refutable hypothesis' (Chomsky, 1980a, p. 80). It cannot be dismissed by pure counter-argument. The discussion in this book interweaves general aspects of the theory with specific examples of its actual content because Chomsky's general ideas are based on specific claims about language and cannot be adequately understood without looking at these claims. A principle of language is not a proposal for a vague abstraction but a specific hypothesis about the facts of human language, eventually coming down to precise claims about the grammaticality or ungrammaticality of specific sentences, as with structure dependency. UG is a scientific theory based on specific evidence about language.

2 Concepts of Government/ Binding Theory

The Framework of Government/Binding Theory

The different periods in Chomskyan thinking have become known by the names of particular books or concepts. The original model, *Syntactic Structures*, was called after Chomsky (1957), which established the notion of generative grammar itself. This was superseded by the model first known as *Aspects* after Chomsky (1965), later called the *Standard* Model, which was distinctive for its separation of deep from surface structure. During the 1970s this led to the *Extended Standard* Model, refining the types of rules that were employed, which developed into the *Government/Binding* Model, named after *Lectures on Government and Binding* (Chomsky, 1981a, i.e. LGB). Some parts of this syntactic model have since been modified in *Knowledge of Language* (Chomsky, 1986a, i.e. KOL) and *Barriers* (Chomsky, 1986b). The present book is essentially within the Government/Binding Model presented in Chomsky (1981a), with some use of *Barriers* syntax. Government/Binding Theory is however simply a convenient label for this model, used here because of its widespread currency. Chomsky himself finds the label misleading because it gives undue prominence to the two elements of Government and Binding whose status 'was not fundamentally different from others that entered into the discussion, or others that did not' (Chomsky, 1987). This chapter gives an overview and an informal presentation of some key areas; chapters 4–6 give a fuller, more technical account. The approach adopted in this book is to describe the current model without reference to its historical origins; while the account is usually based on Chomsky's own writings, it should not be forgotten that these build on and incorporate the work of many other linguists.

The classic Chomskyan models express the insight that language is a relationship between sounds and meanings. Sounds are the physical forms of speech, meaningless in themselves: *Good morning* means nothing to a speaker of Japanese, *Ohayoh gozaimasu* nothing to a speaker of English. Meanings are the abstract mental representations, independent of physical form: the meaning of *Good morning* and *Ohayoh gozaimasu* is the same and is separate from the words that are said in the two languages. If language could be dealt with as pure sound or pure meaning, its description would be comparatively simple. The difficulty of the task is due to the complex links between them.

To describe a sentence such as:

Gill teaches physics.

the grammar must show how the sentence is pronounced – the sequence of sounds, the stress patterns, the intonation, and so on; what it actually means – the individual words, the syntactic structures, and so on; and how these are related via various syntactic devices. It therefore needs a way of describing actual sounds, a phonetic representation; it needs a way of representing meaning, a semantic representation; and it needs a way of describing the syntactic structure that connects them, a syntactic level of representation. Syntactic structure plays a central mediating role between physical form and abstract meaning. Figure 2.1 depicts the bridge from sound to meaning.

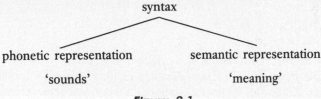

Figure 2.1

GB embodies a slightly different relationship between **'phonetic form'** (**PF**), realized as sound sequences, and **'logical form'** (**LF**), representations of syntactic meaning, mediated through 'syntax', as shown in figure 2.2.

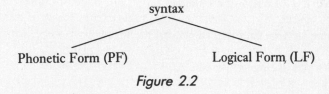

Figure 2.2

Phonetic Form and Logical Form have their own natures, for which distinct PF and LF components are needed within the model. They form the contact between the grammar and other areas, at the one end physical realizations of sound, at the other further mental systems: 'PF and LF constitute the "interface" between language and other cognitive systems, yielding direct representations of sound on the one hand and meanings on the other as language and other systems interact . . .' (KOL, p. 68). Most research in GB has concentrated on the central syntactic component rather than on PF or LF. Given that syntax is a bridge, independent theories of PF or LF are beside the point: however elegant the theory of PF or LF in itself, it must be capable of taking its place in the bridge between sounds and meanings. Similarly with language acquisition: the central problem is how the child acquires the syntactic interface rather than phonology or meaning. Phonetic Form and Logical Form are treated in this book as incidentals to the main theme of syntax. The bridge between sounds and meanings is not fully made in figure 2.2, unlike figure 2.1. LF still represents essentially 'syntactic' meaning. 'By the phrase "logical form" I mean that partial representation of meaning that is determined by grammatical structure' (Chomsky, 1979b, p. 165); it is not a full semantic representation in itself but represents the structurally determined aspects of meaning that form one input to a semantic representation.

The syntactic level is further elaborated in GB through the concept of movement; the last chapter talked of the original form of the sentence before movement takes place and the derived form after it happens:

The hospital is where?

compared with:

Where is the hospital?

Hence GB requires two levels of syntactic representation: **d-structure** at which all the elements in the sentence are in their original location, and **s-structure** at which they have been moved. Thus the d-structure:

You are seeing what at the cinema?

is connected to the s-structure:

What are you seeing at the cinema?

by movement of *what* and *are*, shown by the arrows:

What are you seeing at the cinema?

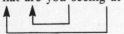

While the terms d- and s-structure originated in 'deep' and 'surface' structure respectively, they are now specialized in their scope. The essential bridging level between sounds and meaning is s-structure, leading on the one hand to Phonetic Form, on the other to Logical Form. S-structure is related by movement to the underlying d-structure that expresses the key structural relationships in the sentence. But s-structure still needs to indicate the original locations of the elements that are moved, as we shall see later; otherwise the semantic and phonological interpretations would go awry. This is achieved by **'traces'**, symbolized as *t*, which mark the original places in the sentence from which elements have been moved. The fuller s-structure of the sentence, keeping to the movement of *what* for simplicity, is:

What are you seeing *t* at the cinema?

including *t* to mark the position from which *what* has moved. S-structure is not just the 'surface' structure of the sentence but is enriched by traces of movement showing the original locations for elements that have moved. GB requires a level of syntactic representation where the effects of movement can still be seen as this is necessary for determining both the phonetic form of the sentence in the PF component and its logical form in the LF component.

This can now be assembled into what is known as the T-model, shown in figure 2.3:

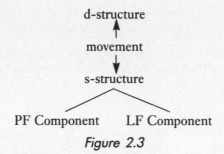

Figure 2.3

D-structure is related to s-structure by movement: s-structure is interpreted by both PF and LF components in their respective ways. In GB the grammar is a continuous interaction between components and sub-theories embodying different principles and parameters. They will be briefly presented here to give an overview; their nature is spelled out in greater depth in later chapters.

D-structure requires an account of the phrase structure, achieved by the sub-theory of X-bar syntax; this is named after its reliance on lexical categories such as Noun (N) with different numbers of **'bars'**, N′, N′′, and so on, explained in chapter 4. One of the principles of X-bar syntax has already been introduced, namely that the location of heads within phrases can be specified once in the grammar of each language by setting the value for the head parameter. X-bar syntax also integrates the lexicon with the syntax; on the one hand it is concerned with the characteristics of the lexical categories, Nouns, Verbs, Adjectives, and Prepositions; on the other the syntactic structure of the sentence reflects the properties of the lexical items of which it is composed; a Verb *like* must be followed by an NP for instance. The Projection Principle that projects the characteristics of lexical entries onto the syntax links d-structure to s-structure and LF to the lexicon by specifying the possible contexts in which a particular lexical item can occur. Already a complex network is building up, seen in the fuller diagram of the T-model in figure 2.4.

Syntax is also concerned with the functional relationships between the parts of the sentence – who is doing what to whom – called in GB θ-**roles (theta roles** or **thematic roles)**. A sentence such as

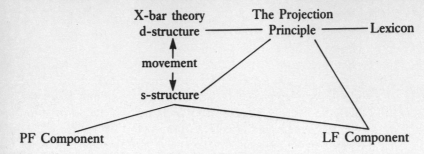

Figure 2.4

Sally gave Jim a record.

has three θ-roles: *Sally* refers to the person who is carrying out the action, *the record* to the object affected by it, *Jim* to the person who receives it. GB handles θ-roles in θ-**theory**. Again θ-theory takes into account how lexical items behave: *give* always has a recipient:

She gave the money to charity.

but *sleep* does not:

*He is sleeping it to someone.

Interacting with X-bar syntax and the Projection Principle, θ-theory assigns θ-roles to elements of the structure of the sentence. A Verb such as *drive* assigns two θ-roles to NPs:

He drove him to the station.

θ-roles express certain relationships between elements, a type of meaning directly relevant to the LF component and indirectly to the semantic component as shown in figure 2.5. It is also important that each Noun Phrase

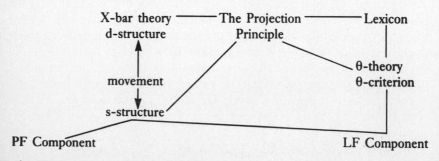

Figure 2.5

has only one such relationship, one θ-role, guaranteed by a requirement of θ-theory known as the θ-criterion.

The relationship of movement between s- and d-structure is restricted in terms of what can be moved, where it can be moved *from*, where it can be moved *to*, and how far it can be moved. This involves not only movement and structure-dependency but also **Bounding Theory** that limits the distance that an item may move. To add one further sub-theory, **Case Theory** deals with the assignment of particular 'cases' to Noun Phrases in the sentence according to their position in the d-structure or s-structure, accounting inter alia in English for the eventual difference between the surface forms, *she, her, hers,* and so on. Case Theory is linked to d-structure and s-structure.

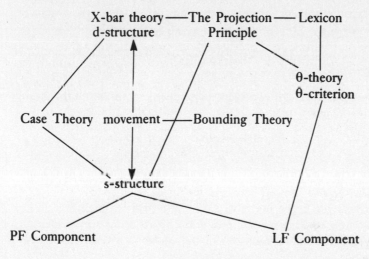

Figure 2.6

In addition to these sub-theories we shall later examine **Binding Theory**, which explains how the reference of various types of Noun Phrase can be linked to other Noun Phrases, for example the link between *James* and *himself* in:

James watched himself in the mirror.

and **Control Theory**, which deals with the subjects of infinitival clauses, for example the invisible subject of *leave* in:

She wanted to leave.

The overall theory consists of an interlocking network of sub-theories in which each interacts with all the others. The analysis of any sentence or 'rule' inherently involves the whole theory; a sentence such as:

Twenty-five demonstrators were arrested.

needs X-bar theory to account for its d-structure; movement and Bounding Theory to show the links between d- and s-structure; Case Theory to describe the Cases involved; θ-theory to account for the possible θ-roles assigned to the NPs; and so on. The sentence cannot be simply described as 'passive', or the construction as the product of a passive rule. The over-riding goal of GB is never to deal with isolated phenomena but always with a continuous interaction of principles and sub-theories; 'small changes in the characterization of the principles and concepts have wide-ranging and complex consequences for some particular language under investigation and for others as well' (KOL, p. 128).

THE GOVERNMENT/BINDING FRAMEWORK

GB describes knowledge of language as an interlocking set of sub-theories consisting of principles and parameters, as shown in figure 2.6.

X-bar syntax describes the structure of phrases, for example the head parameter (chapter 4)

The *Projection Principle* requires all the levels of syntax to observe the specifications for each lexical item given in its entry in the *lexicon* (chapter 4)

Movement is the relationship between two levels (chapter 5):
  – *d-structure* where the underlying structure of the sentence is given
  – *s-structure* where the related form of the sentence after movement is described, including traces (*t*) of the underlying positions of the items

Bounding Theory prevents the relationship of movement from extending too far in the sentence (chapter 5)

θ-Theory deals with the assignment of semantic roles (θ-roles), such as 'recipient', to elements in the sentence, constrained by the θ-criterion (chapter 4)

Case Theory assigns Cases to Noun Phrases in the sentence (chapter 5)

Binding Theory concerns the reference relationships of Noun Phrases (this chapter and chapter 6)

Control Theory deals with the subject of infinitival clauses (chapter 6)

The *Phonetic Form (PF) Component* interprets s-structure to represent it as sounds

The *Logical Form (LF) Component* represents the sentence as syntactic meaning, one aspect of semantic representation

Government

Some principles of language have effects that are confined to a particular sub-theory. Others however affect every part; for example, while structure-dependency is particularly relevant to movement, it enters into virtually all aspects of language. Even more widespread is the concept of **government**. This refers to a particular syntactic relationship of high abstraction between a 'governor' and an element that it governs. A Preposition such as *to* governs a Noun Phrase. For instance in the Preposition Phrase:

to her

the Preposition *to* governs the NP *her*. A Verb governs the NP object; in the sentence:

He likes Coltrane.

the verb *like* governs the NP *Coltrane*. The list of governors includes the lexical categories Noun, Verb, Adjective, and Preposition – everything that can be the head of a phrase. This chapter illustrates the idea of government and some of its uses; a technical definition awaits the discussion in chapter 6. The term 'government' is derived from the familiar usage of traditional grammar for example, 'Nouns are governed, as it is called, by verbs and prepositions' (Cobbett, 1819, p. 67).

If the relationship of government obtains between two elements in the sentence, they influence each other in various ways. So the fact that the Preposition *to* governed the NP above meant that it had the form:

to her

rather than:

*to she

In other words government ensures that the word gets an appropriate Case. The Verb also governs an NP that follows it; in the sentence:

Sarah consoled her.

the Verb *console* governs the NP *her*. Not only does government ensure that the NP gets the right Case, *her* rather than *she*, but also the actual presence of an NP, derived by the Projection Principle from the entry for the Verb, follows from government; the Verb governs the elements that it projects onto the sentence.

The theory pays particular attention to the subject of the sentence. In traditional grammar subjects govern Verbs; it is a thorny problem whether something governs the subject. One possibility is the abstract element in the sentence called **Inflection (INFL)**. The syntactic categories used so far, such as Noun or Preposition, are all 'concrete' and 'lexical' in that they relate to actual words in the sentence and in the dictionary. However some properties of the sentence are not allocated to a single word but are spread across different locations, in particular tense and number. INFL represents these properties as a single abstract constituent that does not itself usually occur in the surface sentence or in the lexicon.

First any sentence must be either *past* or *present* in tense; i.e.:

Mervyn played the piano very well.

versus:

Mervyn plays the piano very well.

To represent this, the tense is detached from the verb and made into a separate constituent which is part of INFL. D- and s-structures show the tense of the sentence separately from the actual Verb:

Mervyn past play the piano very well.

or:

Mervyn present play the piano very well.

The s-structure of the sentence contains abstract features such as *past* and *present*. The PF component interprets them as actual sound sequences; the s-structure item *past* is turned into the appropriate past tense form, whether /t/, /d/, or Id/, or as an irregular past, having been attached to the end of *like* via a type of movement we will ignore for present purposes. The syntactic description requires an abstract element of Tense that may be either *past* or *present*. Tense is a technical notion that refers only to the *past* versus *present* distinction, sometimes abbreviated to TNS.

A sentence can also be either singular or plural in number:

The boy falls over the step.

versus:

The boys fall over the step.

This aspect of the sentence, traditionally called number, is treated by GB as an abstract feature called **agreement (AGR)** that indicates whether singular or plural is required. The two s-structures are, using brackets to link the Verb and its number:

The boys (plural fall) over the step.

and:

The boy (singular fall) over the step.

Again the PF component interprets which form of *singular* or *plural* to use with the Verb, whether the regular /s/, /z/ or ɪz/, or an irregular plural, and it is attached to the end.

Both Tense and AGR form part of the same abstract element INFL (Inflection). The information about Tense and number is concentrated in a single non-lexical constituent, INFL. So the sentence:

They shout at each other.

can be represented as:

They INFL (Tense AGR) shout at each other.

Coming back to government, in GB it is the AGR feature of INFL that may govern the Verb and assign it Tense and number: here INFL(AGR) governs the Verb *shout* and makes it *plural* and *present*. To take a second example, the d-structure:

The dustmen INFL (past plural) come this morning.

represents the sentence:

The dustmen came this morning.

where INFL (past plural) governs *come* and gives it the plural past form which the PF component in due course turns into *came*. To sum up, the constituent INFL in the sentence is made up of two features: Tense which may be *past* or *present*; and AGR which may be *singular* or *plural*. The effects of these features spread through the sentence by government.

The Pro-drop Parameter

While the principles of UG lay down absolute requirements that a human language has to meet, the parameters of UG account for the syntactic variation between languages. English does not just instantiate UG principles; it also has particular settings for all the UG parameters; it selects a particular type of movement and sets the head parameter one way. 'The grammar of a language can be regarded as a particular set of values for the parameters, while the overall system of rules, principles, and parameters, is UG which we may take to be one element of human biological endowment, namely the "language faculty" ' (Chomsky, 1982a, p. 7).

Let us illustrate how parametric variation works through **the pro-drop parameter**. This concerns whether a language has declarative sentences without apparent subjects, known as null subject or subjectless sentences. A starting point can be the Beatles' line:

I am the walrus.

In Italian this would be translated as a null-subject sentence:

Sono il tricheco. (am the walrus)

But in English the null-subject counterpart is ungrammatical:

*Am the walrus.

A pro-drop language such as Italian can have subjectless declarative sentences; a non-pro-drop language such as English cannot (putting aside the entirely different imperative construction which can also be subjectless). This difference applies to a range of sentences e.g. Italian:

Parla. (speaks)

or the familiar notice on trains:

E pericoloso sporgersi. (is dangerous to lean out)

Needless to say, exceptions can be found in English. Some dialects may permit subjectless sentences; the opening page of a Trinidadian novel, *The Dragon Can't Dance*, includes the sentence:

Is noise whole day.

(Lovelace, 1985)

The performance tendency to omit initial words from sentences in casual speech may also clip a first person pronoun from the beginning of an utterance as in:

Flew in from Miami Beach.

It is important to theories of language acquisition whether children learning English produce null subject sentences and whether native speakers of Italian use them in English, as we shall see in subsequent chapters.

In Italian it is also possible to say:

Cade la notte. (falls the night)

But English speakers cannot say:

*Falls the night.

with the meaning 'Night falls'. English declarative sentences have the order subject-Verb; inversion of subject and Verb is usually kept for questions. Italian can have the order Verb-subject even in declaratives. Languages with null subject sentences such as Italian and Spanish also permit Verb-subject order; the languages that behave like English do not. Again there are certain exceptions in English; the order Auxiliary-subject is needed when certain 'triggers' are used:

Scarcely had he gone when . . .

Adverbials also occasionally appear in the subject position as in:

Here comes the sun.

However interesting these differences between English and Italian may be, they would not be important if they could not be generalized to Universal Grammar. The group of pro-drop or 'null subject' languages, to which Italian and Spanish belong, permits both subjectless sentences and inverted declaratives. The other group of non-pro-drop languages, such as English and French, does not allow declarative sentences without subjects or with Verb-subject order. Other languages can be assigned to these two groups; Chinese for example appears to be a pro-drop language; if asked:

Shi shen mo? (what are you?)

it is possible to answer:

Shi ge haixiang. (am the walrus)

without an initial *wo* (I) as subject. Pro-drop is therefore a generalization about human languages, a parameter of UG on which they vary. The main aspects of language affected by the pro-drop parameter are the two features mentioned, although other features have also been claimed to belong to the same phenomenon, such as the possibility in Italian, but not in English, of saying:

Chi credi che verrà?
*Who do you believe that will come?

The information about pro-drop is summarized in the following chart.

Differences between pro-drop and non-pro-drop languages

		Subject Verb	Null-subject	Verb Subject Inversion
Italian	pro-drop	*lui parla*	*parla*	*parla lui*
Arabic	pro-drop	*huwa yatakalamu*	*yatakalamu*	*yatakalamu huwa*
Chinese	pro-drop	*ta shuo*	*shuo*	**shuo ta*
German	non-pro-drop	*er spricht*	**spricht*	**spricht er*
English	non-pro-drop	*he speaks*	**speaks*	**speaks he*
French	non-pro-drop	*il parle*	**parle*	**parle il*

Discussing the pro-drop parameter through specimen sentences from different languages exemplifies it rather than explains it. Several different explanations have been put forward in GB; the one used here is chosen because it illustrates the importance of government. A division was made earlier between lexical categories such as Noun and Verb and non-lexical categories such as INFL. A further type of category crucial to the operation of Government/Binding theory needs to be introduced, namely the **empty category**. The symbol **e** represents an empty category in general; we have already seen one specific type of empty category, namely *t*, the trace of movement. Though pro-drop languages have declarative sentences without apparent subjects, as in the Chinese:

shuo (speaks)

GB treats such sentences as having an empty subject position; the basic assumption is that all sentences have subjects but that these may not be 'visible' in pro-drop languages; while the structure of the sentence requires a subject, in pro-drop languages this may be left empty. Similarly in the Verb-subject inversion sentences such as the Italian:

Cade la notte. (falls the night)

GB sees the subject position as empty but nevertheless still there in the s-structure for reasons that will later become apparent. The empty subject category is called **pro**. The d-structure for the Chinese sentence is then:

pro shuo

pro is an empty category that does not appear in the surface. So the d-structure for the Italian sentence is similarly:

pro cade la notte.

with *pro* marking the empty subject position.

In the list of governors given earlier, INFL stood out from the rest, N, V, A, and P, in not being a lexical category, i.e. an actual word with a lexical entry. Government theory is extended through the principle of **proper government** which holds that lexical categories govern properly, non-lexical categories do not. The Empty Category Principle is then:

An empty category must be properly governed.

In pro-drop languages a sentence may have a null subject; it follows that in these languages the empty category *pro* is properly governed and so INFL is a proper governor and must therefore have lexical properties; the empty category of subject is 'licensed' by the AGR feature of INFL. In the s-structure:

pro INFL shuo.

the INFL category must be a proper governor for the empty category *pro*. In non-pro-drop languages, a sentence may not have a null subject; the empty category *pro* is not properly governed, and so INFL is *not* a proper governor. The English s-structure:

pro INFL speak

is ungrammatical because the INFL constituent cannot properly govern *pro*, it does not have lexical properties. The values for the pro-drop parameter amount to a choice of whether INFL is a proper governor or not – whether it acts like a lexical category. Another way of putting it is that in pro-drop languages INFL can behave like a lexical category such as N; in non-pro-drop languages, it cannot: 'the pro-drop parameter amounts to the choice at the level of the grammar between having AGR with or without nominal features' (van Riemsdijk and Williams, 1986, p. 303). The choice whether INFL has lexical properties accounts for the whole complex of phenomena associated with pro-drop in human languages.

Many pro-drop languages have a rich system of inflectional elements while many non-pro-drop languages do not; in the Latin sentence:

amata est (is loved)

the form of the participle *amata* (loved) indicates that the subject is singular and feminine, although no subject is actually present in the sentence. An English sentence minus its subject does not provide any of this information. Intuitively languages compensate for the lack of information consequent on having null Subjects by having richer information elsewhere. Unfortunately the null subject language Chinese has no inflections; so this intuition is not entirely correct; Chinese also only has Verb-subject order with certain verbs such as *lai* (come):

> lai le ren
> (come aspect-particle person)
> someone came

but not with *shuo* (speak), as we saw on the earlier chart:

> *shuo ta
> (speaks he)

Whether there is a null subject depends partly on discourse processes (Huang, 1984). Hence Chinese may not be fully a pro-drop language. Nor is the reverse prediction correct; as Bouchard (1984) points out, languages with 'rich' morphology such as French, are not necessarily pro-drop.

THE PRO-DROP PARAMETER

The pro-drop parameter, sometimes called 'the null subject parameter' 'determines whether the subject of a clause can be suppressed' (Chomsky, 1988, p. 64).

Definition: a parameter with two settings
  either INFL is a proper governor
  or   INFL is not a proper governor

The Empty Category Principle: an empty category must be properly governed.

Examples:

English	*he speaks*	*speaks*	*speaks he*
Italian	*lui parla*	*parla*	*parla lui*

Gloss: a language that has INFL as a proper governor will permit null subjects (since the empty category *pro* is properly governed); a language that does not have INFL as a proper governor will not (as *pro* will not be properly governed).

Extensions: chapter 6 (sources given there)

Binding Theory

Government Theory contributes one half of the Government/Binding Theory label, **Binding Theory** the other. Binding Theory deals with whether expressions in the sentence may refer to the same entities as other expressions. As with pro-drop the following introductory discussion necessarily distorts the picture by isolating Binding from the other principles of UG; it is put in a wider context in chapter 6.

One of the topics in traditional grammar was how pronouns related to their antecedents. As Cobbett puts it, 'Never write a personal pronoun without duly considering *what noun* it will, upon a reading of the sentence, be *found to relate to*' (Cobbett, 1819, p. 73). Binding Theory is basically concerned with the same issue of how pronouns and other types of noun relate to each other but extends the antecedent/pronoun relationship to other categories in a rigorous fashion; Binding Theory 'is concerned with connections among noun phrases that have to do with such semantic properties as dependence of reference, including the connection between a pronoun and its antecedent' (Chomsky, 1988, p. 52). Take a sample sentence:

McCabe shot him.

This implies that there is some entity in the real world to which *McCabe* may be used to refer; the noun *McCabe* relates a piece of language to a postulated piece of the world. This person is not otherwise mentioned directly in the sentence. To know who is being talked about means knowing which person called McCabe is referred to from other information than that contained in the sentence. The same applies to *him*, known as a **pronominal**; another person is being talked about who is not mentioned; we have to deduce for ourselves who was shot. But we are clear that *McCabe* and *him* do not refer to the same person. Some relationship, or lack of relationship, between *McCabe* and *him* prevents them referring to the same entity.

Let us extend the discussion to *himself*, known as an **anaphor**. In the sentence:

McCabe shot himself.

while *McCabe*, as before, refers to someone outside the sentence, *himself* refers to the same person as *McCabe*. This information depends not on knowing who McCabe is but on knowing the syntactic relationship between *McCabe* and *himself*, that is, on the internal structure of the sentence. Binding Theory accounts for the differences in the interpretations of *McCabe*, *him*, and *himself* – how the speaker knows when two such expressions may refer to the same person and when they may not. The convention to show that two expressions corefer is to assign them the same 'index'. The fact that *McCabe* and *himself* may refer to the same person is shown by giving them both the index i:

McCabe$_i$ shot himself$_i$.

Binding Theory describes when different expressions may be coindexed – when *him* or *himself* may refer to the same person as *McCabe*. If an expression is in a certain structural relationship to another and is coindexed with it, it is 'bound' to it. In the examples *himself* is bound to *McCabe* and has the same index; *him* is not bound to *McCabe* and has a different index. All syntactic theories will therefore need to account for the types of relationship seen here – to have a Binding Theory – although the terminology and framework may differ.

One possible way of explaining Binding is to consider the class of word involved. Three word-classes are relevant: **referring expressions, anaphors** and **pronominals**. Nouns such as *McCabe* are classed as referring expressions (r-expressions) in that their reference is necessarily to something in the world outside the sentence rather than to some other element in the sentence. The word *himself* belongs to the class of anaphors, made up of subgroups such as reflexives – *herself, themselves*, and so on – and reciprocals such as *each other*. The word *him* belongs to the class of pronominals among which are also numbered *she, him, them*, and so on.

The reference possibilities for r-expressions are straightforward since they always refer out of the sentence (with one or two exceptions); *McCabe* indicates there is supposed to be someone called McCabe existing outside the sentence. Anaphors, however, always have antecedents in the sentence rather than outside it; the anaphor *himself* must be bound to the noun *McCabe*, yielding the possible sentence:

McCabe$_i$ shot himself$_i$.

Pronominals do not have antecedents that are nouns within the same sentence; *him* cannot refer to the same person as *McCabe*. The difference between:

McCabe shot him.

and:

McCabe shot himself.

is that the former contains a pronominal *him* with no antecedent in the sentence, the latter an anaphor *himself* that has an antecedent. This explains for example why *Jane* and *her* do not refer to the same person in:

Jane sponsored her.

but *Jane* refers to the same person as *herself* in:

Jane*ᵢ* sponsored herself*ⱼ*.

But this analysis falls down when confronted with more complex data, such as:

McCabe said that Jensen shot himself.

where *himself* does not refer to the same person as *McCabe* despite being in the same sentence. To get round this problem we need to use the term 'sentence' to refer both to main sentences and to the embedded sentences that occur within main sentences, that is to say 'clauses'. A sentence such as:

McCabe said that Jensen shot himself.

will be treated as having two sentences – the main sentence *McCabe said . . .*, and the embedded sentence *. . . that Jensen shot himself.* Similarly:

The policeman asked the demonstrators to move on.

has a main sentence *The policeman asked . . .*, and an embedded sentence *. . . the demonstrators to move on.* This analysis can be shown through the convention of **'bracketting'** – enclosing constituents in brackets to show what goes with what. Bracketting will be used for the moment only to draw attention to the boundaries of the embedded sentence, i.e. the brackets in:

McCabe said (that Jensen shot himself).

indicate the embedded sentence.

What happens to Binding when there is an embedded sentence? In:

McCabe said (that Smith shot him).

the pronominal *him* has two possible references; on the one hand it may be bound to *McCabe*, the subject of the main sentence:

McCabe*ᵢ* said (that Smith shot him*ᵢ*).

On the other hand it may refer to someone else altogether. But it may not have *Smith*, the subject of the embedded sentence, as an antecedent. Pronominals such as *him* are ambiguous since they either have an antecedent within another sentence or refer outside it altogether. They are said to be 'free' outside their own sentence since their reference must always go outside it. However, in:

McCabe said (that Jensen shot himself).

the anaphor *himself* refers to the same person as *Jensen*, the subject of the embedded sentence; it may neither be bound to *McCabe*, the subject of the main sentence, nor refer to someone not otherwise mentioned:

McCabe said (that Jensen$_i$ shot himself$_i$).

Unlike pronominals, anaphors must have antecedents within their own sentence; they are 'bound' within it.

So pronominals seem to be free to refer outside their own sentence in either of two ways; anaphors seem to be bound within the sentence in which they occur; and referring expressions seem to be free at all times. Binding Theory needs to specify the structural area within which Binding may or may not take place according to the category of word employed; this area within which the Binding Principles apply is called the **local domain**. The example of local domain used here is the sentence in which the word occurs, whether an embedded or a main sentence, but this will need later modification. What has been said so far can be summed up as three **Binding Principles**;

A: **An anaphor is bound in a local domain.**
B: **A pronominal is free in a local domain.**
C: **A referring expression is free.**

This is one form of the Binding Principles used in KOL (p. 166), with the omission of a bracketted qualification from Principle C; slightly more informal versions of A and B are given in Chomsky (1988, pp. 52, 76). Let us work through some example sentences to see how these principles operate. In:

Jane wanted (the girl to help herself).

Principle A applies because *herself* is an anaphor and it is therefore bound to *the girl* within the local domain of the embedded sentence, not to *Jane* in the main sentence. Principle C also requires the referring expression *Jane* to refer to someone outside the sentence. So the sentence can be shown as:

Jane wanted (the girl$_i$ to help herself$_i$).

To take a second sentence, in:

Kate asked (the woman to see her).

principle C again requires the referring expression *Kate* to be free and hence to refer outside the main sentence. Principle B requires the pronominal *her* to be free in its local domain (the embedded sentence); it may either take *Kate* in the main sentence as its antecedent, as in:

Kate$_i$ asked (the woman to see her$_i$).

or refer to someone not otherwise mentioned at all. A third example sentence is:

McCabe said (he shot himself).

By Principle A the anaphor *himself* is bound to *he* within the embedded sentence:

McCabe said (he$_i$ shot himself$_i$).

By Principle B the pronominal *he* is free and so may corefer with *McCabe* outside the embedded sentence or with someone else not mentioned. To find which expression binds another in a sentence, the speaker must know not only the syntactic category to which the words *her* or *himself* belong but also the relevant local domain. Though the concepts required are abstract, they are necessitated by the data; they are hypotheses that may be refuted by better data.

The reason why 'local domain' is used in the definition of the Binding Principles rather than 'sentence' can be seen in sentences such as:

Henry believed (himself to be innocent).

On the analysis given so far, the main sentence is *Henry believed* . . ., and the embedded sentence . . . *himself to be innocent*; *himself* is an anaphor and so by Principle A it should be bound within the local domain of the embedded sentence. Yet this is clearly not the case, as the coindexing shows in:

Henry$_i$ believed (himself$_i$ to be innocent).

himself is in fact bound to *Henry* which is outside the embedded sentence. Either Principle A is wrong or some subtle difference in the type of embedded sentence used needs to be taken into account in the definition of local domain. Later chapters explore the precise characteristics of the sentence that are involved in Binding, pinning the concept of local domain down more closely by utilizing aspects of Government Theory, in particular, whether or not the main verb *believe* 'governs' the apparent subject of the embedded sentence *himself*.

As always GB theory integrates the principles with the lexical specification.

The principles depend upon a knowledge of which words are anaphors, and which are pronominals. The lexical entries in the speaker's lexicon must indicate which category each item belongs to, effectively yielding a list such as:

> he   [+pronominal]
> himself   [+anaphor]
> each other [+anaphor]

And so on. Additionally the lexical entries for certain verbs such as *believe* need to specify the type of sentence that may follow them, in ways to be developed later.

Binding Theory is typical of the approach in several ways. Firstly, it exemplifies the close relationship between syntax and lexical items already seen in the Projection Principle; a full knowledge of Binding Theory in the speaker's mind involves the interaction of syntactic and lexical knowledge. Syntax is not a separate area from vocabulary but is interwoven with it; abstract principles relate to actual lexical items. Secondly, it drives home that the theory is not about rules – the properties of isolated syntactic constructions – but about principles that apply to many constructions. Binding Theory is not concerned just with *himself*, or with reflexives; it applies to many areas, among which are reflexives, pronominals, nouns, and so on. Thirdly, Binding demonstrates the interconnectedness of the theory. Structure-dependency comes into play, for example, as the speaker needs to relate structural constituents in the sentence. In particular the Binding Principles cannot be stated in isolation from the notion of subject and from Government, as we shall see in chapter 6.

Finally Binding Theory demonstrates that UG is not concerned with information specific to one language, say English; the Binding Principles are couched at a level of abstraction that may be used for any human language. Though the actual sentences of Chinese, Arabic, or Russian may be very different, they are all covered by the same Binding Principles. Binding is a property, not of English alone, but of all languages. So in the Arabic sentence:

> Qālat Fātma anaa Huda qatalat nafsaha.
> (said Fatimah that Huda killed herself)
> Fatimah said that Huda killed herself.

nafsaha (herself) as an anaphor may be bound to *Huda* within the local domain, but not to *Fātma*. In Chinese, too, in the sentence:

> Hailun renwei Mali hui gei taziji chuan yifu.
> (Helen consider Mary for herself put on clothes)
> Helen thinks that Mary dresses herself.

the anaphor *taziji* (herself) is bound to *Mali* in the same local domain, by Principle A.

Languages differ over the lexical items that may be used as anaphors or pronominals, and in the details of the syntax, but each of them nevertheless observes Binding. Rather than a statement about a single construction in a single language, we have arrived at some principles of language. Of course these principles may be wrong; some other more inclusive explanation may subsume Binding; the aim is to make statements about language that are precise enough to be tested. The purpose is always to see any construction in any language as a variation on a theme set by UG. The relationship between UG and the grammar of a particular language is that between an abstract set of principles that can be realized in different ways and a particular example of their realization. The waltz rhythm for example is realized differently in Strauss' *The Blue Danube*, the Beatles' *She's Leaving Home*, and Max Roach's *The Drum Also Waltzes*; despite their superficial differences, they have an underlying similarity. English grammar incorporates structure-dependency in one way, Italian in another, Chinese in another, but all of them are alternative versions of the same principle. The realization of Binding Theory in English defines it in terms of English sentence structure; it includes unique lists of English words that are anaphors and pronominals. Italian may have a slightly different version defined in terms of Italian sentence structure; it has totally different lists of anaphors and pronominals. Binding Theory nevertheless forms part of both languages. The speaker's knowledge of English or Italian is a knowledge of how they fit UG. A grammar is a realization of the resources

---

BINDING THEORY

'The theory of *binding* is concerned with the relations, if any, of anaphors and pronominals to their antecedents' (Chomsky, 1982a, p. 6).

Binding Principles (KOL, p. 166 adapted):
  A: An anaphor is bound in a local domain
  B: A pronominal is free in a local domain
  C: A referring expression is free

Examples:
  (1) *McCabe said that Jensen$_i$ shot himself$_i$.*
  (2) *McCabe$_i$ said that Smith shot him$_i$.*

Gloss: in (1) the anaphor *himself* must refer to the same person as *Jensen* because it is within the same local domain, (Principle A); in (2) the pronominal *him* may refer to the same person as *McCabe* because it is in a different local domain, (Principle B).

Extension: chapter 6

of UG – structure-dependency, the head parameter, and so forth; it is one of the possible permutations of UG; languages vary in the ways they use the principles but not in the principles themselves. Part of the human language faculty consists of knowledge about how a language uses the Binding Principles.

Core and Periphery

UG asserts that at some fundamental level all human languages conform to a particular pattern: even the variations in the pattern are systematic. Their conformity is not due to common historical origins, nor to the communicative needs of the user, but to the properties of the language faculty, the UG at the heart of grammatical competence. Knowledge of a language means knowing how it fits the general properties of UG with which the mind is equipped. We don't know English as such or Arabic as such: we know the English version of UG or the Arabic version of UG. UG is 'a system of subtheories, each with certain parameters of variation. A particular (core) language is determined by fixing parameters in these sub-theories' (Chomsky, 1982a, p. 2).

Logically, the potential number of human languages is infinite; the permutations and combinations could vary without rhyme or reason. This has indeed been taken as axiomatic by some linguists; 'language is a human activity that varies without assignable limit' (Sapir, quoted in KOL, p. 21). In terms of UG theory such apparent diversity conceals an underlying identity; all languages are similar at the abstract level of principles such as Binding or vary within tight limits, as with the head and pro-drop parameters. These common characteristics might be coincidence, no more than statistical accidents. Or they might reflect the nature of the mind that knows them. UG theory specifies not so much what a human language may be like as what it may *not* be like. One way of viewing UG is, in a way, not as permitting various types of language but as preventing various types of language. The principle of structure-dependency excludes from the class of human languages those that are structure-independent. The examples in this chapter suggest that if a language breached the Binding Principles or Government it would not be a human language at all. Each of the principles and parameters of UG constrains the possibilities of human language. UG 'permits only a finite number of core languages (apart from the lexicon): there are finitely many parameters and each has a finite number of values' (KOL, p. 149). One of the powerful consequences of the framework is that the number of possible languages could now in principle be counted. UG puts severe limitations on what a human language may be; there are only a certain small number of languages possible because the combinations of the different values for the various parameters are limited; each possible human language must have one of these combinations. Human languages are limited to the 'finitely many (in fact relatively few) possible core grammars' (Chomsky, 1982b, p. 17).

So the language faculty itself only accepts languages that conform to the requirements of UG. In particular this limits the scope of language acquisition; learners do not need to investigate a vast number of possible grammars for the language they are learning because they can safely assume that it will have the characteristics of UG. The principles and the range of values for each parameter effectively rule out many of the possibilities in advance. Again the presence of UG in the mind does not so much facilitate learning as limit the learner's choice to a small subset of possibilities out of the vast number that are logically possible; languages that contravene UG principles cannot be conceived by the human language faculty. To sum up, 'UG now is construed as the theory of human I-languages, a system of conditions deriving from the human biological endowment that identifies the I-languages that are humanly accessible under normal circumstances' (KOL, p. 23).

UG theory also recognizes that various aspects of a language may be untypical and unconnected to UG. As an example, English is normally taken to have compulsory verbs in declarative sentences. It is possible to say:

Molly is the singer in a band.

but not:

*Molly the singer in a band.

(though it is possible in some versions of English, or indeed in languages such as Arabic). But:

The more the merrier.

has no Verb; it should not be English. It might be that proverbs preserve older forms of the language; or proverbs may be used precisely because of their distinctive language.

However it is also possible to say:

The sooner the better.

which seems the same construction; it is not confined to one isolated proverb. Indeed, novel sentences can be created on the same lines, as in:

The more of these, the merrier the linguist.

taken from Fodor (1983, p. 26). Or, as a colleague said on reading the above:

The older the idiom the less you can mess about with it.

The description of competence needs to include the possibility of such curious verbless sentences; they are part of English since they can be used creatively, even if in a very limited way.

The knowledge of any speaker contains masses of similar oddities that do not fit in with the overall pattern of the language. 'What a particular person has in the mind/brain is a kind of artifact resulting from the interplay of accidental factors . . .' (KOL, p. 147). UG theory avoids taking them all on board by raising a distinction between **core** and **periphery**. The **core** is the part of grammatical competence covered by UG; all the principles are kept, all the parameters set within the right bounds. The **periphery** includes aspects that are not predictable from UG. Some are survivals from earlier periods; *The more the merrier* reflects a common comparative construction in Old English. Others are imports from other languages; the fact that *police* does not rhyme with *nice* indicates it was a late borrowing from French after other words with *i* had changed their pronunciation. Still others are idiomatic expressions that have meanings quite different from their literal content – *It's raining cats and dogs* or *He went for a Burton*. Some are sheer accidents: the radio programme *The Goon Show* added the expression *the dreaded lurgy* to British English, Lewis Carroll's *Jabberwocky* the word *chortle*. It is unrealistic to expect a UG theory to account for myriads of such unconnected features of language knowledge. It deals instead with a core of central language information and a periphery of less essential information; 'a core language is a system determined by fixing values for the parameters of UG, and the periphery is whatever is added on in the system actually represented in the mind/brain of a speaker-hearer' (KOL, p. 147). The theory of UG is far from a complete account of the speaker's entire knowledge of language; it deals with the core aspects that are related to UG, not with the periphery that is unrelated to UG.

As structure-dependency, for instance, is an aspect of core grammar, all languages must observe it. But this does not imply that no peripheral aspects of the language breach it, hard as they may be to imagine. Similarly a non-pro-drop language does not necessarily have a subject in every sentence. A further glance at Beatles' songs quickly produces

Can't buy me love.

with no apparent subject, and

In the town where I was born lived a man who sailed to sea.

which seems to have Verb-subject order. There are also apparent exceptions to the Binding Principles in:

Footballers like myself have a hard time with referees.

where it is far from clear how an anaphor *myself* is bound within the sentence by Principle A, or

I looked at my son and I saw *me*.

where the same principle predicts *myself*. It may be that the explanation for these is the processes of performance, or that the complex of reference possibilities of the last two require a more subtle interpretation of Binding. But in principle core grammar would not have to be reformulated to accommodate these even if they were true exceptions; they can be left on the periphery. UG does not pretend to account for the whole of knowledge, only the core; it idealizes away from the totality of language knowledge to those parts that humans share.

Such idealization involves the methodological danger of providing an easy way to dispose of inconvenient counterexamples: if some feature of a language seems to contravene our concept of UG, it can be put down to peripheral rather than core grammar, and the UG proposal maintained despite exceptions. Earlier, similar escape routes were used when arguing that, despite examples of verbless sentences, English sentences need a verb; despite examples of subjectless sentences, English is a non-pro-drop language; and, despite certain apparent breaches of Binding Principles, English nevertheless maintains them. This increases the problem of finding appropriate evidence; actually occurring sentences can be dismissed not just because they are performance but also because they are peripheral. The laudable aim is to concentrate on the key points that languages have in common, on the central features of the language faculty. But such abstraction brings the danger of insulating the theory from relevant as well as irrelevant evidence.

The distinction between periphery and core is not absolute but a continuum of 'markedness'. Some aspects of grammar are totally derived from UG, some less derived, some quite unrelated. 'Markedness' means departure from the usual 'neutral' form in one way or another; the black sheep is marked, the white sheep unmarked because sheep are expected to be white; the albino crow is marked because crows are expected to be black. The more something departs from UG the more it is marked; the central core is unmarked – the neutral, expected form of human language. The unmarked version of the head parameter is that all phrases consistently have their heads on the same side; a completely marked language would vary head position inconsistently. A language may have an unmarked core where the head position is consistent but more peripheral elements where it varies, English being a case in point. So one form of markedness is simply whether the parameter applies in the way laid down by UG. It might be that a language does not completely fit, at a cost to be seen later. Chinese for instance has null subject sentences and so should be a pro-drop language; it only has Verb-subject order with certain verbs; it might then be described as marked so far as the pro-drop parameter is concerned.

But another sense of markedness refers to the choice between settings for a parameter. One interpretation of the pro-drop parameter is whether INFL is a proper governor; it is a switch with two settings, each of which might be equally part of UG. Or one setting might be closer to the core, one more peripheral. How could a choice be made between these two possibilities? Once again we come back to language acquisition. Language learners have the pro-drop switch ready in their minds. The switch might be initially neutral, in which case neither setting is more marked than the other; it makes no difference which language they are learning as it is equally easy to switch in either direction. Or they might start with the switch set one way; depending on the language they encounter, they have either to keep it the same way or turn it the other way. If the switch is initially set to pro-drop, learners acquiring Spanish have nothing to acquire since Spanish is a pro-drop language; those learning English have to acquire something extra and vice versa if the switch is initially set the other way. How can we tell which is the case? One way is to see whether the child learning English ever uses null subject sentences, as is indeed true. This suggests that the initial setting is pro-drop. A complementary approach is to consider the types of evidence that the child requires in order to set the switch; the less evidence that is required the easier the parameter is to set and the least marked the setting. Thus markedness is linked to learnability.

Finally it will have become apparent that much of the discussion is not about language as such but about grammar. The speaker knows a core grammar that incorporates the principles of UG and has particular values for the parameters, conforming to English or French, or whatever language it may be. The speaker's language knowledge extends far outside these limits, and includes marked peripheral information. While 'grammar' is a precise definite term, 'language' is a looser weaker concept that relates to it in some way. Chomsky calls language an epiphenomenon; 'the notion "language" itself is derivative and relatively unimportant. We might even dispense with it with little loss . . . the fundamental concepts are *grammar* and *knowing a grammar* . . .' (Chomsky, 1980a, p. 126). What the speaker knows is a grammar, not a language; the term 'language' is an artefact derived from more basic issues; 'The grammar in a person's mind/brain is real; it is one of the real things in the world. The language (whatever that may be) is not' (Chomsky, 1982b, p. 5). Hence UG theory tends to use the term 'grammatical' competence rather than 'linguistic' competence.

3 First Language Acquisition

Plato's Problem

A central issue addressed by Chomsky is 'Plato's problem' – 'How do we come to have such rich and specific knowledge, or such intricate systems of belief and understanding, when the evidence available to us is so meager?' (Chomsky, 1987). Our knowledge of language is complex and abstract; the experience of language we receive is limited. Our minds could not create such complex knowledge on the basis of such sparse information. It must therefore come from somewhere other than the evidence we encounter; Plato's solution is from memories of prior existence, Chomsky's from innate properties of the mind. This 'poverty of the stimulus' argument has a clear and simple form: on the one hand there is the complexity of language knowledge, on the other the impoverished data available to the learner; if the child's mind could not create language knowledge from the data in the surrounding environment, given plausible conditions on the type of language evidence available, the source must be within the mind itself.

Language acquisition is conceptualized by Chomsky in terms of initial and final 'states' of the mind. At one extreme is the newborn baby who knows no language, termed the **initial zero state**, or S_0. At the other extreme is the language knowledge of the adult, which is, to all intents and purposes, static; the speaker may become more or less efficient at using language, or vocabulary items may be learnt or forgotten, but competence is essentially complete and unchanging. The adult native speaker's knowledge is termed the **steady state**, or S_S for short – fully developed unchanging competence. Acquiring language means progressing from not having any language, S_0, to having full competence, S_S; 'a person proceeds from a genetically determined initial state S_0 through a sequence of stages S_1, S_2 ..., finally arriving at a "steady state" S_S which then seems to change only marginally' (Chomsky, 1980b, p. 37). A theory of acquisition must show how the child progresses from S_0 to S_S. To establish the innate properties of the mind we need to discover what could not be contributed by the environment during this progression from S_0 to S_S.

An E-language approach would interpret this as an invitation to follow large numbers of children from S_0 to S_S, for example, the 128 children involved in the Bristol study outlined in Wells (1985). An I-language approach sees language acquisition as a logical problem that can be solved without necessarily looking at the development of children. The final state S_S consists of a core grammar instantiating the principles and parameters of UG, which is the common possession of all human beings, and peripheral grammar and a mental lexicon of idiosyncratic items, which are more variable. It is possible to work back from S_S to S_0 to see how the child might have acquired full competence; to postulate an element of grammatical competence is to propose something that is learnt by the human mind and necessitates an explanation of how it could be acquired; if structure-dependency, say, is part of language knowledge, it must have a source. Most models of language learning that have been put forward can be given short shrift because in principle they cannot account for the acquisition of the types of knowledge postulated by UG theory from the evidence available to the child.

The Chomskyan models have always tried to place linguistic theory within the context of acquisition; the linguist is concerned not only with describing language knowledge but also with accounting for its origin. The earlier models conceptualized acquisition in terms of the **Language Acquisition Device (LAD)**. The child's mind is a black box whose internal workings cannot be inspected. Into it go the language data, samples of performance, out of it comes grammatical competence, S_S; the child's LAD takes in input and produces output. If something is found in the output that cannot be derived from the input, it must have come from the LAD itself; 'Having some knowledge of the characteristics of the acquired grammars and the limitations on the available data, we can formulate quite reasonable and fairly strong empirical hypotheses regarding the internal structure of the language acquisition device that constructs the postulated grammars from the given data' (Chomsky, 1972a, p. 113). The relationship between knowledge and acquisition was established through the goal of 'explanatory adequacy' that a linguistic theory had to meet. Two different descriptions of competence might be equally successful, and so be 'descriptively adequate'. The choice between them should be made according to which best fits the input/output model. The preferred description of the output, whenever a choice is available, is that which children can learn most easily from the language data available to them; 'a linguistic theory that aims for explanatory adequacy is concerned with the internal structure of the device . . .; that is, it aims to provide a principled basis, independent of any particular language, for the selection of the descriptively adequate grammar of each language' (Chomsky, 1964, p. 29).

But the concept of explanatory adequacy seemed like an optional extra; only after linguists had produced competing descriptions, did it come into play. As most energy went into the descriptions themselves, there was seldom a straightforward choice between rival descriptions that could be settled through explanatory adequacy. The current UG theory however integrates acquisition with the description of grammar at every point; the principles and parameters of UG are proposals for the contents of the initial state S_0. Standard introductory textbooks on Government/Binding syntax, such as van Riemsdijk and Williams (1986), constantly allude to acquisition. Rather than an ultimate long-term goal, acquisition is part of the working discussion, as has been evident throughout this book. Given that a grammar is an I-language mental reality that instantiates UG in a particular way, the question of how it is acquired has a bearing on every syntactic issue.

The overall model of language acquisition proposed by Chomsky can be put quite simply. Universal Grammar is present in the child's mind as a system of principles and parameters. In response to evidence from the environment the child creates a core grammar that assigns values to all the parameters, yielding one of the allowable human languages – French, Arabic, or whatever. To start with, the child's mind is open to any human language; it ends by acquiring a particular language. The principles of UG are principles of the initial state. The Projection Principle, Binding, Government, and the others, are the built-in structure of the language faculty in the human mind. No language breaches them; since they are underdetermined by what the child hears, they must be present from the beginning. They are not learnt so much as 'applied'; the child's grammatical competence automatically incorporates them. The resemblances between human languages reflect their common basis in principles of the mind; Japanese incorporates the Binding Principles as do English or Arabic, because no other option is open to the child. While we are concentrating here on acquisition of syntax, Chomsky extends the argument to include 'fixed principles governing possible sound systems' (Chomsky, 1988, p. 26) and 'a rich and invariant conceptual system, which is prior to any experience' (Chomsky, 1988, p. 32), which guide the child's acquisition of phonology and vocabulary respectively.

Parameter-setting allows the child to acquire the circumscribed variation between languages. A speaker of English has set the head parameter to head-first, a speaker of Japanese to head-last. Acquiring a language means setting all the parameters of UG appropriately. As we have seen, they are limited in number but powerful in their effects. To acquire English rather than Japanese the child must set the values for pro-drop, the head parameter, and a handful of others. The child does not acquire rules but settings for parameters, which, interacting with the network of principles, create a core grammar. Rather than a black box with mysterious contents, Chomsky is proposing a carefully specified system of properties, each open to challenge.

In addition to the core grammar, the child acquires a massive set of vocabulary items, each with its own pronunciation, meaning, and syntactic restrictions. While the acquisition of core grammar is a matter of setting a handful of switches, the child has the considerable burden of discovering the characteristics of thousands of words. 'A large part of "language learning" is a matter of determining from presented data the elements of the lexicon and their properties' (Chomsky, 1982a, p. 8). So the child needs to learn entries that specify that *sleep* is a Verb which requires a subject; that *give* is a Verb that requires a subject, an object, and an indirect object; that *record* is a Noun that requires a determiner; and so on, for all the items that make up the mental lexicon of a speaker of English.

As well as the aspects derived from UG principles the child acquires parts of the language that depart from the core in one way or another along a continuum of markedness, for example constructions such as *The more the merrier*. Grammatical competence is a mixture of universal principles, values for parameters, and lexical information, with an additional component of peripheral knowledge. Some of it has been present in the speaker's mind from the beginning; some of it comes from experiences that have set values for parameters or led to the acquisition of lexical knowledge. To sum up in Chomsky's words, 'what we "know innately" are the principles of the various subsystems of S_0 and the manner of their interaction, and the parameters associated with these principles. What we learn are the values of the parameters and the elements of the periphery (along with the lexicon to which similar considerations apply)' (KOL, p. 150).

Let us see what this entails through two examples. Native speakers of English know that

His father plays tennis with him in the summer.

is a possible sentence. What have they acquired? First they have set the head parameter to head-first, so that *play* appears to the left of *tennis*, *in* to the left of *the summer*. This setting was presumably acquired by noticing that English phrases have a head-first tendency. They also know that the verb *play* can be followed by an object NP. This comes from the built-in Projection Principle and from the lexical entry for *play*, which is derived from observations of sentences. They also know that an actual lexical subject – *his father* – must be included; they have set the value of the pro-drop parameter to non-pro-drop, possibly based on their observation that null subject sentences do not occur in English. The fact that *him* must refer to someone other than *his father* derives from their built-in knowledge of Binding Principles, together with the specific lexical knowledge that *him* is a pronominal, acquired from experience.

Now take the Japanese sentence:

Kare wa tegami o eki   de yomimasu.
he   letter   station on read

Japanese speakers have set the value for the head parameter to head-last, as seen in the Verb *yomimasu* (read) occurring to the right of *tegami o eki de* and in the Postposition *de* (on) occurring to the right of *eki* (station). They have learnt that the verb *yomimasu* requires a subject and an object. Government and Case Theory have been learnt in relationship to the case particles *wa* (subject) and *o* (object) which are assigned to the appropriate constituents. Japanese learners have followed the same route as English learners but with a different result. (It should perhaps be noted that the analysis of Japanese is controversial and that this discussion does not take into account the notion that Japanese may be 'non-configurational', an additional parameter of UG.)

The Evidence Available to the Learner

A constant theme in Chomsky's writing is the nature of the evidence available to the child, taking up arguments suggested by Baker (1979), Gold (1967), and others. Children have to acquire the grammar from the evidence they encounter. Without any evidence they will acquire nothing; with evidence they will learn Chinese or Arabic or any human language they encounter. The 'logical problem of language acquisition' hinges upon the types of evidence they meet and the uses they put it to. This can be illustrated by looking at how one might learn to play games such as snooker and pool. After years of watching snooker on television, I know from observation some of the sequences of colours in which balls are hit. If I started to play tomorrow, I could copy the sequences I have already observed, but I would not know if a new sequence was illegal. I have no idea what sequences are impossible because I have only seen sequences in which the rules are obeyed rather than those in which they are broken. While I might pass for a snooker player for a few minutes, an adequate knowledge of snooker involves knowing what *not* to do as well as what to do. To learn snooker properly, I would require some other type of evidence. One possibility is to see players breaking the rules, unlikely in television snooker because of the high standard of professional play. Furthermore, to recognize a sequence as a mistake, something must indicate that it is wrong, such as a penalty from the referee or the hissing of the crowd; otherwise it is another permissible sequence to add to my stock. A further possibility is to learn from the mistakes I make while actually playing; I hit a black ball followed by a red and see if my opponent tells me it is wrong. Or I might deduce from the fact that I have never seen a particular colour sequence, say two reds in succession, that it is illegal; this would not help me to distinguish sequences that are impossible from those that are rare or unlikely. Finally I might buy a guide to snooker and read up the actual rules given there; this solution however is no use if I am unable to read or cannot grasp the type of information given in the rule. Overall it would be impossible for me to learn colour sequences solely from watching games.

This analogy illustrates the general properties of the evidence that are necessary for acquisition. On the one hand there is *positive* evidence of actually occurring sequences, i.e. sentences of the language. On the other is evidence such as explanations, corrections of wrong sequences, or ungrammatical sentences, that shows what may *not* be done. A knowledge of correct snooker sequences appears to be unlearnable from positive evidence alone but needs evidence of impossible sequences, correction, ability to read the rule book, and so on. But these possibilities are not available in first language acquisition; except for positive evidence, the other forms detailed above are seldom encountered by the child. The foundation of UG accounts of language acquisition is that evidence other than positive evidence by and large cannot play a critical role; the child must learn chiefly from positive examples of what people actually say rather than examples of what they don't say. Again, this comes back to the poverty of the stimulus argument; to acquire language knowledge from experience, the mind needs access to evidence other than actual sentences; as this is not available, the knowledge cannot be acquired but must already be there.

Chomsky (LGB, pp. 8–9) recognizes three types of evidence for acquisition. First comes 'positive evidence (SVO order, fixing a parameter of core grammar; irregular verbs, adding a marked periphery)'. The occurrence of particular sentences in the speech children hear tells them which sort of language they are encountering and so how to set the parameters; hearing sentences such as:

The hunter chopped off the wolf's head.

they discover that English is head-first; hearing sentences such as:

Mukashi ojihisan to obaasan ga koya ni sunde imashita.
(once upon a time old man and old woman cottage in lived)
Once upon a time an old man and an old woman lived in a cottage.

they discover Japanese is head-last. Positive evidence can set a parameter to a particular value.

Chomsky's second type of evidence is 'direct negative evidence (corrections by the speech community)'. The child might conceivably say:

Man the old.

and a parent correct:

No dear, in English we say 'The old man'.

The third of Chomsky's types is 'indirect negative evidence'; the fact that certain forms do *not* occur in the sentences the children hear may suffice to set a parameter. An English child is unlikely to hear many subjectless declarative sentences:

*Speaks.

or subject Verb inversion:

*Speaks he.

save for performance mistakes. At some point the cumulative effect of this lack makes English children decide that English is a non-pro-drop language. Chomsky claims that 'There is good reason to believe that direct negative evidence is not necessary for language acquisition, but indirect negative evidence may be relevant' (p. 9). While this division into three types of evidence will be used in the later discussion, there are some terminological difficulties: explanation of grammatical rules is not positive evidence of what actually occurs but neither is it negative evidence of what doesn't occur; it is evidence of another sort altogether, which might be termed 'explanatory evidence'.

I see the argument as partly depending on two requirements which, though Chomsky does not name them explicitly himself, I shall call **occurrence** and **uniformity**. It is not enough to show that some aspect of the environment logically could help the child's acquisition; we must show that it does occur. Parental explanation of the Binding Principles might be highly useful to the child; it is inconceivable that it actually occurs. If a model of acquisition depends crucially on children hearing a particular structure or being corrected by their parents, it is necessary to show that this actually happens; to meet the **occurrence** requirement, speculations about the evidence that children might encounter need support from observations of what they do encounter.

All children with very few exceptions learn language. Suppose a learning theory suggests acquisition depends upon the provision of particular types of evidence and that observations of children confirm these do occur. This explanation would still be inadequate if a single child is found who acquires language without this type of evidence. If some children are corrected by their parents, some are not, yet all acquire language, so acquisition cannot crucially depend upon correction. Since language knowledge is common to all, the **uniformity** requirement stipulates that a model of acquisition must only involve properties of the situation known to happen to all children. Uniformity is a stronger form of occurrence; it is not enough to show that a certain type of evidence is available to one child; it must be available to all children. A model of language acquisition cannot rely on a particular feature of the environment unless it is available to all children. Children are capable of acquiring their first language despite wide differences in their situations within a culture and across cultures. Baby-talk words such as *puff-puff* or *bow-wow* are used by some parents in England and shunned by others; some children are told *Open the window*, some asked *Could you open the window?*; yet, although children differ in the extent to which they are able to use language, they nevertheless appear to attain the same grammatical competence. So long as the environment contains a certain amount of language, it appears not to be crucial to the acquisition of grammatical competence what this sample consists of; any human child learns any human language, whatever the situation. As Gleitman (1984, p. 556) succinctly puts it, 'Under widely varying environmental circumstances, learning different languages, under different conditions of culture and child rearing, and with different motivations and talents, all non-pathological children acquire their native tongue at a high level of proficiency within a narrow developmental time frame.'

Some Insufficient Ways of Acquiring Language

Let us go through some alternatives to the innate UG position. This section brings together various points against non-UG positions, derived from Chomskyan thinking in general rather than a specific source. To give concreteness, wherever possible the discussion uses examples of the language of young children and their parents taken from the Bristol transcripts, made available as part of the project described in Wells (1985).

1   *Imitation*

Children might learn by imitating the behaviour of those around them. Children brought up among Italian-speaking people speak Italian not English; their knowledge of language reflects their experience. If this counts as imitation, the child learns by imitating. However often the term 'imitation' has been applied more specifically to speech exchanges in which children repeat the speech of adults (e.g. Clark and Clark, 1977, p. 334), as in:

TV: It's Tuesday.
Child: It's Tuesday.

The basis of this acquisition model is that children parrot what is said to them.

In terms of the present discussion children can only imitate what they actually hear. Imitation provides only positive evidence, with all its deficiencies; principles such as Binding could not be learnt by imitation because children would never discover what *not* to say. Furthermore speakers can produce new sentences that have never been produced before or understand sentences that they have never met before: language knowledge is creative. However often children imitated the speech of others, they would be unable to produce new things they had never heard before. Imitation in this sense cannot account for the vital creative aspect of language use. The defence to this charge is that children in some way generalize to new circumstances they have not met before; Chomsky insists that generalization is not an adequate explanation because it conceals 'a vast and unacknowledged contribution . . . which in fact includes just about everything of interest in this process' (Chomsky, 1959, p. 58). Imitation seems to be rare in transcripts of English-speaking children, but is common for example among the Kahuli of Papua New Guinea (Ochs and Schieffelin, 1984); the occurrence requirement seems culturally determined, and so the uniformity requirement is not met.

Direct imitation in the form of repetition of adult sentences is unlikely to lead to acquisition. However, to some extent this may be a straw man argument; staunch supporters of direct imitation are thin on the ground. Deferred imitation in which the child repeats an adult remark some time later may have a greater frequency in the child's speech than direct imitation and hence meet the occurrence requirement, though it may be hard to detect in the child's speech. Nor is frequency in itself necessarily important; even if the child only imitated once a day, it might still be the key to acquisition. Nevertheless it is still true that children cannot imitate what they do not hear; if they never hear relevant sentences, they will never be able to imitate them.

2 Explanation

Logically speaking, the Binding Principles, for example, could be taught to the child through parents explaining that there are two classes of words, anaphors and pronominals, which behave in different ways. Explanatory evidence in principle could counteract the inadequacy of positive evidence. The minds of students learning foreign languages or computing languages are often presumed to work in this way by their teachers. But it is totally implausible for first language acquisition. Firstly, such conscious knowledge of language, essentially similar to the linguist's knowledge, is different from unconscious competence and the property of some other faculty of the mind. It is also doubtful whether young children could acquire such abstract and complex conscious knowledge: a child that is old enough to understand the explanation is hardly in need of it. Secondly, the occurrence requirement requires a search for such explanations in the speech of parents to children. Not only have few instances of syntactic explanation by parents been found, but also most parents do not possess sufficient conscious knowledge of abstract UG principles to be able to give explanations of them. Chomsky's point about second language learning is equally applicable to first language acquisition: 'one does not learn the grammatical structure of a second language through "explanation and instruction" beyond the most elementary rudiments, for the simple reason that no one has enough explicit knowledge about this structure to provide explanation and instruction' (Chomsky, 1972a, pp. 174–5). Finally, the uniformity requirement requires all children to encounter syntactic explanation, which seems unlikely. So, while some aspects of language might well be learnt through explanation, its difficulty and its rarity suggest it is hardly the prime means of learning principles of syntax.

3 Correction and approval

Adults might, however, provide negative evidence by explicitly correcting the child's malformed sentences. A child might say:

Book the blue.

and the parent might dutifully correct:

No we don't say that. We say 'the blue book'.

Like explanation, correction could in principle compensate for deficiencies in the positive evidence; even if parents themselves don't supply negative evidence, they might react to the child's own mistakes. This view of language acquisition as a process of teaching by adult correction is one that, in my experience, is commonly held by parents.

For correction to be feasible, the occurrence requirement has to be met by evidence that children produce ungrammatical sentences, and that adults correct them. Starting with the children's speech, examples can be found such as:

I broked it in half.
She be crying because her fur will get wet, wouldn't she?
What did my mummy do at you?

Since these are ungrammatical in terms of adult competence, the sheer occurrence of ungrammatical sentences is demonstrated. If children learn the head parameter for the order of elements in phrases by correction, however, they must produce sentences that specifically violate the appropriate setting. The child would have to make mistakes such as the concocted example:

Man old the go will.

so that the adult can point out:

No. You should say 'The old man will go.'

While the real children's sentences above are typical and familiar to every parent, sentences that go against the typical order within the phrase are hard to find; Roger Brown (1973, p. 77) for example comments that 'the child's first sentences preserve normal word order.' Put conservatively, children do not seem to make many mistakes with UG principles; from the first time they use a principle, they get it right. While the occurrence requirement is met in that children do produce ungrammatical sentences, they have not been shown to produce sentences that actually violate UG. I searched the Bristol transcripts in vain for a single example of a structure-dependency violation. The closest I have come is a student of mine who reported observing a child saying:

What does sheep make a noise?

Part of the constituent *what* seems to have moved rather than the whole constituent *what noise*. Chomsky indeed asserts 'Though children make certain kinds of errors in the course of language learning, I am sure that none make the error of forming the question "Is the dog that in the corner is hungry?" despite the slim evidence of experience and the simplicity of the structure independent rule' (Chomsky, 1972c, p. 30). Though it is impossible to prove the negative point that relevant mistakes never occur, they are, to say the least, extremely hard to find. This conclusion may be overturned by new evidence; Platt and MacWhinney (1983) for example demonstrate that four-year-old children are more tolerant of their own mistakes than those of others or of babies, though again the mistakes studied do not appear typical of UG principles. But, as we shall see below, it is not crucial to UG theory whether any of the child's interim grammars breach its principles.

Even if the occurrence requirement were met in the child's speech, the occurrence of correction in the parents' speech still has to be shown. A preliminary point is that if parents are to correct the mistake, they have to be able to detect it. But some mistakes are not apparent to the listener. If the child said:

Peggy hurt her.

with the meaning:

*Peggy₁ hurt her₁.

the fact that *her* was incorrectly being used as an anaphor could not be detected if the listener finds an alternative plausible interpretation which happens not to be the one intended. Berwick and Weinberg (1984, p. 170) make the same point in terms of parsing: 'If an antecedent can be found, the sentence will be grammatical, otherwise not: in both cases the sentence will be parsable.'

Let us start by using correction to refer to explicit comments by the adult on the form of the child's speech. Take the following exchange between a Bristol mother and child:

Child: I yeard her.
Mother: You *heard* her.
Child: Yeard her.
Mother: Not yeard. Heard.

Such examples bear witness that correction does indeed occur; the problems are how often it occurs and what is corrected. The above example was one of only five I could find in six transcripts amounting to some three hours of recording of diverse activities. A second example was:

Child: I'm calling it a flutterby.
Mother: That's wrong, isn't it?

The remaining three concerned *please* and *thank you* as in:

Child: Find some more.
Mother: Please. Ask him properly and he might.

In only one of these five does an adult directly point out what is wrong with the syntax of the child's speech and even that may be simply correction of pronunciation; if this is typical, explicit correction of syntax is a rare phenomenon. Brown (1973, p. 412) comments 'in general the parents seemed to pay no attention to bad syntax, nor did they even seem to be aware of it.' When Brown and Hanlon (1970) correlated the grammaticality of the children's speech with approval or disapproval by the mother, they found that some sentences were frowned on:

Child: And Walt Disney comes on Tuesday.
Mother: No he does not.

and other sentences were praised:

Child: Draw a boot paper.
Mother: That's right. Draw a boot on paper.

But often grammatical sentences are corrected, and ungrammatical sentences approved, as my own examples also show; only one correction out of five applied to an ungrammatical sentence. Hirsh-Pasek, Treiman and Schneiderman (1984) found a ratio of 3 to 1 for approval of well-formed versus ill-formed sentences and 5 to 1 for disapproval of well-formed versus ill-formed, suggesting that something other than grammaticality is involved.

However again there is a straw man element in the argument: even if parents seldom correct the syntactic structure of their children's sentences overtly, correction could take other forms. It may be, as Hirsh-Pasek et al. (1984) suggest, that it is more subtle. The child's sentence given above for instance:

Draw a boot paper.

was expanded by the mother rather than corrected directly:

That's right. Draw a boot on paper.

Indirect correction may be far more frequent than hitherto supposed. A type of exchange familiar to every parent is repeating the child's ungrammatical sentence; a person who denies the value of direct correction will point to the apparent approval conferred on the sentence by the adult. Hirsh-Pasek et al. (1984) found that ill-formed sentences were about twice as likely to be repeated by parents as well-formed ones. The very fact that a sentence is repeated singles it out to the child as needing attention, let alone the intonation pattern used by the mother. Nor should the apparent infrequency of correction itself be a reason for dismissing it, a confusion of quantity with quality. The real argument once again is whether the type of knowledge postulated in UG is learnable through correction; in principle, this still seems unlikely. Chomsky originally stated that 'It is simply not true that children can learn language only through "meticulous care" on the part of adults who shape their verbal reportoire through careful differential reinforcement ...' (Chomsky, 1959, p. 42). Provided that the word 'language' is clearly restricted within the UG scope, this seems still tenable. Perhaps as a postscript it should be noted that a questionnaire that formed part of the Bristol research showed that the more that parents believed they corrected, the slower the language development of their children (Wells, 1985, p. 351).

4 Social interaction

The interaction between the child and the parents has often been seen in recent years as the mainspring of language acquisition. Correction, approval, or imitation are different types of social exchange between the child and the parent; even if these do not carry sufficient weight separately, perhaps the child learns through a number of such routines. Jerome Bruner for instance attaches particular importance to 'formats'; a format is 'a standardized initially microcosmic interaction pattern between an adult and an infant that contains demarcated roles that eventually become reversible' (Bruner, 1983, pp. 120–1), an example being the complex evolution of peekaboo games. Or take the following Bristol exchange:

Father: Are you a mucky pup?
Child: No.
Father: Yes you are.
Child: No.
Father: Yes you are.

This seems a well-practised routine; the child may learn question formation in English by seeing how the question:

Are you a mucky pup?

relates to the declarative sentence:

Yes you are.

Many, if not most, researchers into child language in the past decade have connected the child's linguistic development on the one hand to the development of semantic meanings, on the other to social interaction. Bruner (1983, p. 34) talks of 'two theories of language acquisition; one of them, empiricist associationism, was impossible; the other, nativism, was miraculous. But the void between the impossible and the miraculous was soon to be filled in', in his view by showing how the child mastered 'the social world as well as the physical' (p. 39).

The arguments against social routines providing adequate evidence will be familiar by now; they provide positive evidence rather than negative evidence; there is a leap from routines to the creative use of language. This is not to deny that such exchanges are vital for building up the use of language, pragmatic competence; 'it would not be at all surprising to find that normal language learning requires use of language in real-life situations, in some way' (Chomsky, 1965, p. 33). But UG theory aims to explain grammatical rather than pragmatic competence; principles of UG are incapable of being learnt by social interaction. Whatever degree of importance one assigns to principles such as structure-dependency or Binding, it is clear they are not learnable through routines, however elaborate.

The 'poverty of the stimulus' argument, which maintains that the evidence is inherently too impoverished for the child to be able to acquire UG principles, should be distinguished from an earlier claim made by Chomsky, namely the 'degeneracy of the data'. Language acquisition is made more difficult by the fact that children hear performance, which may contain a high proportion of mistakes, slips of the tongue, and so on; part of the positive evidence is misleading and has to be ignored by the learner. A model of language learning cannot be predicated on children hearing only grammatical sentences; it has to be able to tolerate a certain amount of ungrammaticality. However, the claim that the data is degenerate has to be modified in the light of the research of the 1970s into language addressed to children, which showed that it was highly regular; Newport (1977) found that only 1 out of 1500 utterances addressed to children was ungrammatical. Such regularity, however, applies only to the language addressed directly to the child; children also overhear adult performance addressed to fellow adults, with the usual quota of deviancies. Nevertheless, the main argument has to concentrate on the impoverished nature of the data rather than its degeneracy. Many claims and counterclaims about speech addressed to children have indeed been made in recent years. To take Bruner again as a representative, he postulates a Language Acquisition Support System in parents' minds that enables them to provide the appropriate linguistic environment for their children; 'Language is not encountered willy-nilly by the child; it is shaped to make communicative interaction effective – fine-tuned' (Bruner, 1983, p. 39). Even if such fine-tuning or indeed any other linguistic behaviour by the parent could teach the principles of UG, it would still have to meet the uniformity requirement that all parents use it, which seems unlikely.

5 Dependence on other faculties

The other major alternative is that language acquisition depends upon general cognitive development. The basic issue is the autonomy of the language faculty. It is not denied that in actual use the production and comprehension of language depends upon other mental faculties and physical systems, although, as we see later, it is tricky to disentangle them. What *is* denied is that language acquisition depends upon other faculties. Piaget typically claims that the symbolic function of language depends upon the general semiotic function that develops out of the sensorimotor stage of cognitive development. The book *Language and Learning* (Piattelli-Palmarini, 1980) provides a useful debate between Chomsky and Piaget on the issue of autonomy. Chomsky points to the complexity of the knowledge that is learnt – structure-dependency and *each other* – and denies that this could be the product of sensorimotor intelligence or of general learning theories. 'The common assumption to the contrary, that is that a general learning theory does exist, seems to me dubious, unargued, and without any empirical support or plausibility at the moment' (Chomsky, 1980b, p. 110). His usual argument is that, whatever else cognitive development can account for, it cannot explain the acquisition of language knowledge; as no one has proposed a precise way in which principles such as structure-dependency are acquired, they must be learnt in a manner specific to language. If one accepts Chomsky's premise that language consists of abstract principles such as structure-dependency and Binding, an attempt to show they are derived from other faculties must show their existence elsewhere and show how they are acquired, which he claims has not been done. The insufficiency of general cognitive development as a basis for language acquisition is demonstrated not so much by direct evidence but by challenging its advocates to show how language knowledge is learnable by such means.

The discussion has sketched standard arguments against five alternatives to the UG position. The positions outlined are of course considerably more sophisticated than the brief versions given here. But overall the discussion has found no way in which principles of UG are learnable from the environment. The chart below summarizes the argument. Positive evidence alone is insufficient to acquire the principles of UG. The alternatives to innateness are insufficient because they rely on positive evidence, or they occur too rarely or inconsistently, or they cannot explain creativity, or they cannot handle the type of knowledge that is acquired. UG theory, however, is only concerned with core grammar, not with the many other aspects of language the child has to acquire. The arguments apply to the acquisition of the syntactic core: peripheral grammar, pragmatic competence, social competence, communication skills, and so on, may well be acquired by, say, the formats of Bruner. Indeed in some way these complement Chomsky's approach by showing how the ability to use language may be acquired: 'The study of grammar will ultimately find its place in a richer investigation of how knowledge of language is acquired' (Chomsky, 1972b, p. 119).

Some insufficient ways of acquiring UG principles from the environment

	positive evidence	other evidence	occurrence	uniformity
imitation	+		–	–
explanation		+	–	–
correction		+	–	–
social interaction	+		+	–

So where does UG come from? Apart from oddities like telepathy or morphic resonance, the remaining possibility is that UG does not come from *anywhere*; it is already there. Important aspects of language are not acquired from experience; they are already present in the mind. 'The solution to Plato's problem must be based on ascribing the fixed principles of the language faculty to the human organism as part of its biological endowment' (Chomsky, 1988, p.27). The distinctive quality of Chomsky's theory compared with other models is not innateness as such. Even a theory that children learn by associating pairs of words and objects attributes to them the ability to form such associations. 'Every "theory of learning" that is even worth considering incorporates an innateness hypothesis' (Chomsky, 1976, p. 13). The differences between language learning models lie in the nature and extent of the properties they attribute to the initial state. Chomskyan theory asserts that UG is innate; rather than a black box with mysterious contents, the mind contains UG principles and parameters.

The claim for innateness could be refuted in several ways. One is to deny the poverty of the stimulus argument itself. But, so long as some aspect of language is known but not acquired from the world, the argument holds. A weaker attack is to deny that particular aspects of language are present in S_S, to reject, say, structure-dependency or Binding as part of the speaker's competence. However, structure-dependency is simply an explanation why:

   *Is the teacher who here is good?

is wrong; the only valid way of rejecting it would be to propose an alternative explanation; until that happens it is the best explanation that is available. If a better proposal is made, then it will be superseded. It seems doubtful whether any alternative principles that could account for this knowledge could be learnt either from positive evidence or from the likely non-negative evidence the child meets. The same is true of other principles. No one claims that the present principles represent the last word. But, to avoid the poverty of the stimulus argument, the alternative principles would have to be learnable in one of the ways outlined above, which seems unlikely.

A further possibility is to accept that a given aspect of language is present in S_S but to demonstrate that it could have been acquired from experience or from some other faculty in the mind. Structure-dependency might be shown to arise naturally from some environmental factors, unlikely as this may seem. Or indeed it might come from other faculties of the mind, as Anderson (1983) suggests. But dismissing a particular grammatical point from S_S does not defeat the argument itself, which could only be gainsaid by showing it applied to *no* aspect of language. Claims about innate ideas in UG theory can always be found to be wrong; contrary evidence may show up and cause specific claims to be abandoned or modified. 'An innatist hypothesis is a refutable hypothesis' (Chomsky, 1980b, p. 80). A theory based on evidence changes as more evidence comes to light, as do theories in other disciplines; UG theory is not an unsubstantiable conjecture about the mind, but a hypothesis that is open to refutation and modification. Chomsky's argument that children are born equipped with certain aspects of language is justified by precise claims based on evidence about language knowledge; each piece of final knowledge that is not derived from experience is innate – structure-dependency, Binding, or whatever. To defeat the argument involves explaining how each and all of these principles could have been acquired from experience or from other faculties.

Grammatical competence was presented as knowledge of how the principles and parameters of UG are reflected in a particular language; knowledge of English is knowledge of how English utilizes UG. This chapter has taken UG as the initial state of the language faculty, S_0; it comes from within not from without. Acquiring English means discovering how it fleshes out the properties of UG which are already present. 'A study of English is a study of the realization of the initial state S_0 under particular conditions' (KOL, p. 37). The steady state is reached by the mind using evidence to discover how UG is reflected in a particular language. When installing a new video recorder, though the clock and tuner are built-in to the machine, they still need setting to local circumstances – the time of day and the appropriate wavelengths. The final state S_S is one of the possibilities inherent in S_0, as are all the possible human languages; the contribution of experience is to decide which of these possibilities is actually realized, which wavelength is tuned to. S_0 'projects' onto the final state S_S, as a frame in a film projects onto the screen. 'We can think then of the initial state as being in effect *a function that maps experience onto the steady state*' (Chomsky, 1980b, p. 109).

Children acquire structure-dependency in English by fitting what they hear to the preexisting principle in their minds. They acquire Binding by using the principles they know and learning which words are anaphors and which are pronominals. 'Language learning, then, is the process of determining the values of the parameters left unspecified by universal grammar' (Chomsky, 1988, p. 134). They need to hear some examples of English sentences;

otherwise they have no reason for learning English rather than Japanese. The evidence encountered by the child need not be very extensive; a handful of English sentences could show how the head parameter applies, which words are anaphors, and whether the language is pro-drop. Positive evidence 'triggers' acquisition rather than being needed in large quantities; some language is necessary to set the process off, to show how the principle applies or the parameter should be set. But, unlike an E-language model, this experience does not form the primary source of information about language; a loud noise may trigger an avalanche but the noise is not part of the falling snow. Experience sets off a complex reaction in the organism; 'a central part of what we call "learning" is actually better understood as the growth of cognitive structures along an internally directed course under the triggering and partially shaping effect of the environment' (Chomsky, 1980a, p. 33). Thus, although an I-language theory, it has a place for experience in language learning – otherwise all children would end up speaking the same language. 'The environment determines the way the parameters of universal grammar are set, yielding different languages' (Chomsky, 1988, p. 134). Provision of appropriate input is completely necessary; indeed with certain rare constructions accelerated learning may take place if suitable triggering is provided; Cromer (1987) shows that children given ten examples of the construction seen in *The wolf is easy to bite* every three months were, at the end of the year, on average way ahead of those not given this exposure.

The last chapter stressed the view of UG as limitations on language; it cuts down the potentially infinite number of languages to the smaller number of possible human languages by imposing strong restrictions on their syntactic form. UG is a collection of restrictions on core grammar; the grammar of English consists of one combination of these restrictions, the grammar of Chinese another. Children narrow down the infinite possibilities of human language to the one that they actually learn via UG. Given that a language could be anything at all, untold millions of children each year choose English, or French, or whatever language they are learning, out of the diverse possibilities; 'the system of UG is so designed that given appropriate evidence, only a single candidate language is made available . . .' (KOL, p. 83). Hence the reason why children learn language speedily, easily, and uniformly, and apes and computers do not, is that UG narrows down the choices open to them.

The Physical Basis for Universal Grammar

Acquisition of language is, to Chomsky, learning in a peculiar sense: it is not acquisition of information from outside the organism, as we acquire, say, facts about geography; it is not like learning to ride a bicycle where practice develops and adapts existing skills. Instead it is internal development in response to vital, but comparatively trivial experience from outside. To make an analogy, a seed is planted in the ground, which grows and eventually flowers; the growth would not take place without the environment; it needs water, minerals, and sunshine; but the entire possibility of the plant is inherent in the seed; the environment only dictates the extent to which its inherited potentialities are realized. Knowledge of language needs experience to mature; without it nothing would happen; but the entire potential is there from the start. Chomsky argues that language acquisition is more akin to growing than to learning; it is the maturing of the mind according to a preset biological clock. 'In certain fundamental respects we do not really learn language; rather grammar grows in the mind' (Chomsky, 1980a, p. 134). Language is part of the human inheritance; it is in our genes. As Lenneberg (1967) pointed out, to become a speaker of a human language does not require a particular size of brain – dwarfs speak perfectly normally; it does not require a particular type of interaction with adults. The requirements for learning a human language are to be a human being and to have the minimal exposure to language evidence necessary to trigger the various parameters of UG.

The physical basis of UG means that it is part of the human genetic inheritance, a part of biology rather than psychology; 'universal grammar is part of the genotype specifying one aspect of the initial state of the human mind and brain . . .' (Chomsky, 1980a, p. 82). Like other inherited attributes this does not rule out variation between individuals. Most introductory linguistics books assert that all human children can learn all human languages. An 'English' child transported to Japan, a 'Japanese' child transported to England, grow up with competences identical to those of children born of Japanese or English parents. If this is due to common genetic inheritance, some individual variation might be expected; all human beings have eyes but some are brown, some blue, some green. At the moment the common features of UG in all human minds need to be established before variations that show up between individuals can be investigated. It is how the human eye works that is of basic importance, not minor variations of colour. 'The main topic is the uniformity of development . . . it could ultimately be an interesting question whether there is genetic variation that shows up in language somewhere' (Chomsky, 1982c, p. 25). While the bulk of UG seems common to all human beings, this assumption is not based on proof that, say, 'English' native speakers of Japanese have identical competences to 'Japanese' speakers of Japanese.

The language organ is also held to be the property only of human brains: people speak; dogs do not. Various attempts have been made to refute Chomsky's claim that the language faculty is species-specific. The usual approach is to teach another species a simplified form of English, using some other means of expression than the vocal apparatus such as gestures, or visual signs. Gardner and Gardner (1971) taught a chimpanzee, Washoe, sign language to a level where she reacted differently to the signed sentences:

baby mine

and:

mine baby

Patterson (1981) taught sign language to a gorilla, Koko, so that she could create new sentences such as the signed equivalent to:

cookie rock

to describe a stale bun. Does this not show that other species can learn language?

One objection is that the languages involved do not contain anything resembling the principles of UG; whatever the ape has acquired, it is not core grammar. The ape's knowledge might be peripheral or it might be functional knowledge of how to achieve things through questions but it is not language knowledge as a UG system. Chomsky's ingenious rebuttal to this argument is to consider teaching human beings to fly; perhaps 'the distinction between jumping and flying is arbitrary, a matter of degree; people can really fly, just like birds, only not so well' (Chomsky, 1976, p. 41). Chomsky's main objection is that the learning described does not resemble language acquisition in children because it is taught rather than 'picked up'. Children learn language from positive evidence rather than reinforcement by their parents. The apes, however, are all *taught* language; in the wild, apes do not develop language for themselves. The child 'does not choose to learn, and cannot fail to learn under normal conditions' (Chomsky, 1976, p. 71). The role of the environment to the child is triggering; it sets things off rather than provides precise controlled instruction. Even if the attempt to *teach* language to apes were successful, it would not prove how animals could *acquire* language. To sum up, 'the interesting investigations of the capacity of the higher apes to acquire symbolic systems seem to me to support the traditional belief that even the most rudimentary properties of language lie well beyond the capacities of an otherwise intelligent ape' (Chomsky, 1980a, p. 239). Nor do the accounts of ape language demonstrate that even this level of language is attained, as argued in a review article (Seidenberg, 1986).

Parameter-setting

Let us look more closely at how children acquire settings for parameters, so that they learn that Spanish is a pro-drop language, French is not; English is head-first, Japanese is head-last; and so on. The parameters in the child's mind can be thought of as built-in switches, each to be turned to suit the language that is heard. 'The transition from the initial state S_0 to the steady state S_S is a matter of setting the switches' (KOL, p. 146). Acquiring the grammar of English means setting all UG parameters the English way. Continuing to use pro-drop as an example, the setting of the switch is triggered by evidence. The evidence that English children hear enables them to discover it is a non-pro-drop language; the evidence that Spanish children hear enables them to discover it is a pro-drop language. Somewhere in what children hear is the trigger that sets the value for the parameter. Children must be learning either from positive evidence alone or from indirect negative evidence – the lack of null subject sentences in English. This is possible only if their choice is circumscribed; if they know there are two possibilities, pro-drop or non-pro-drop, they only require evidence to tell them which one they have encountered. Hearing a few sentences is sufficient to set the parameter one way or the other. The logic of indirect negative evidence, as Chomsky sees it, is 'if certain structures or rules fail to be exemplified in relatively simple expressions, where they would be expected to be found, then a (possibly marked) option is selected excluding them in the grammar, so that a kind of "negative evidence" can be available even without correction, adverse reactions, etc.' (LGB, p. 9). Indirect negative evidence does not circumvent the poverty of the stimulus argument because it relies on the child's expectation of certain principles; in other words it presupposes innateness.

We can distinguish three logical possibilities for parameters in the initial state S_0:

1 The switch is in a neutral position; the child is equally prepared for pro-drop or non-pro-drop. In this case the interim stages in the child's development of grammar might have either setting for pro-drop; children learning Spanish and English would have no common sequence of acquisition but would set the parameter appropriately from whenever they first use it.

2 The switch is set to non-pro-drop. The child initially assumes that INFL governs the subject in all languages and so needs evidence to set it differently in pro-drop languages; children learning English would use one setting from the beginning and would have no need to change it; children learning Spanish would start with a non-pro-drop setting and would change with time, triggered by evidence.

3 The switch is set to pro-drop, the reverse position; those learning non-pro-drop languages are now the ones who require evidence; those learning Spanish need no extra evidence, those learning English do.

The most extensive study of child language within the current GB model is Nina Hyams' book *Language Acquisition and the Theory of Parameters* (Hyams, 1986), which is specifically concerned with pro-drop. By analysing published examples of children's language, she found that English children at the earlier stages indeed produced null subject sentences such as:

Read bear book.

and:

Want look a man.

These were not due to the children's limited capacity to handle information since at the same time they could produce equivalent sentences with subjects such as:

Gia ride bike.

and:

I want kiss it.

Nor was it a performance clipping of the initial *I* since the children also had null subjects which were not at the beginning of the sentence. Hyams concluded that the third of the above alternatives is correct for pro-drop: children start from the setting for the parameter that allows null-subject sentences whether they are learning English, German, or Spanish. English and German children go on to learn that their languages are non-pro-drop, setting the switch away from its initial value.

There is still no explanation for how the child does this. Let us look at the evidence available to the child. It might seem that indirect negative evidence suffices to acquire pro-drop; noticing a lack of null subject sentences, the child switches to non-pro-drop. However, this involves the child keeping track not just of those sentences that occur but also of those that do not; when, say, 500 sentences have been heard and not one null subject sentence is among them, the switch reverses. Apart from the difficulties with the occasional subjectless sentence the child will hear for accidental or dialectal reasons, this involves a striking feat of memory.

Nina Hyams presents a solution in which the child learns from positive evidence, using a slightly different syntactic analysis from that given here. This rests on a further property of non-pro-drop languages alluded to briefly in chapter 2, namely the presence of 'expletives' such as *there* and *it* as subjects. A non-pro-drop language such as English uses an impersonal indefinite *it* in constructions such as 'weather' sentences:

It's raining.

Italian cannot use *it* in this way but must have a null subject sentence:

Piove. (rains)

Similarly English has 'existential' sentences with *there* such as:

There's a tide in the affairs of men which taken at the flood leads on to fortune.

which also has a meaningless 'dummy' *there* in subject position. In other words it is a sign of a non-pro-drop language to have lexical expletives like *there* and *it* acting as subject; Hyams suggests that the trigger to tell the child to set the parameter away from the initial pro-drop value is the presence of such expletive subjects. When English children hear:

Once upon a time there were three bears.

or:

It's time for bed.

they realize that English is non-pro-drop and this affects the whole complex of syntactic phenomena covered by the parameter. Hyams supports this by showing that English children acquire expletive subjects at about the time they acquire full lexical subjects. Thus the child is setting the switch from positive evidence alone, namely the use of *there* and *it* as subjects, rather than from the indirect negative evidence of the lack of null subject sentences.

Other parameters have not been extensively studied in first language acquisition, with the exception of **Principal Branching Direction (PBD)** derived from Chomsky (1964) – 'the branching direction which holds consistently in unmarked form over major recursive structures of a language' (Lust, 1983), i.e. on which side of the head certain constructions such as relative clauses appear in the phrases of a language – a variation on the head parameter. PBD is thus an aspect of the head parameter applying to the embedding of subordinate clauses. It is phrased in terms of branching direction to right or left; confusingly a language with a right PBD will be head-first, and vice versa. English has the relative clause to the right of the Noun, as in:

The child who eats the rice is crying.

where the relative clause *who eats the rice* appears to the right of the head N *child* within the NP. English also typically has the subordinate clause after the main clause as in:

The child drank the milk after he ate the rice.

The Principal Branching Direction of English is therefore Right. Japanese on the other hand has the relative clause on the left of the noun, as in:

Go han o tabete iru ko ga naite imasu.
(rice eating is child crying is)

and the subordinate clause before the main clause:

Kodomo ga gohan o tabete kara okahsan wa sooji shita.
(child rice eating after mother cleared up)

The PBD of Japanese is therefore Left (again the equivalent to saying its setting for the head parameter is head-last). PBD is, according to Lust, 'a principle of natural language variation with extensive consequences for a language' (Lust, 1983, p. 141). She claims that children from the start are sensitive to the PBD of the language they are learning. Thus English children are more successful at imitating:

John ate and read.

which conforms to its Right PBD by omitting the subject on the right:

John ate and (John) read.

than they are at imitating:

John and Mary ate lunch.

which goes against the PBD by omitting the Verb Phrase on the left, i.e.

John (ate lunch) and Mary ate lunch.

However Japanese children are better at imitating:

Zubon to seitaa o kiru
(pants and sweater put on)

where the omission is on the left:

(pants (put on) and sweater put on)

than:

Onigiri o tsukutte taberu.
(riceball make and eat)

where the omission is on the right:

(riceball make and (riceball) eat)

They too prefer sentences that conform to the PBD of their language. With PBD the initial setting appears to be neutral; evidence switches it to the left or the right.

Using a limited number of such parameters, UG cuts down on the possible core grammars the child can choose from. Ideally, given the evidence that the child has available, UG should narrow the possible grammars down to one; 'the system of UG is so designed that given appropriate evidence, only a single candidate language is made available, this language being a specific realization of the principles of the initial state S_0 with certain options settled in one way or another by the presented evidence (e.g., the value for the head parameter)' (KOL, pp. 83–4). The evidence for fixing parameters need only be sufficient to trigger them and may be readily available. 'The parameters must have the property that they can be fixed by quite simple evidence, because this is what is available to the child; the value of the head parameter, for example, can be determined from such sentences as *John saw Bill* (versus *John Bill saw*)' (KOL, p. 146). The effects of such parameters are sweeping; they are not confined to one rule or construction but apply anywhere in the grammar. Thus the pro-drop parameter is a choice in the theory of government, a principle that pervades the grammar, not just an explanation for the occurrence of null subject sentences in some languages.

The discussion of acquisition is no longer concerned with what happens in a single language; the interest lies in finding how the child's UG can cope equally well with different languages. Most experimental or observational work with children has dealt with the acquisition of particular rules in a language – how the child learns question formation, or passives, or relative clauses. From a UG perspective such work is at best partial. Rules such as question formation are not 'pure' discrete phenomena that can be studied in their own right but involve many principles, each of which has some contribution to make; rule-based research is misleading. Research needs to examine how a principle or a parameter is employed across the board in the child's grammar. Even the examples used here run some risk of becoming construction specific; the discussion of null subject sentences may seem to concern a single sentence type rather than an underlying principle that manifests itself in this sentence type as well as elsewhere. So far, work that directly tackles the implications of the principles model for development has hardly been tackled in the context of first language acquisition, with the exception of that cited by Hyams and Lust. First language acquisition studied in a UG context needs both to encompass a variety of languages and also to deal with principles and parameters rather than rules.

Markedness and Language Development

UG is concerned with core grammar rather than with the periphery. The logical argument of acquisition deals primarily with the core, with the elements that are directly related to UG. Peripheral elements can be learned in ways that are unlinked to UG. Politeness formulas such as *please* and *thank you* may well be learnt through active correction by the parents;

historical accidents such as *The more the merrier* are not necessarily learnt through UG or entirely from positive evidence. The same idealizations are involved in acquisition as in the description of competence; it is grammatical knowledge that is being discussed, not language performance or language use; within language knowledge the crucial areas are those that are universal.

Within the core, one possibility is that certain parameter settings are more marked than others; languages that have syntactic movement for instance may be closer to UG than those that do not, making English unmarked, Japanese marked. With the opposite assumption, English is marked, and Japanese is not. Going back to pro-drop, the conclusion that all children start with a pro-drop setting means that non-pro-drop is more marked. Children start off with the unmarked setting for the parameters; they have to reset those which are more marked in the language they are learning.

Markedness also relates to the problem of evidence available to the child. One interpretation is that the unmarked settings of parameters are those that the child can learn from the least amount of positive evidence. Spanish learners need no evidence to set pro-drop; they have the right setting from the start. Children learning English need evidence to turn the switch away from its initial unmarked setting, if we accept Hyams' account. Children need evidence to move from unmarked to marked settings. Hence marked elements of UG need more evidence, or different types of evidence, than unmarked elements. Elements of peripheral grammar may need totally different types of evidence; for example the *was/were* distinction in English might need specific negative correction from parents.

Complementary to this approach to markedness is the **Subset Principle**:

> **if a parameter has two values + and −, and the value − generates a proper subset of the grammatical sentences generated with the choice of value +, then − is the "unmarked value" selected in the absence of evidence.** (Chomsky, KOL, p. 146).

Roughly speaking, children choose the setting for a parameter that fits the evidence with the least possible assumptions. The children's choice is conservative in that it stays as close to the data they hear as possible. They prefer a language that is a 'subset' of a larger language rather than leaping immediately to the 'larger' version. This is slightly difficult to accommodate within the discussion here since it concerns the 'languages' the children learn rather than 'grammars'. Wexler and Manzini (1987) show how the Subset Principle deals with the learning of the Binding Principles but feel it does not apply to the type of evidence for pro-drop presented by Hyams (1986).

There are general problems in interpreting data from the actual language development of children in relation to markedness. The study of children's speech is potentially misleading for the logical problem of acquisition. As with adults, grammatical competence is imperfectly reflected in speech performance; children too can run out of breath, or make mistakes, or change their minds. The psychological processes used in speech comprehension and production are indirectly and partially linked to their grammatical competence. To study the competence of adults, an alternative source of evidence is available in the form of judgements about sentences, a device used frequently in this book. Such judgements are hardly feasible with small children. However large the sample of children's utterances, it is still an inaccurate source of information about their competence.

In addition the processes involved in language performance are themselves developing at the same time as competence. Filtering out the effects of performance processes from actual samples of speech is doubly difficult with children since it cannot be assumed that only language develops. The child starts by saying one word at a time:

Mine. Bath. Yes. Car. Carses. Hiding.

and goes on to a two-word stage:

That baba. All gone. A lion. Little girl. See Mary.

Both stages may be the by-product of short-term memory restrictions that limit the number of items in the child's utterance rather than of anything directly to do with language acquisition; 'it might be that he had fully internalized the requisite mental structure, but for some reason lacked the capacity to use it' (Chomsky, 1980a, p. 53). The apparent progress from one word to two words may have little to do with language acquisition, more to do with the growth of 'channel capacity'. The expansion of children's general cognitive capacity allows them to produce longer and more complex sentences, but this is caused by relaxing constraints on performance rather than by increased competence. In Chomsky's words, 'much of the investigation of early language development is concerned with matters that may not properly belong to the language faculty ... but to other faculties of mind that interact in an intimate fashion with the language faculty in language use ...' (Chomsky, 1981b, p. 36). Acquisition considered as a logical problem is an abstraction from such features of development. The history of speech developing in the child reflects factors that are nothing to do with acquisition.

I shall make a distinction between language **acquisition** – the logical problem of how the mind acquires S_S independent of intervening stages – and language **development** – the history of the intervening stages; the distinction reflects Chomsky's thinking, even if he does not make it in these terms. Acquisition is an idealized 'instantaneous' model in which time and experience play minimal roles; the crucial factor is the relationship between S_0 and S_S. Development reflects the complex interaction of language with the other faculties of mind that are maturing at the same time. Research into both acquisition and development is concerned with evidence, the former with evidence of what speakers know, the latter with evidence from what children say. Acquisition theory does not necessarily need support from actual studies of children's language; 'behavior is only one kind of evidence, sometimes not the best, and surely no criterion for knowledge' (Chomsky, 1980a, p. 54). While some studies such as Hyams' have attempted the complex task of linking development with acquisition, there is no compelling reason why the theory should accept them as more than supplementary evidence.

It is then possible to assign markedness as a *post hoc* consequence of developmental studies. If the pro-drop setting is used first, then, everything else being equal, this is a reason for preferring pro-drop as the unmarked setting. But everything else rarely is equal because of the complexity of actual development. 'We would expect the order of appearance of structures in language acquisition to reflect the structure of markedness in some respects, but there are many complicating factors: e.g., processes of maturation may be such as to permit certain unmarked structures to be manifested only relatively late in language acquisition, frequency effects may intervene, etc.' (LGB, p. 9). Assigning markedness on the basis of developmental stages is circular if there is no other reason for a setting to be unmarked than its earlier occurrence; without a syntactic rationale, markedness amounts to saying 'whatever is learnt first is learnt first'.

It might also be that the language faculty itself matures. Babies have lungs and hearts that function from the time that they are born; however the first teeth appear around seven months, and are replaced by others around six years; wisdom teeth appear much later. This does not mean that teeth are not biologically determined; they appear at particular stages of maturation even if absent at the beginning; 'genetically determined factors in development evidently are not to be identified with those operative at birth' (KOL, p. 54). UG might be like the heart – complete and functional at birth – or like teeth – coming into operation bit by bit; these alternatives are called by Chomsky the 'growth' theory and the 'no growth' theory (Chomsky, 1987). So far as acquisition is concerned, UG is neutral between the two possibilities; the relationship between the two states, S_0 and S_S is not affected by whether UG is initially present or not. It is however vital to the development argument.

Let us borrow the term **wild grammar** from Helen Goodluck (1986) to refer to a grammar that does not conform to UG, by, say, breaking the principles or having illegal parameter settings. If UG is present and functioning from the start, children would never entertain wild grammars; children would not stray outside the bounds of UG at any stage of development; their learning would be error-free so far as UG is concerned. A UG principle such as structure-dependency will be used at all stages of development. This is not to say it initially figures prominently in their speech; it may be precluded for performance reasons of sentence length or complexity; a principle of Binding for example can hardly be used in one-word to two-word sentences. But, if there are no wild grammars, none of the children's grammars should violate structure dependency or Binding at any stage; all of their interim grammars should be possible human languages.

Research into language development to investigate this is necessarily complex and tentative. Anecdotal observations suggest that children rarely produce sentences that breach UG. But this is hardly surprising in view of the complexity of the sentences that are needed to show many UG principles combined with the constraints on the child's performance; there are no opportunities for breaking structure dependency with one word sentences, for example.

More concrete work has been carried out by Matthei (1981). He used an earlier version of the Binding Principles in which the grammaticality of:

The men like each other.

but not:

*The men want John to like each other.

was explained in terms of a 'clausemate condition' that *each other* must corefer within the same tensed clause with a specified subject. If children never possessed wild grammars, and Binding were in operation from the beginning, they would make no mistakes with such sentences. Alternatively 'the appearance of this mental characteristic may be delayed many years after birth, and may be conditional on the triggering effect of relevant experience' (Chomsky, 1980b, p. 43). Matthei considered not only the no wild grammars possibility but two versions of wild grammars: in one, children learn how the principle applies by making use of other information in the sentence; the presence of *that* or of an *ed* ending may be crucial. In the other, children have to learn the specific piece of information that *each other* is an anaphor rather than a pronominal. He asked seventeen children aged between four and six to show their comprehension of sentences such as:

The horses said that the cows jumped over each other.

by demonstrating who jumped over whom. The results showed that they could entertain wild grammars in that they often made the horses jump over the cows, i.e. the coreference for *each other* goes out of the local domain, contrary to Principle A of Binding Theory. Their comprehension was not helped by the presence of *that* or *ed*; nor did they suddenly discover that *each other* was an anaphor, and consistently get it right. Thus none of his three suggestions were completely confirmed. Though the results show little positively, they indicate a possibility that wild grammars exist in the child's development, and hence that some aspects of UG develop with time.

It is perfectly plausible that UG matures. Lila Gleitman has often argued for a biologically determined maturational transition from a semantic phase of language to a syntactic phase; at the first stage the child produces sentences to convey meaning without regard to their syntax; at the next stage the child

abruptly switches to syntactic organization. Her evidence is based on a variety
of forms of acquisition including acquisition by Down's syndrome children,
blind children, deaf children and premature children (Gleitman, 1982).
Chomsky's view that early stages of development are nothing to do with
acquisition supports the possibility of a presyntactic phase; UG may simply
not be available to the very young child, who gets by on semantics alone.
Chomsky separates this line of thinking firmly from the logical problem of
language acquisition; 'there is good reason to believe that the language faculty
undergoes maturation – in fact, the order and timing of this maturation appear
to be rather uniform despite considerable variation in experience and other
cognitive faculties – but this does not bear on the correctness of the empirical
assumption embodied in the idealization to instantaneous learning . . .' (KOL,
p. 54). The further possibility that UG becomes unavailable after a certain age
will be discussed in chapter 7.

Let us review briefly the main argument for the innateness of UG. The first
step is to recognize the complex and abstract grammatical competence
possessed by the native speaker. The distinctive nature of this knowledge
rules out its acquisition through imitation, correction and approval, social
routines, or other mental faculties; grammatical explanation is ruled out for
other reasons. Unless the principles and parameters of grammatical
competence can be shown to be learnable by one or other of these means,
they must be innate. This central argument is bolstered by other arguments
about the common possession of language by the whole human species, the
uniformity of acquisition despite the variety of situations, the lack of key
mistakes in children's speech, and the inability of other species to acquire
language. But the crucial step is the first one; once it is conceded that
language knowledge is defined in terms of a grammatical competence of this
kind, everything else follows.

How does it relate to other approaches to language acquisition? The UG
position that has been presented is, broadly speaking, popular among linguists
rather than those primarily interested in studying first language acquisition in
children. Actual research into child language from a UG perspective has not
been carried out on a wide scale compared to the masses of studies of
discourse interaction, etc; apart from the books mentioned by Hyams and
Lust and three collections edited by Tavakolian (1981), Goodluck and Solan
(1978), and Otsu et al (1983) the remaining literature is chiefly unpublished
PhD theses.

The reasons for this neglect are that firstly, in a sense the study of children
is unnecessary in UG theory since all that the linguist needs to do is to work
backwards from S_S, the final state. The primary work is the linguistic
description and the use of learnability arguments to motivate the description.
E-language research with large numbers of children is secondary though it
can provide some supporting evidence, if it is properly evaluated. Secondly,
experimental or observational research on UG issues is hard to carry out. The
necessity of separating competence from performance and acquisition from

development means on the one hand that actual observations of children are flawed, on the other appropriate methodologies for experiments are extremely hard to devise. Matthei's experiment presents three hypotheses for example, none of which is confirmed by the results, not a very satisfactory experimental design.

The impression one is left with is that most workers in child language are not prepared to take the first step of accepting that the essential part of language is grammatical competence. They may concede that it is a quaint logical problem, but claim that what really interests them is how children form social relationships, how their thinking influences their language, how children with language problems can be helped, all side-issues to UG theory. To those with primarily sociological or educational or indeed E-language aims in general, UG theory has comparatively little to offer; it is concerned with mental man rather than with social man, and with what human beings have in common rather than their differences. In my view UG indeed provides a core test case of the essential quality of human minds; the type of knowledge revealed as part of the structure of the brain is fascinating and profound. Supporting it with research into children's language is a valuable exercise. UG theory has a unique central place in first language acquisition studies. But it is only part of the broad picture. UG theory is concerned with the acorn rather than with the tree in all its complexity; vital as the acorn may be as the source of growth and development, for many purposes the leaves, the wood, the fruit, or the eventual coal are more important. The danger is to see UG as a threat to other ideas of language development, rather than as a complementary theory that accounts for a specific area of vital concern to those interested in the unique properties of the human mind but of less relevance to those, say, who are encouraging the speech of a language-delayed child.

4 X-bar Theory and θ-Theory

Chapters 4 to 6 present the technical details of the principles and parameters theory, illustrated through English. Certain adaptations have been made for ease of exposition; in particular *Barriers* (Chomsky, 1986b) yielded several major alterations to the theory, whose significance and durability is not yet altogether clear; while certain of these innovations are adopted here, some compromise has been made to give the reader access to the more standard ideas. It should also be pointed out that syntactic trees are used as diagrams to help the reader visualize aspects of the sentence, but cannot be fully accurate representations of the principles and parameters model, as argued in Chomsky (1982a, pp. 14–15). The most logical order of presentation would be to treat each component separately. However, since the theory is an interlocking arrangement of principles and sub-theories which interact in many different ways, no part can be considered in isolation from the rest. Nor can the theory be tackled through particular grammatical rules such as 'passive' or 'questions', since these represent the interaction of principles rather than being syntactic areas in their own right. Inevitably a certain initial suspension of disbelief is required until all the parts of the theory are assembled together. This chapter starts with the general idea of phrase structure, which leads in to the X-bar theory of constituent structure; it goes on to the interaction of syntax and the lexicon via the Projection Principle, and to the aspects of meaning covered in θ-theory; it concludes with some recent extensions to the theory of X-bar syntax.

Phrase Structure

Before looking at syntax in detail, we need to review the concept of **phrase structure**, which comes at its heart. Phrase structure is a way of capturing the structural relationships of the sentence through the concept 'consists of'. A phrase consists of one or more constituents; a phrase A may consist of the constituents B and C as seen in the following tree diagram:

These constituents may in turn be made up of others, say B consisting of D and E.

The phrase structure of the sentence is a hierarchy that proceeds from the largest constituent in the sentence downwards, each constituent successively consisting of other constituents, until only single items are left. The 'consists of' relationship can be put in tree diagrams or expressed as rewrite rules – a formal statement that the constituent on the left consists of the constituents on the right:

$$A \rightarrow B\ C$$

means that A has two parts, B and C, with the arrow replacing 'consists of'. Or the same structure can be shown as labelled bracketting:

$$[_A\ [_B\ D\ E]_B\ C]_A$$

While each of these three possibilities conveys the same insight about the phrase structure, one of them may be more convenient for tackling a particular area of the theory than the others.

Turning to an English example, the sentence (S):

The baby likes the toy.

consists of a Noun Phrase (NP) and a Verb Phrase (VP), i.e.:

$$S \atop {NP \quad VP}$$

or, put as a rewrite rule:

$$S \rightarrow NP\ VP$$

The NP *the baby* consists of a **determiner (det)** and a **Noun (N)**:

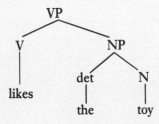

The VP *likes the toy* consists of a Verb (V) and a further NP, which also consists of a *det* and an N:

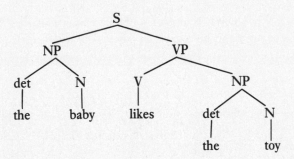

The phrase structure for the whole sentence can be shown as:

An item that comes above another item in the tree is said to 'dominate' it; in the second tree A dominates everything in the tree – B, C, D, and E; B only dominates D and E; C dominates nothing. In the last tree S again dominates everything in the sentence; the NP dominates *det* and N; the VP dominates V, NP, *det* and N. When the item is immediately above another this is termed 'immediate domination'; while S dominates everything in the tree, it immediately dominates only NP and VP; VP dominates V, NP, *det* and N, but immediately dominates only V and NP.

This analysis embodies a decision about syntax that is crucial to later discussion, namely the division of S into NP and VP rather than into NP, V, and NP. Translated into traditional grammatical terms, it divides the sentence into subject and predicate, rather than into subject, verb, and object. The reason for preferring a two-way split between NP and VP over a three-way split between NP, V, and NP is that the relationship between the subject NP and the verb is different from that between the object NP and the verb; for example subjects and verbs agree in number but objects and verbs do not.

This 'asymmetry' between subjects and objects enters into many areas of syntax. Chomsky points out that the NP VP division 'is empirical, therefore controversial, but it appears to be well supported by cross-linguistic evidence of varied types' (KOL, p. 59). Indeed he claims that children could not learn the NP VP division from positive evidence, and so it must be innate: 'UG must restrict the rules of phrase structure so that only the VP analysis is available at the relevant level of representation' (KOL, p. 62).

S-structure is the keystone of the bridge linking sounds and meanings in the GB model. The s-structure of:

Jane hated coffee.

can be shown as:

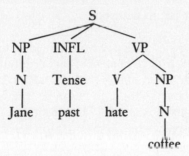

This representation incorporates the element INFL (Inflection) which does not appear as an actual word in the sentence but consists of Tense, which in turn consists of *past*, and other features not show here. At the moment Tense appears in the wrong place in the tree, and needs to be attached to the end of the Verb; this is handled by a type of movement to be seen later. The Phonetic Form component turns *past* into the appropriate past tense form; *hate past* becomes *hated* and *hate present* becomes *hates*. INFL includes features such as AGR (Agreement) and modal auxiliaries such as *will*. While INFL can be shown in the form of a tree, in many ways it behaves as if it were a complex of features rather than branching into separate constituents. The constituents of S are NP, INFL, and VP, i.e.:

S → NP INFL VP

So far, the description of the sentence has employed S as its top category. GB syntax however recognizes two types of sentence, S and S' (S-bar). The bracketting convention introduced earlier now needs to be expanded to include **labelled bracketting**, that is to say giving not only the bracket surrounding the constituent but also the name of the syntactic category. S' contains a constituent called COMP which is not found in S; COMP may be filled by complementizers such as *that, for,* or *whether*, as in:

They said [$_{S'}$ that she was happy].
They asked [$_{S'}$ for her to pass].

and:

They wondered [$_{S'}$ whether she would pass].

S on the other hand does not have a COMP constituent, and so has no possible complementizer. It is possible to say:

They believed [$_S$ her to be happy].

but not:

*They believed [$_S$ that her to be happy].

since the S here has no COMP for *that* to belong to (although of course *believe* can also be used with S′ sentences that rightfully contain *that*).

The definition of S′ does not require COMP necessarily to be filled; although COMP is always present in S′, it can be 'empty'. The main sentence itself is in fact an S′ with an empty COMP constituent. The rule given earlier can now be revised to read:

S′ → COMP S
S → NP INFL VP

The tree of the sentence:

Jane hated coffee.

is now:

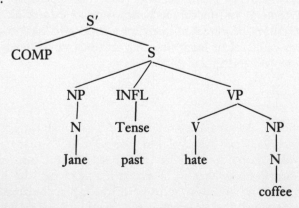

Although COMP is empty, it is still there in the structure of the sentence.

The usefulness of such empty COMPs, particularly for the movement of questioned elements, will not be apparent till later.

The PF component describes how s-structure is realized, how it gets a representation in terms of sounds; it takes:

Jane hated coffee.

and specifies how *Jane*, *hate*, and *coffee* are pronounced, and whether *ed* is realized as one of the regular endings /t/, /d/, or /ɪd/, or as an irregular form such as *went* or *hit*. Such details are irrelevant so far as syntactic description is concerned; for s-structure it does not matter how *Jane* is pronounced or which form of *past* is used; it is the presence of the word *Jane* and of the abstract element *past* that needs to be taken into account, not the details of how *past* is conveyed. The component of Logical Form on the other hand acts as an interface between the s-structure and the semantic component; it puts the syntactic meaning of the sentence in an appropriate form so that a semantic representation for the sentence can eventually be found, giving the meanings of *Jane*, *hate*, and *coffee*, the relationship between *Jane* and *coffee*, the meaning of *past*, and so on. The details of phonetic representation are unimportant so far as LF are concerned. The PF and LF components interpret s-structure by giving it different representations. They add nothing to the s-structure but 'interpret' it for their own ends.

GB theory also requires a d-structure level at which properties of the sentence are stated that are obscured in the s-structure. Questions with wh-words such as *what*, or *who* reflect the movement of a questioned constituent (a wh-phrase) to the front of the sentence. To talk about movement at all implies movement *from* somewhere *to* somewhere; as well as s-structure there must be an underlying form of the sentence, the d-structure, at which movement has not taken place. The d-structure of:

What will Steve have?

is, ignoring the movement of *will* for purposes of discussion:

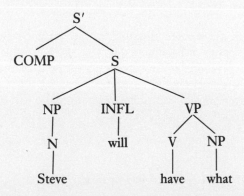

The relationship between s-structure and d-structure is movement: s-structure equals d-structure plus movement; d-structure exists to indicate where items in the s-structure have come from. The sign that movement has taken place is the presence of *t* (trace), which marks the location in s-structure from which something has been moved. The tree of the s-structure of:

What will Steve have?

is:

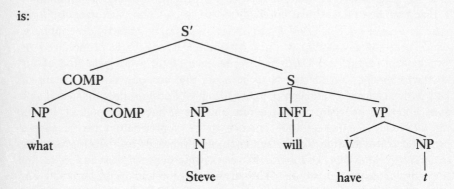

The function of *t* is to show where the wh-phrase *what* has been moved from. It can now be seen that one of the uses of COMP is, roughly speaking, to provide a place in the structure of the sentence for a questioned element to move to. The wh-phrase is attached to COMP by creating a new branch from COMP to which it can be attached alongside a new example of COMP; this analysis, technically called 'Chomsky-adjunction', is necessary given the phrase structures used so far but will not be developed here since it is superseded within a more complex framework in chapter 5. The point is to demonstrate that the description of syntax needs to indicate not only unfilled positions in syntax such as those shown by *pro* but also empty positions from which things have been moved; thus the s-structure is:

What will Steve have *t*?

t leaves no sign in the surface structure of the sentence; the PF component does not need to assign it a sequence of sounds. Nevertheless movement in GB requires the presence of an 'empty category' *t* in the s-structure, for reasons we shall see later.

There is however an odd exception to its normal cloak of invisibility. The written question:

Who do you want to play?

is ambiguous and could result in two answers:

I want to play Jim.

a player's answer selecting an opponent, and:

I want Jim to play.

a manager's answer selecting a player for the team. The original sentence could therefore have two s-structures:

Who do you want to play *t*.

and:

Who do you want *t* to play.

who has moved from two different places in the d-structure, leaving *t*s behind. The PF component turns these into the same surface sentence.

Or does it? It is claimed that the pronunciation of *want to* in the two sentences is potentially different. Both sentences can be said with the full form *want to*:

Who do you want to play?

but only one can be said with the contracted form *wanna*:

Who do you wanna play?

The latter is only possible if the speaker intends the s-structure:

Who do you want to play *t*.

If an otherwise invisible *t* still separates *want* from *to* in the s-structure, *want to* cannot be reduced to *wanna*; in Chomsky's words, 'at the point in the PF component where the contraction rule ... applies, the trace of wh-movement is present so that "want" and "to" are not adjacent and the rule is blocked' (KOL, p. 163). Hence:

Who do you wanna play?

is impossible with the s-structure:

Who do you want *t* to play.

in which the team player rather than the opponent is being discussed. Put another way, when it moves from object position *who* leaves no trace that affects the pronunciation of the sentence; when it moves from subject position, it leaves a trace that prevents *want to* reducing to *wanna*. While too much should not be made of the pronunciation of a particular verb *want* in a particular construction *want to* in English, it is nevertheless one indication that the invisible *t* is actually there.

X-bar Theory

Within the theory, phrase structure is a comparatively simple system derived from a few principles and the setting of certain parameters. The form of phrase structure employed is **X-bar syntax**, a model of syntax not exclusive to GB but used widely, within, for example, Generalized Phrase Structure Grammar (Gazdar et al., 1985). As always the emphasis is on expressing general principles of Universal Grammar rather than peculiarities of a particular language or of a particular rule. X-bar syntax replaces large numbers of idiosyncratic 'rules' with general principles; it captures properties of all phrases, not just those of a certain type; and it bases the syntax on lexical categories that link with entries in the lexicon.

A phrase in X-bar syntax always contains at least a head as well as other constituents; it is 'endocentric'. Thus a Noun Phrase such as *the man* contains a head *man*, a Verb Phrase *sees the woman* contains a head *sees*. An essential requirement of X-bar syntax is that the head of the phrase must belong to a particular category related to the type of phrase. A Noun Phrase always contains a Noun, i.e.:

$$NP \rightarrow \ldots N \ldots$$

and a Verb Phrase always contains a Verb:

$$VP \rightarrow \ldots V \ldots$$

never vice versa, as seen in the ungrammatical sentence:

*The see womans the man.

The head of a phrase is not related arbitrarily to the phrase type; it is not chance that an NP contains an N rather than a V. This general principle that all phrases contain a particular type of head can be formalized as:

$$XP \rightarrow \ldots X \ldots$$

where the X in both places stands for the same one of the four lexical categories, N (Noun), V (Verb), A (Adjective), and P (Preposition); any phrase

XP must have a head X of the same type. Thus VPs contain Vs, NPs Ns, APs As, and PPs Ps.

Furthermore the types of head are related to the major word-classes. Four types of phrases used in X-bar syntax are **Verb Phrase**, **Noun Phrase**, **Adjective Phrase**, and **Prepositional Phrase**. Each of these contains the appropriate V, N, A, or P, that is to say a lexical category corresponding to a major word-class in the lexicon. Hence phrases in the syntax eventually have heads that are lexical categories linked to lexical entries. In a sense the phrase structure consists of arrangements of lexical categories at different levels of abstraction. The phrases in the sentence are tied in to the lexicon via their heads. Let us take an example sentence:

The detective confronted Philby with the evidence.

having the s-structure:

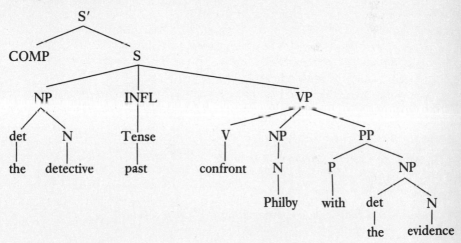

The first NP contains a head N, which is the lexical item *detective*. The VP contains a head V, the lexical item *confront*. The PP contains a head P, the lexical item *with*. From the top of the sentence down the syntax is linked to the lexicon, not just because the sentence eventually consists of actual words, but because the four word-classes are reflected in the heads of each phrase within the sentence. An NP is an expression containing a head N; a PP is an expression containing a head P; and so on. In some ways this resembles a traditional analysis in terms of parts of speech in that the sentence is made up of four lexical categories from top to bottom.

To make this explicit, X-bar theory revises the terminology for phrases. The lexical categories remain as the basic symbols N, V, A, and P. The phrases in which they are incorporated are shown by the addition of 'bars' to the original symbol; a bar is shown by '. Let us exemplify this from the four phrase types, distinguishing for the moment between single-bar categories

(N', P', etc.) and categories with no bars (N, P, etc.). Thus the lexical category *child* is N̂; the phrasal category *the child*, which includes N, is an N':

```
              N'
            /    \
         det       N
          |        |
         the      child
```

The same bar convention applies to the other phrase types. The VP *drink milk* has a V *drink* nestling within a V' *drink milk*:

```
              V'
            /    \
         V         N'
         |         |
       drink       N
                   |
                  milk
```

A PP *from a bottle* has a P *from* within a P' *from a bottle*:

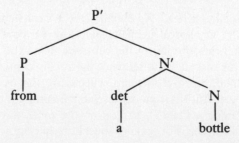

Putting these together with other elements into a sentence we get:

The child drinks milk from a bottle.

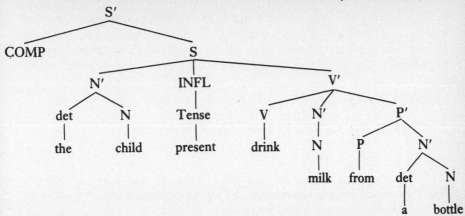

The links between syntax and lexicon are consistently maintained from top to bottom of the tree through the bar notation. The bar system resembles army uniforms; sergeants have more stripes than privates; top-ranking American generals more stars than those below them.

So far the discussion has looked only at the heads of the phrase; now it needs to take in some of the other elements that can be found in the phrase. Let us use the sentence:

A man played the flute.

as an example to illustrate various points. Some elements in the phrase called 'complements' are closely connected with the lexical category itself – the transitive verb (V) *play* is closely related to a following object in the VP such as *the flute* describing what is played; 'phrases typically consist of a head . . ., and an array of complements determined by the lexical properties of the head' (KOL, p. 81). Complements usually consist of a complete phrase in themselves, the NP *the flute* is a complement in the V' *played the flute* – or a sentence. Hence the X-bar structure of the phrase needs to include one level at which the close relationship between heads and complements can be captured. This is expressed as:

X' → X complements

or:

X' → complements X

depending on the relative position of the head and complements. It is a principle of Universal Grammar that all phrases have heads of a related type and possible complements; 'Along with some others like it, it specifies the general properties of the phrases of a human language' (Chomsky, 1988,

p. 68). Languages have four phrase types related to lexical categories, 'parts of speech' – Verb Phrase, Noun Phrase, Preposition Phrase, and Adjective Phrase. The head/complement principle applies to all four phrase types; the Verb Phrase can be seen as having a Verb head and a complement:

played the flute

The Noun Phrase has a Noun head and a complement:

proof of his guilt

The Preposition Phrase likewise has a Preposition head and a complement:

with a stick

Finally the Adjective Phrase too can have an Adjective head and a complement:

full of himself

The head parameter from chapter 1 can now be set within X-bar syntax. The principles for expanding phrases had to be given in two forms to show that complements could occur before or after the head. The choice between these two is between *head-first* and *head-last* in the phrase, precisely the difference in word order captured by the head parameter. To say that English is *head-first* means that the verb V occurs on the left of the complements in the V':

bought a newspaper

It means that the preposition P occurs on the left of the complements in the P':

on the boat

It means that the adjective A occurs on the left in the A':

open to offers

And it means that the noun N occurs on the left of the complements in the N', as in:

claim that the earth is flat

The *head-last* setting for the head parameter found in Japanese means that the

V will be on the right of the complements within V′, the P on the right in the P′, the A on the right in the A′, and the N on the right in the N′, as seen in the examples in chapter 1. If a language is consistent, that is to say all its phrases have the same setting, a major part of its phrase structure can be described by stating whether its setting for the head parameter is *head-first* or *head-last*; 'the order of head and complements is one of the parameters of universal grammar' (Chomsky, 1988, p. 70).

A second type of element in a phrase is called a 'specifier'; typically this is not related to the lexical category so closely and it does not always consist of a complete phrase in its own right. The determiner *a* in *a man* for example is acting as a specifier in the NP and consists of a single lexical item *a*. So far each type of phrase has been treated as having X′ (single bar) and X (zero bar), that is to say:

$$X' \rightarrow \ldots X \ldots$$

To accommodate specifiers requires a second level of structure, which can be captured by:

$$X'' \rightarrow X' \text{ specifier}$$

or:

$$X'' \rightarrow \text{specifier } X'$$

Let us flesh this out with the English NP:

the claim that the earth is flat

This is an N″ having a specifier consisting of a determiner *the*, and an N′, *claim that the earth is flat*; this N′ consists of an N, the lexical item *claim*, and a complement, the embedded S′ *that the earth is flat*. Both the specifier and complement positions in the phrase are filled, as seen in:

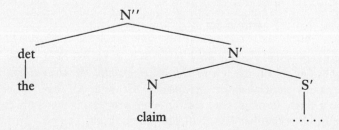

All NPs have the same two-bar level structure, even if specifiers and complements are not actually present.

Putting the levels of specifier and complement together, the structure of a phrase consists of two levels, arbitrarily using particular specifier and complement positions:

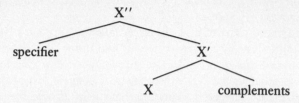

GB claims that these two levels are necessary for all types of phrase. The NP, as we have seen, is a double bar, N''; this contains a head N' and possible specifiers; the N' consists of a head N, the lexical category itself, and possible complements. Similarly the VP is V'', which contains V' and specifiers, which in turn has V and complements; the AP is A'' which contains A' and specifiers, which in turn has A and complements. While the terms Noun Phrase, Verb Phrase, Preposition Phrase and Adjective Phrase are still used for the sake of convenience, they are shorthand for lexical categories with the maximum number of bars, i.e. two: NP means N'', AP means A'', and so on. X-bar theory proposes that all phrases in all languages share a simple cell-like structure with two levels, one of which (X'') consists of the head (X') and possible specifiers, the other of which (X') consists of the head (X) and possible complements. Specifier and complement are not themselves syntactic categories but functional labels for parts of the structure of the phrase that may be filled by actual syntactic categories.

The question of specifier/head order has not been described here. One possibility is that this is a separate parameter, as essentially argued by Huang (1984) for Chinese; in which case the order of head and complements could be set separately from the order of head and specifiers. Or it is possible that specifier/head order derives from the head parameter in that specifiers commonly occur on the opposite side of the head to the complements, as seen in the English Noun Phrase:

the claim that the earth is flat

where the complement *that the earth is flat* occurs on the right of the N *claim* and the specifier *the* on the left of the N' *claim that the earth is flat*.

The separate principles for expanding X'' and X' may be combined together in a single formula. One conventional proposal is that a phrase always had a head that is one bar less than the phrase itself, i.e.;

$$X^{\text{bar } n} \rightarrow X^{\text{bar } n-1}$$

as given for instance in Jackendoff (1977, p. 30) and Huang (1982, p. 34). Thus the two-bar N'' *the proof of his guilt* has a head with one bar less, the N' *proof of his guilt*; the single-bar N' has a head with one bar less again, the zero-bar N *proof*; the V' *drink milk* contains a head with one bar less, the V *drink*; and so on for the other categories. This formulation, though useful and widespread, is inadequate (inter alia) since natural languages permit 'recursion' in which one category becomes one or more categories of the same kind. A simple example is two NPs coordinated with *and*, as mentioned in Jackendoff (1977, p. 53). In:

The old man and the sea

both *the old man* and *the sea* are apparently N'', since they have specifiers; the N'' must have two N'' heads rather than the expected N' head, as seen in the tree:

$$
\begin{array}{c}
\text{N''} \\
\diagup \mid \diagdown \\
\text{N''} \quad \text{and} \quad \text{N''}
\end{array}
$$

The way of accommodating this within the formula that is adopted in Radford (1988) for example is to express it as:

$$X^{\text{bar } n} \rightarrow X^{\text{bar } m}$$

where m is less than or equal to n.

So far the bar notation has been applied only to the four lexical categories. X-bar theory also uses bars for S, as has already been seen in the distinction between S and S'. Since S' includes S and is the same type of category, the extra bar makes it fit in with the general X-bar principles and permits the rule:

S' → COMP S

Let us combine the different areas of phrase structure looked at up to now by giving a complete tree for:

Jane hated coffee.

using all the bar levels and types of sentence.

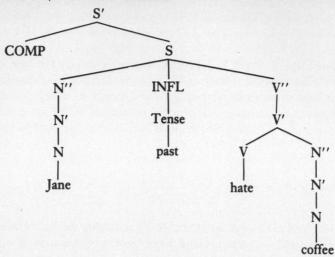

The extension of bars to the non-lexical categories S and S' raises some problems in making them conform to the usual X-bar principles, particularly over what constitutes the head of S and whether more bar-levels are needed to include specifiers and complements at this level of the sentence. These will be put aside for the moment to concentrate on some other areas.

In general X-bar syntax within Chomskyan theory strives for the maximum generality. It makes statements about phrase structure that are true for all phrases rather than for one rule or one phrase type. Thus it expresses cross-category generalizations about the need for a head and for a particular type of head independently of whether the phrases are Noun Phrases, Verb Phrases, or other types of phrase. The order of elements within the phrase is generalized so that a single statement specifies on which sides of the head complements and specifiers occur in all phrases of the language. The fact that P comes before NP in a PP *on the train*, and that V comes before NP in the VP *liked whisky*, are covered by the generalization that heads come before complements in English. Once the parameters of X-bar theory have been set one has captured the phrase structure of the language: rather than a list of rules, the phrase structure consists of settings for parameters and some account of 'language-specific idiosyncracies' (Chomsky, 1982a, p. 10). Because of its principles and parameters nature, it is not clear that the theory can be properly represented in tree diagrams of the type used here (Chomsky, 1982a, pp. 14–15); they will however continue to be employed for expository reasons.

C-selection and the Projection Principle

The route followed so far has been from the syntax to the lexicon; this section reverses direction to see how the lexicon influences syntax. Looked at from

X-BAR THEORY

Definition: A theory of the phrase structure of the d-structure of the sentence.

Principles: XP → ... X ... (a phrase always contains a head of the same type)

X'' → specifier X' (a two-bar category consists of a head that is a single-bar category and a possible specifier)

X' → X complements (a one-bar category contains a head that is a lexical category and possible complements)

Lexical categories: N Noun, V Verb, A Adjective, P Preposition

Parameter: the head parameter distinguishes languages that incorporate the above principle with complements (maximal bar categories) to the right or left of the head, i.e. as:

X' → X complements

or:

X' → complements X

Extensions: discussed in the last section of this chapter

Sources: apart from the Chomskyan references, the main recent contributions to X-bar theory have been Stowell (1981) and Huang (1982); for a discussion of the exceptions to the head parameter and an alternative explanation see Hawkins (1982)

syntax, V'' has a head V' which has a head V which leads to a lexical entry; looking at it from the lexicon means considering how the lexical entry for a V affects the V' and the V'', how the entry:

drive [__ NP]

requires a V' with an NP complement. The lexical entry is said to 'project' onto the structure of the sentence; it defines the possible complements within the phrase. Its influence ceases at the double bar level; hence V'' (VP), N'' (NP), A'' (AP), and P'' (PP) are known as **maximal projections** – levels beyond which the properties of the lexical entries for the heads no longer apply. Thus the specifications for the lexical entry for an N project up to N'', i.e. the Noun Phrase, for P up to P'', the Prepositional Phrase, and so on. The Projection Principle from Chapter 1 can now be reintroduced in the form given in Chomsky (LGB, p. 29).

Representations at each syntactic level (i.e., LF, and D- and S-structure) are projected from the lexicon, in that they observe the subcategorization properties of lexical items.

(Note that Chomsky uses 'D- and S-structure'; however, the forms 'd- and s-structure' are used in this book except where quoting direct from Chomsky's work.) For the properties of lexical entries to project onto the syntax, there must be a means for this to take place. Let us take the lexical entry for the verb *deplore*:

deplore [___ NP]

The square brackets contain an underlined gap to show the location of the item and an NP to show it must be followed by an NP. Thus the entry for *deplore* means that the sentence:

Mary deplores violence.

has to have an NP following *deplore* at d-structure:

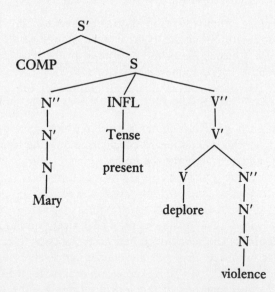

a sentence containing *deplore* without an NP is ungrammatical, for example:

*Mary deplores.

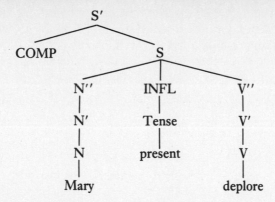

Since no movement takes place, the s-structure of this sentence is equally ungrammatical. It is not just that:

*Mary deplores.

is malformed; it does not make sense without supplying what it is that Mary deplores. The LF representation needs *inter alia* the properties of the Verb to be taken into account. Thus the characteristics of the verb *deplore* project onto the three levels of d-structure, s-structure, and, through Logical Form, onto semantics.

The lexical entry **c-selects (category selects)** the categories that go with it. The entry:

deplore [__ NP]

c-selects an NP to follow the Verb. In the more complex entry:

give [__ NP_1 NP_2]

the verb c-selects two NPs to follow it, as in:

Coffee gives people insomnia.

The entry claims that sentences where *give* is followed by only one NP are ungrammatical:

*Coffee gives people.

It is not just a matter of whether Verbs are transitive or intransitive, i.e. whether they need a following NP. Some also require a following Prepositional Phrase. The entry for:

fly [__ PP]

indicates that *fly* c-selects a PP:

He flies to London.

not:

*He flies.

Some Verbs c-select a following Sentence S', for instance:

hope [__ S']

as in:

I hope that this is true.

Others c-select both NP and S':

promise [__ NP S']
I promise you that this is true.

The combination of X-bar theory and the Projection Principle welds syntax and the lexicon together. The types of phrase structure that are used are comparatively simple – four lexical categories with various bars and some non-lexical categories. Rather than numerous rules describing how Verbs may be followed by NPs, PPs or Ss, with complicated exceptions and restrictions, the lexical entry for each verb permits only certain possibilities. Compared with

---

C-SELECTION

The Projection Principle: 'representations at each syntactic level (i.e., LF, and D- and S-structure) are projected from the lexicon, in that they observe the subcategorization properties of lexical items.' (LGB, p. 29)

Gloss: the entries for each lexical item contain not only details of its lexical category, meaning etc, but also specifications of the syntactic categories (complements) that it projects onto the structure of the sentence. E.g.:

give [__ NP$_1$ NP$_2$]

means that the V *give* needs a V' in which there are two complement NPs earlier forms of generative grammar, the balance has shifted from constituent structure to the lexicon, as it has done in other contemporary theories such as Generalized Phrase Structure Grammar or Lexical Functional Grammar. Knowledge of language that would once have been regarded as syntactic is now seen as the projection of lexical entries. As we saw in the last chapter, much of the burden of language acquisition is acquiring the specifications of large numbers of lexical items.

Grammatical Functions

Most theories of grammar have used the notion of the **grammatical functions (GFs)** of subject and object of the sentence. X-bar theory defines these as particular configurations of constituents in the sentence rather than independently. The subject of a sentence is the NP in the following configuration:

$$
\begin{array}{c}
\text{S} \\
\diagup | \diagdown \\
\text{N''} \quad \text{INFL} \quad \text{V''} \\
| \\
\end{array}
$$

The GF subject is the NP (N'') immediately dominated by S, that is to say the '*NP of S* (i.e., NP immediately contained in S)' (KOL, p. 59). The subject is defined in terms of grammatical configuration rather than in its own right. The GF object may be defined similarly as the NP (N'') dominated by VP, i.e. '*NP of VP*' (KOL, p. 59). However the word *immediately* has vanished from the definition because this NP is a complement of the V, as seen in:

$$
\begin{array}{c}
\text{V''} \\
| \\
\text{V'} \\
\diagup \diagdown \\
\text{V} \quad \text{N''} \\
\cdots
\end{array}
$$

and so occurs alongside the V rather than the V'. Hence the definition must take this difference into account; 'We can now define the grammatical *object* to be the NP of X' and the grammatical function *subject* to be the NP of X''' (KOL, p. 161); subject is defined at a two-bar level, object at a single-bar level. The concept of object also extends to the GF object of preposition, defined as the NP dominated by PP, as in:

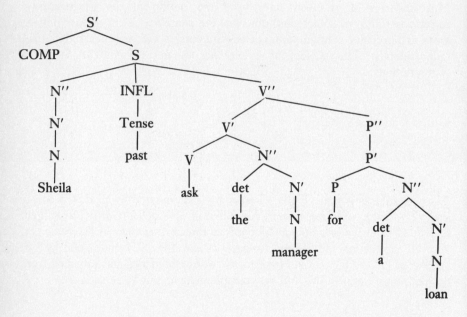

Here again the N'' is alongside the P rather than the P'. The grammatical functions of subject and object are combined in the tree for the sentence:

Sheila asked the manager for a loan.

The GF subject is the NP *Sheila* since it is the N'' immediately dominated by S: the GF object is the NP *the manager* since it is the N'' immediately dominated by V'; the NP *a loan* is a GF object of Preposition since it is the N'' immediately dominated by P'. The definitions of Grammatical Functions in terms of configurations are crucial to the following discussion. Loose ends that still remain to be tied up are the question of bar levels for COMP and INFL and their relationship to the categories S and S'.

We now need to return briefly to the movement relationship between d-structure and s-structure. The question:

Who will Jim marry?

is in part a projection of the lexical entry for *marry*:

marry [___ NP]

which requires *marry* to be followed by an NP. However, as the question has no NP after *marry*, why is it grammatical? The Projection Principle requires an NP to be present at all syntactic levels to meet the specifications of the lexical entry. Questions are derived by movement from the d-structure in which the element is present in a different location. For the moment the discussion will be concerned only with movement of the NP, not of the Verb. The d-structure is:

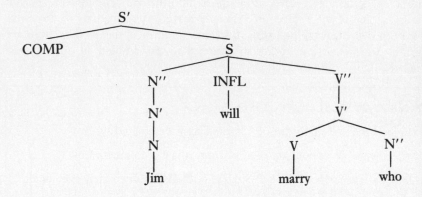

This satisfies the lexical entry for *marry* by supplying the missing NP in the right place in the sentence. Leaving aside the details of movement and COMP till later, in the s-structure *who* comes at the beginning of the sentence in COMP but leaves a trace *t* where it was.

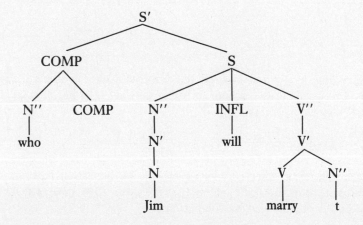

This satisfies the projection of *marry* at s-structure by having the dummy entry *t* in the correct place, standing for the moved NP. *t* is a by-product of the Projection Principle; without a marker for the element that has been moved, the projection from the lexical entry would not apply to s-structure. The Projection Principle does *not* apply to the PF component; while the specifications of lexical entries affect the sentence at all syntactic levels, they do not influence the phonetic representation. This s-structure therefore contains elements that do not appear in the actual sentence. NPs that appear in the s- or d-structure may in fact be 'empty', and so not appear in the surface; 'if some element is "understood" in a particular position, then it is *there* in syntactic representation, either as an overt category that is phonetically realized or as an empty category assigned no syntactic form' (KOL, p. 84). The insistence of the Projection Principle that all specifications of the entry must be observed, combined with movement and trace, means that there are positions in d-structure and s-structure that are unfilled in the surface sentence.

GRAMMATICAL FUNCTIONS

Subject: the NP of S; the N'' immediately dominated by S

Object: the NP of VP, i.e. the N'' immediately dominated by V'

Object of Preposition: the NP of PP; i.e. the N'' immediately dominated by P'

Gloss: grammatical functions (GFs) are defined in terms of configurations in the phrase structure; the subject is the 'NP of S'. There are no independent GFs in their own right.

Source: largely KOL.

S-selection and θ-Theory

It is traditional in grammar to see the sentence as containing relationships such as who is doing the action and who or what is being affected by the action. A sentence such as:

Peter cooked spaghetti.

expresses who (*Peter*) affected what (*spaghetti*). Such relationships should not be confused with the GFs subject and object that have already been introduced, as can be seen by comparing:

Miles Davis played the opening solo.

in which *Miles Davis* is the GF subject and also the person doing the action, and:

The opening solo was played by Miles Davis.

in which *the opening solo* is the GF subject in s-structure but does not refer to the person doing the action.

θ-theory (theta theory) is the part of the theory that handles such relationships. They are part of the contents of the lexical entry for an item, which get assigned to a relevant NP in the sentence; 'We call the semantic properties assigned by heads *thematic roles* (θ-roles)' (KOL, p. 93). The lexical entry for a Verb needs to specify the θ-roles that go with it. A sentence such as:

Bob rides horses.

c-selects an NP (*horses*) as a projection of the lexical entry:

ride [__ NP]

But this does not say anything about the relationship between *ride* and the NP *horses* or between the subject NP *Bob* and *likes*. One way of capturing this is to put it as a logical formula:

ride (Bob, horses).

which states that there is a relationship *ride* between two items *Bob* and *horses*, or, more technically, *ride* has two arguments. Other relationships between Verbs and NPs can be put in the same way; the Verb *exists* requires only one relationship:

Eldorado exists

i.e. one argument:

exist (Eldorado).

The Verb *present* requires three relationships, three arguments:

John presented Bill with a prize.

that is to say:

present (John, Bill, with a prize).

Such relationships can be captured in formal logic; the above expressions are in fact clauses of the computer language PROLOG. The relationships that go with a Verb are its 'arguments'; *Bob* and *horses* are arguments of *rides*; *John*, *Bill*, and *with a prize* arguments of *present*; and so on. Some Verbs such as *exist* have only one argument; some such as *like* have two; others such as *present* have three. As well as NPs, propositions can also be arguments. The Verb *believe* for instance, as in:

I believe he is here.

relies on the relationship:

believe (I, he is here).

in which the second argument is the proposition *he is here*.

The number of θ-roles is not agreed by everyone, let alone their names. One is the *Agent θ-role*, meaning roughly 'person or thing that carries out the action of the Verb'; another the *Patient θ-role* meaning 'person or thing affected by the action of the Verb'. Thus:

Conrad plays trombone.

has a θ-role Agent *Conrad* referring to the person who carries out *playing* and a θ-role Patient *trombone*, referring to the thing affected by *playing*. Most Verbs specify an Agent, as does *play* with the lexical entry:

play [__ NP] <Agent, Patient>

(It should be noted that there is no standard convention for using brackets in lexical entries; the use of square and pointed brackets will be maintained here to distinguish c-selection from s-selection, described below.) Transitive Verbs require a θ-role Patient but intransitive Verbs do not:

Peter fainted.

Other θ-roles may also be specified. The role of Goal or 'recipient of the object of the action' is necessary for example in:

He dedicated the book to his mother.

where *his mother* has the θ-role Goal. Similarly a PP with *for* can express a Goal:

He made a meal for his children.

To reiterate, θ-roles such as Patient should not be confused with GFs; a Patient may be assigned anywhere in the appropriate projection, not just to the GF object position.

It should be stressed that the theory is not particularly concerned with the differences between θ-roles. The important issues are their existence and their integration with the rest of the theory rather than how, for example, Patient differs from Goal. So, in addition to c-selection of syntactic categories, there is also *s-selection* (semantic selection); there are θ-role restrictions on the projections from the Verb as well as syntactic restrictions. The Verb *like* has the entry:

like [__ NP] <Agent, Patient>

This indicates that at d-structure there must not only be a following NP but the sentence must also involve two θ-roles.

June likes beer.

is grammatical because it has an NP *beer* and because there are two θ-roles, Agent and Patient. However:

*June likes.

is ungrammatical, not just because the NP is missing, but also because it is a θ-role short; no meaning can be given to a sentence with *like* which does not indicate both a person who does the liking, the Agent, and an object that is liked, the Patient.

θ-roles can be assigned to **A-positions** – positions which may in principle be filled by arguments laid down in lexical entries. The grammatical function of subject is one A-position, to which an Agent can be assigned. The grammatical function of object is also an A-position. So in the sentence:

Alec watched television.

Alec is an NP in subject position to which the θ-role Agent can be assigned; *television* is an NP in object position to which the θ-role Patient can be assigned.

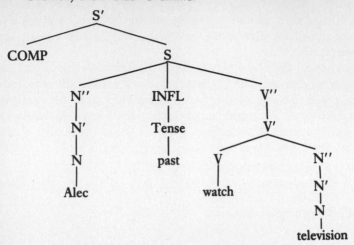

Similarly the Grammatical Function of object of preposition is an A-position as in:

She went to the theatre.

Each of the A-positions is defined in terms of grammatical functions; a lexical entry can assign θ-roles only to those positions that conform to particular grammatical configurations of subject or object. An A-position is a GF position such as subject or object at d-structure; θ-roles are only assigned to A-positions. Non-A-positions (usually smbolized as 'Ā-positions' but spelled out in full here) such as specifier and COMP cannot be assigned θ-roles, as we shall see later.

An important difference between c-selection and s-selection is that one θ-role in the lexical entry of Verbs is assigned outside their maximal projection. While the entry for *eat* c-selects the contents of the VP, its maximal projection, it s-selects part of the contents of the S, beyond the maximal projection of the V:

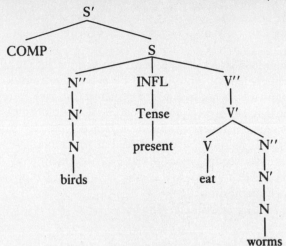

The Agent is an **external** θ-role that goes outside the maximal projection of the verb; other θ-roles such as Goal or Patient are **internal** within the maximal projection. The Projection Principle is confined to the maximal projection of the head; the assignment of θ-roles affects a broader domain. Hence the Projection Principle needs to be modified with a codicil called the **Extended Projection Principle (EPP)** (Chomsky, 1982a, p. 10) to the effect that all sentences have subjects, defined in terms of grammatical function as earlier.

The subject GF is also different from the other A-positions in that a θ-role may be assigned to it but need not be. In English we have the expletive subjects *there* and *it* which are assigned no θ-role:

There is a fly in my soup.

or:

It seems that Sarah has resigned.

Although Verbs such as *seem* have at least one internal θ-role, they do not assign an external θ-role. Assignment of external θ-roles is different from assignment of internal roles with respect to the subject position, again linked to the subject/object asymmetry. Because the subject A-position is not necessarily assigned a θ-role, the notion of θ-**marking** is required; there are A-positions to which θ-roles have been assigned which are θ-marked and there are A-positions to which θ-roles have not been assigned which are not θ-marked. All θ-roles are assigned to A-positions but not all A-positions have θ-roles.

The correspondence between c-selection and s-selection is maintained by the θ-**criterion**:

Each argument bears one and only one θ-role, and each θ-role is assigned to one and only one argument. (LGB, p. 36)

The same A-position in d-structure can only have one θ-role: an NP cannot have two θ-roles simultaneously. Putting the EPP and the θ-criterion together means that there must be an argument in d-structure for each θ-role in the lexical entry. Because it can project an external θ-role, s-selection is broader than c-selection; the complements within the maximal projection must be c-selected and the arguments must be θ-marked; but the subject NP need not be θ-marked. These two requirements – that each argument shall have one and one only θ-role and that θ-marking assumes c-selection but not vice versa – are crucial to later chapters.

Let us recap by looking at a whole sentence:

Keith lent the book to Harry.

with the d-structure tree:

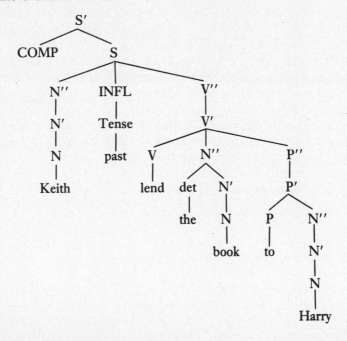

The lexical entry for the Verb is

lend [__ NP, NP/PP] <Agent, Patient, Goal>

The entry c-selects an NP to follow *lend*, namely *the book*, and an NP or a PP to follow that, *to Harry*. The entry s-selects three θ-roles and consequently needs three A-positions in d-structure to assign θ-roles to. The first one assigns Agent to the NP in subject position in the sentence; the second assigns Patient to the NP in object position in the Verb Phrase; the third assigns Goal to the NP in object position in the PP. The relationships have been mapped on to the syntax; syntax and θ-roles are now integrated. So far has the integration gone that c-selection is now a kind of s-selection. If every θ-role has a particular syntactic category that goes with it, such as NP or S, and if each argument has one and only one θ-role assigned to it (the θ-criterion), c-selection is predictable from s-selection (KOL, pp. 86–7).

θ-THEORY

'θ-theory is concerned with the assignment of thematic roles such as agent-of-action, etc.' (LGB, pp. 5–6)

θ-criterion: 'each argument bears one and only one θ-role, and each θ-role is assigned to one and only one argument' (LGB, p. 36)

θ-roles:
Agent: the person or thing carrying out the action
Patient: the person or thing affected by the action
Goal: the recipient of the object of the action

Gloss: a lexical entry such as:
    like [__ NP] <Agent, Patient>
s-selects two θ-roles which are assigned to A-positions consisting of GFs; internal roles are assigned within the maximal projection, here the VP; an external θ-role such as Agent may be assigned to the GF subject outside the maximal projection.

Extensions to X-bar Syntax

The form of X-bar theory used so far has been essentially the mainstream within which most of the theory can be understood and used. However in recent publications Chomsky has been developing a form that goes beyond that used in *Lectures on Government and Binding* (LGB), most explicitly in *Barriers* (Chomsky, 1986b). Up to now the analysis of the top levels of the sentence has appeared out of step with the rest of X-bar theory. As presented so far, S' consists of COMP and S, while S in turn consists of NP, INFL, and VP, as seen in the tree:

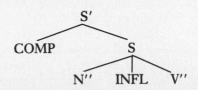

All the sentences used as examples have had this structure. But the phrase structure involved does not fit the principles that underlie the other phrases in X-bar syntax. The phrase S appears odd because it is not a lexical category, and there is no S with a double bar. COMP and INFL also appear anomalous because they have no phrasal projections. Rationalizing these levels of the sentence brings them within the remit of the usual X-bar principles. It also clarifies such notions as the subject/object asymmetry and provides a firmer, more consistent, basis for movement. The basic aims are to show that the phrases S' and S have heads, that there is a continuity between them, and that they have the appropriate specifiers and complements.

A starting point can be INFL – the abstract element that gathers together Tense, AGR, and other features. To bring INFL in line with other categories let us shorten it to I and give it three bar levels, I, I', and I''. The maximal level is I'', which consists of I' and a specifier; it can also be known as IP (Inflection Phrase). I' in turn consists of I and a complement.

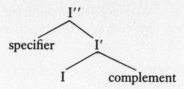

If I'' is equated with S, the top levels of the sentence now have the following structure:

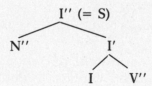

The Noun Phrase (N'') is the specifier of I', as is usual at this level in the phrase; the only oddity is that, according to the Extended Projection Principle, the presence of a N'' specifier in subject position is compulsory rather than optional. The VP (V'') is a complement to I, again in the usual fashion. Each phrase has a head of a related type with one bar less. The jump between I and the rest of the structure does not go against the X-bar principles, since V'', from which the rest of the sentence hangs, is a complement rather than the head of the phrase and does not need to be one bar less. These phrases are now in step with the other phrases, rather than being odd exceptions. As with the other categories it is still convenient to refer to the sentence as S rather than as IP or as I'', and to I as INFL; this usage will be maintained here except when the other terms are needed for a particular point; in trees equivalents between S and I'' will be given in brackets.

There is still the unresolved problem of COMP and S'. Which out of S and COMP can be the head of S' in a bar-relationship to it? The solution is to take COMP as a separate phrase type of its own, C, C', and C'', i.e. CP (Complement Phrase). The top of the tree now looks like:

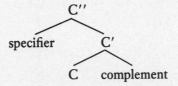

Again the alternative ways of naming the same element can be confusing; at the top is C'' or CP which is equivalent to S'; this consists of a specifier and a C'. The C' consists of C – the old COMP – and a complement. This can be converted into the more usual form as:

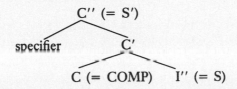

So the new Complement Phrase conforms to the usual X-bar requirements in that it has a head, and it has the right number of bars with appropriate specifiers and complements. The nature of these specifiers will be dealt with in the next chapter. The jump from C to the rest of the sentence does not contravene the principle of one bar less, because S (I'') is a complement rather than a head. The remaining peculiarity of the I and C categories is that they do not appear to be lexical categories like N and V. However, C can consist of *that* or *for*; I can consist of a modal such as *will* or a past tense form *ed*; at least in some respects they have the characteristics of other lexical categories. The top levels of the sentence have been unified with the rest of X-bar theory. In addition, as seen in the next chapter, the account of movement is sharpened by providing a specifier of COMP to which elements can be moved. The term S' will be used here rather than C'' or CP, and COMP rather than C, except when greater precision is required; in trees equivalents will sometimes be given in brackets.

To sum up, let us redo the earlier sentence (see p. 116):

Keith lent the book to Harry.

in these terms, giving equivalents in brackets, i.e. C', V' and N':

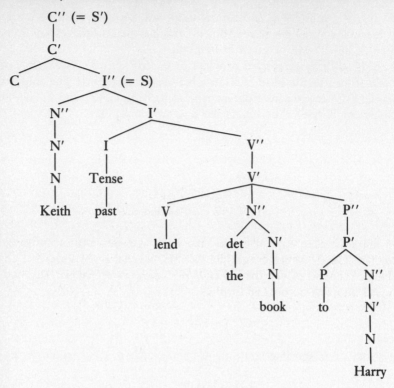

Within this tree we can see the repetition of the same structural pattern of phrases, specifiers and complements. Such trees are duplicating information unnecessarily if they can be reduced to repetition of the same structure through X-bar principles.

This chapter has developed the way in which the complex phrase structure of human languages derives from a small number of X-bar principles with parameters of variation. The central insight is that a sentence consists of phrases with a common structure, just as cells with different functions and locations in the body share the same structure. First comes a maximal phrase containing a related head of the phrase and possible specifiers; this head in turn consists of a final head related to it and possible complements. The final head is a lexical category which links to a lexical entry with idiosyncratic properties that select which complements must occur in the phrase and how many semantic roles need to be associated with it. Language variation comes down to differences in the relative positions of complements and heads. Once the complex apparatus of X-bar syntax is established, the account of phrase structure is simple and all-embracing. The apparent diversity of different languages can be reduced to combinations within this UG system.

5 Movement and Case Theory

This chapter looks at the nature of syntactic movement, in particular **Bounding Theory**, which circumscribes it, and **Case Theory**, which gives it a motivation. Just as the development of X-bar syntax gradually eliminated the peculiarities of individual rules, so the general principle of movement has subsumed many separate rules previously known as transformations. Universal Grammar is seen once again as limiting the ways in which movement can take place, narrowing down the possible human languages. The starting point is to consider that there may be no restrictions on movement at all: any part of the sentence could be moved anywhere. This can be stated as:

Move-α.

where α stands for any constituent category. The theory of movement explores the restrictions that human languages actually place on movement. It is a property of UG that only certain elements may be moved, that they may only be moved to certain locations, and that they may not move more than a certain distance; 'move-α' is tightly constrained. Some of these restrictions apply uniformly to all human languages, some are parameters that vary within limits from one language to another. Chapter 1 introduced the principle of structure-dependency, one of the consequences of which is that the elements which may be moved must be constituents; structure-dependency restricts α in 'Move-α' to standing for constituents. In terms of X-bar syntax, movement involves the maximal projection, e.g. N'' (NP), sometimes the zero projection, e.g. V.

NP-movement

While movement is a general relationship that applies throughout English and other languages, the passive construction in English can be taken as a starting point. The traditional analysis indeed treats the passive as a form of movement in which the subject and object are exchanged:

The policemen chased the bank robbers.

becomes:

The bank robbers were chased by the policemen.

by exchanging *the policemen* and *the bank robbers* and adding *were* and *by*. Although the GB analysis relies on movement, it is not an exchange of this type. Instead the passive sentence is treated as having a d-structure in which the NP occurs after the Verb and is then moved into subject position.

The Projection Principle requires that lexical entries project onto all syntactic levels. The verb *defeat* has the entry:

defeat [__ NP] <Agent, Patient>

It c-selects an NP and s-selects two θ-roles, Agent and Patient. However the passive sentence:

The Saxons were defeated.

seems to contravene the Projection Principle by not having an NP following the Verb. To meet its requirements, the s-structure must supply the missing NP:

The Saxons were defeated *t*.

The s-structure of the passive sentence is now satisfactory in that it incorporates the correct projection of the lexical entry in the form of an NP, even if only as an empty trace *t*.

The d-structure of the sentence locates the NP in its original position before movement takes place:

were defeated the Saxons.

This analysis of the passive allows the d-structure to meet the specifications of the entry that *defeat* c-selects a following NP. But this d-structure is still deficient since there is no subject A-position to fulfil the requirement of the Extended Projection Principle for a subject. Again the solution is to postulate an empty category *e* that occupies the missing position specified by the entry, yielding the d-structure:

e were defeated the Saxons.

e can now be the missing subject. The Extended Projection Principle is thus satisfied at both d- and s-structure by the presence of empty categories, *e* and *t*, to meet the specifications of the lexical entry for a following NP and the need for a subject. The requirement that specifications of a lexical entry be met at all syntactic levels necessitates empty categories at both d- and s-structure to indicate the missing items. The analysis of the passive given here falls in neatly with the Projection Principle in that movement allows the link to the lexical entry to be preserved; the apparent failure of passives to meet the projection from the Verb is solved by deriving them from an underlying form in which the correct elements are present. Movement is then the relationship between the d-structure:

e were defeated the Saxons.

and the s-structure:

The Saxons were defeated *t*.

An element in the d-structure moves to an empty place *e*, leaving behind it an empty place *t*. Movement cannot take place without an empty position into which the element can move.

The distinctive feature of the passive is the past participle of the Verb, combined with a Verb such as *be* or *get*, as in:

The cat was killed.
My key got lost.

and:

The performance will be postponed.

This is referred to as the 'passive morphology'. The type of movement involved in the passive is known as NP-movement since it moves an NP to an NP position; the trace *t* left behind is an NP-trace.

In English the passive morphology is said to 'trigger' movement. A sentence such as:

*Were defeated the Saxons.

is ungrammatical; the passive morphology forces *the Saxons* to move. Passives in other languages need no movement; for example according to Chomsky (1988, p. 119), in the Spanish sentence:

Ha sido devorada la oveja por el lobo.
(It has been devoured the sheep by the wolf)
The sheep has been devoured by the wolf.

the object NP *la oveja* may stay in place after the verb rather than having to move into preverbal subject position. Some languages also permit impersonal passives in which the subject position receives an expletive subject, as in German:

Es wurde getrunken. (it was drunk, i.e. drinking took place).

The triggering of movement in the passive has parameters of variation between languages. To quote Chomsky (LGB, p. 121) 'In the case of passive, languages tend to have devices for suppressing the subject, but these can work out in many ways, depending on how options are selected from the components of UG.'

Movement is also tied in with θ-theory. The d-structure position of *the Saxons* is the Grammatical Function (GF) object. Hence it is an Argument position (A-position) and capable of receiving a θ-role. Movement takes *the Saxons* to the GF position of subject, also an A-position. So NP-movement shifts *the Saxons* from one A-position (the GF object) to another A-position (the GF subject): NP-movement is restricted to movement between A-positions. The θ-criterion however stated that two θ-roles cannot be assigned to the same A-position: the subject *e* cannot have two roles. *The Saxons* can only substitute for *e* if *e* has not already been assigned a θ-role; otherwise the θ-criterion would be breached by the same argument having two θ-roles. It is not just that the position is empty but that it is not already θ-marked. The difficulty is that the entry for *defeat* includes a θ-role which would normally be assigned to the subject and would therefore prevent movement since *e* would be assigned a θ-role. For NP-movement to work, the empty subject *e* must be unavailable for θ-assignment: a second characteristic of the passive morphology prevents the assignment of the external θ-role to the subject, leaving it empty for an NP to move into.

Before developing movement more generally, let us consolidate the analysis of the passive by including 'full' passives with a *by* phrase, as in:

The battle was won by the Normans.

The d-structure is:

e was won the battle by the Normans.

The NP *the battle* is in the A-position of GF object and has the θ-role Patient: the GF subject is filled by *e* and is prevented by the passive morphology from receiving the Agent role. The passive morphology also triggers movement to the empty A-position at the beginning of the sentence, yielding the s-structure:

The battle was won *t* by the Normans.

While the examples given so far all involve the θ-role Agent, it is also possible to have the NPs from other GF positions moving into the subject position, as in:

The complainant was sent a summons.

where the subject *the complainant* is a Goal.

But as always within this model a construction such as passive is treated as the interaction of various principles rather than as a single 'rule'. Hence the idea of NP-movement applies not just to passives but also to phenomena such as the 'raising' that occurs with sentences with *seem*. A sentence such as:

They seem to be competent.

is analysed as having a d-structure in which *they* occurs after the Verb:

e seem they to be competent

They moves to the subject position in the s-structure:

They seem *t* to be competent.

leaving a trace behind. The passive is not a rule of its own; nor are Verbs such as *seem* odd exceptions; 'movement is never determined by specific rule, but rather results from the interaction of other factors' (Chomsky, 1986b, p. 5). Instead such constructions are examples of the general principle of movement 'Move-α' where α is in this case NP. The restrictions on NP-movement are universals that apply to all languages, subject to parametric variation and to the differences in lexical entries.

Wh-movement

A second type of movement is known as **wh-movement** and concerns the movement of wh-phrases. A wh-phrase is one that contains one of the wh-words that include the item *how* as well as words starting with *wh* such as *who*, and *which*; 'We may think of *wh* as a feature that appears in the surface form within a word . . . but is abstractly associated with the NP of which this noun is the head (or the PP containing this NP)' (KOL, p. 69). Two areas of English that have traditionally been seen as involving wh-movement are questions and relative clauses, both of which contain wh-phrases. Let us start with an example question:

Who did he see?

with the d-structure as follows, continuing for the moment to avoid the problem of *did*:

he past see who.

The lexical entry for *see* is:

see [__ NP] <Agent, Patient>

The θ-role Agent is assigned to the GF subject *he*, the θ-role Patient to the GF object *who*. Since both the object and subject are filled, there is no A-position in the d-structure to which *who* can move. One difference between NP-movement and wh-movement must be that wh-movement can move the wh-phrase into a non-A-position.

The resulting s-structure after movement, omitting details of *did*, is:

who he past see *t*

The wh-phrase *who* has moved from the object position to the front of the sentence, leaving a trace *t* behind it; this type of trace is consequently a wh-trace, also known as a variable. But what exactly is the non-A-position to which *who* has moved? It needs an empty position in the d-structure at the beginning of the sentence. The structure of COMP that was introduced in the last chapter now proves its usefulness. While C'' (S') was claimed to have a specifier position, no example was given. The reason was that this position is empty except when a wh-phrase moves into it. Wh-movement takes a wh-phrase from an A-position and moves it to the specifier of C'', which is otherwise unfilled. The abbreviated d-structure of:

he past see who

can be seen in the following tree, which shows the empty specifier position:

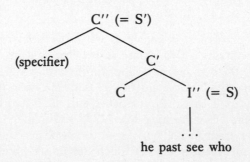

The s-structure after movement is then:

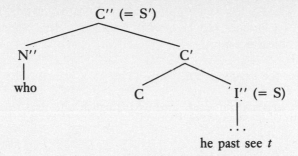

he past see *t*

The wh-phrase *who* has moved into the vacant specifier position. As the specifier of C'' is not an A-position, θ-roles cannot be assigned to it originally; wh-movement goes from an A-position to a non-A-position (Ā-position). This does not violate the θ-criterion that each A-position has only one θ-role since the specifier of C'' does not carry any competing θ-roles. The principle 'Move-α' is constrained in that movement can be either to an empty A-position (NP-movement) or to a non-A-position (wh-movement); it cannot be to an A-position that is already filled and has a θ-role. As with NP-movement, there may be several steps, as in:

What did he believe he saw?

which has the s-structure:

What he past believe t_1 he past see t_2

The original location of *what* is the object A-position of the embedded S'. It moves first to the position of specifier of C'' in this S', a non-A-position. From there it moves to specifier of C'' in the main S', a further non-A-position.

Wh-movement also applies to the wh-phrase in relative clauses. Take the sentence:

The student who the examiner failed was Tom.

The d-structure is:

The student [the examiner failed who] was Tom.

Who is the GF object, an A-position. It moves to the specifier of C'' to get the s-structure:

The student [who the examiner failed *t*] was Tom.

Relative clauses behave like questions in that movement starts from a θ-marked A-position and goes to a position that is not θ-marked.

There are nevertheless some peculiarities to relative clauses in English. The wh-word for instance may be omitted from the surface sentence when it moves out of object position:

The student the examiner failed was Tom.

As well as wh-words such as *who* and *what* English also uses *that* in relative clauses:

The student that the examiner failed was Tom.

This in fact is the complementizer *that* which is characteristic of embedded S' (C'') sentences such as:

I said [that he was right].

Hence *that* is an example of the actual C category, i.e. the head, as in the abbreviated tree of the relative clause:

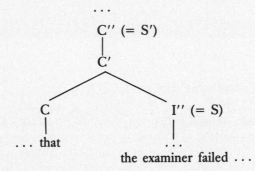

However in English the sentence may *not* contain both a wh-word and *that*:

*The student who that the examiner failed was Tom.

One of them, or both of them, have to be left out. One way of dealing with this is seen in the **Doubly Filled COMP Filter** (LGB, p. 53) which can be paraphrased as:

COMP may not contain both a wh-element and a complementizer.

A filter prevents otherwise grammatical sentences from occurring; it is a restriction on output that excludes certain sentences. The Doubly Filled COMP Filter is not universal; some languages permit both wh-words and complementizers to occur together, as in Dutch:

Ik vroeg him *wie of* hij had gezien.
(I asked him who whether he had seen)

where both *wie* and *of* are in the COMP (van Riemsdijk and Williams, 1986, p. 161). Whether or not this filter is present is a parameter of UG. Its presence in English explains why *who* and *that* cannot be combined; its absence in Dutch permits the juxtaposition of *wie* and *of*. The English setting for the parameter may be unmarked, the Dutch setting marked, in which case Dutch children need positive evidence to set the value for the parameter away from the unmarked position.

V-movement

We can now take up some ordinary properties of English sentences that have deliberately been overlooked in the discussion so far. All the sentences that have been discussed have had s-structures in which INFL (I) and its features come to the left of the Verb:

Susan present singular like tomatoes.

But in a surface sentence of English these features are actually manifested on the right of the Verb:

Susan likes tomatoes.

where the *s* ending of *likes* shows present tense and singular agreement. The straightforward GB account is that 'there is a rule – call it *R* – which assigns the elements of INFL to the initial verbal element of VP' (LGB, p. 256). It is a parameter of UG whether languages use rule R in the syntax or in the PF component. If the latter is the case, rule R changes the order and attaches the appropriate feature to the end of the Verb. However rule R explains nothing; it recognizes the issue but adds an *ad hoc* rule to relocate the features of INFL in the right place.

The *Barriers* account (Chomsky, 1986b, pp. 68–74) reinterprets rule R as movement of the Verb. The V is originally in the VP; it moves to become part of INFL and to incorporate the relevant features, i.e.:

Susan [V_I like present singular] *t* tomatoes.

To show that V has incorporated features of I it is given the symbol V_I. V-movement sorts out the relative positions of INFL and V. It moves a zero bar category, V, rather than the maximal categories moved in *wh*- and NP-movement. It is also movement into a non-A-position, INFL. The s-structure tree is then:

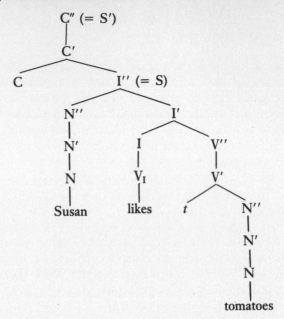

V-movement brings the amalgamation of INFL and V within the theory in a less arbitrary fashion than rule R. One difference from rule R, and from the earlier analyses from which it derives, is that V moves to the left rather than INFL to the right.

So far no acknowledgment has been made here that questions in English involve inversion of auxiliary Verb and subject, either on its own:

Will Judith pass?

or in combination with wh-movement:

When will you leave?

How does the auxiliary get in the right place in the sentence? The *Barriers* account is again based on V-movement. Modals are moved out of the INFL along with its other features. V-movement of the modal from I attaches the features Tense and AGR to the modal rather than to the main Verb and moves it to the position of C, as seen in the abbreviated s-structure tree for:

Will Judith pass?

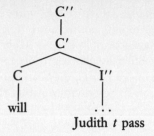

Judith *t* pass

will has moved from its original position in the I'', leaving a trace. This now accommodates the fact that in English tense and number are shown on the auxiliary in initial position in questions rather than staying with the verb.

We can now see where the need for *do* or *did* in questions such as:

Did John see him?

comes from: when there is no modal to 'carry' the features of INFL such as Tense and AGR, 'do-support' comes into operation and supplies the missing auxiliary in the shape of a *do*. This form of V-movement, sometimes known as I-movement (Radford, 1988), takes the zero-bar category V (provided it is an auxiliary) and moves it into the head position of C rather than the specifier position. V-movement may be combined with wh-movement. Take the sentence:

What will Paul wear?

V-movement moves *will* to the head of C, as seen in the abbreviated s-structure tree; wh-movement moves *what* to the specifier of C'':

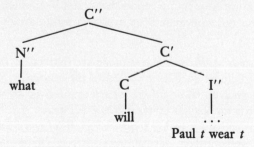

Paul *t* wear *t*

Indeed both types of V-movement may affect the same item; the copula *be* may start at V in the VP, move to I to pick up its features, and finish as head of C', as in:

Is Sheila happy?

To give Chomsky's own words, 'First V(=*be*) moves to the head position I of IP, amalgamating with I, and then this newly formed inflected element V_I moves to C, the head position of CP ...' (Chomsky, 1987, p. 68). Such behaviour may be true of other auxiliaries; while the aspectual elements have been treated here as part of the INFL, they can also be regarded as 'defective verbs' (Chomsky, 1986b, p. 73) originating within the VP and moving in two steps.

The extension of bar-levels to C and I in *Barriers* syntax has allowed the theory to account for inversion questions and the attachment of INFL to V. V-movement and wh-movement, together with the specification of levels for C and I, now account for the elements that occur in front of the subject NP in English, namely wh-phrases and auxiliaries. Nevertheless it should be pointed out that the analysis of V-movement is still far from settled.

MOVEMENT

Principle: '"Move-α" (that is "move any category anywhere")' (Chomsky, 1982a, p. 15)

Types:
NP-movement: movement of NPs from A-positions to non-θ-marked A-positions, leaving NP-trace
Wh-movement: movement of wh-phrases from A-positions to the non-A-position of specifier of C, leaving wh-trace (variable)
V-movement: movement of V to INFL and of V_I to head of C

Restrictions:
 (i) only maximal or zero-level bar categories may move
 (ii) movement must only be from an A-position
 (iii) movement must be to a position that is not θ-marked, i.e. an empty A-position (NP-movement) or a non-A-position (wh-movement)

Examples:
(a) passives such as *The mouse was killed* are derived by NP-movement from d-structures such as *e was killed the mouse*
(b) questions such as *What did the cat kill* are derived by wh-movement from d-structures such as *the cat past kill what*
(c) relatives such as *The mouse which the cat killed was white* are derived by wh-movement from d-structures such as *The mouse the cat killed which was white*
(d) inversion questions such as *Was the mouse killed* involve V-movement of *be* into I and of the resulting amalgamation into head of C

Extensions: see Bounding Theory and LF movement in later sections of this chapter

Bounding Theory

Movement has so far been implicitly assumed to apply step by step from the most embedded constituent, the bottom of the tree, to the least embedded, the top. Take the sentence:

  Who did he say that John liked?

Movement involves hopping from one position to another empty position; *who* does not move from the most embedded object position to the specifier of C′ in the main S′ in one jump; it goes via the specifier of C in the embedded S′ (S′ is used in this section rather than C″ since the *Barriers* revision of this area has not been incorporated.)

  Who did he say t_1 that John liked t_2?

As well as restrictions on what may be moved and where it may be moved from and to, there are also restrictions on the route that movement can follow. 'Local' restrictions on movement stop an element from moving too far in one hop. Bounding Theory claims that movement is prohibited if too many **'bounding nodes'** intervene between the starting and finishing point of each movement. The location from which movement takes place does not have to be **'adjacent'** to the landing site but it must at least be **'subjacent'**, that is to say, not more than one bounding node away. The bounding nodes for English can be taken to be S, S′, and NP. Individually they do not prevent movement; cumulatively they do.

  Let us start with wh-movement in questions. The sentence:

  Which tune did Clifford play?

has the bracketted s-structure:

  [$_{S'}$ which tune did [$_S$ Clifford play t]]

did is the result of V-movement with *do* introduced to carry the features of INFL; *which tune* has moved from object position to the specifier of C, crossing an S boundary. So a single S boundary does not block movement. But take the ungrammatical sentence:

  *Which tune did Harold accept Max's guess that Clifford played?

with the s-structure:

[$_{S'}$ Which tune did [$_S$ Harold accept [$_{NP}$ Max's guess that [$_{S'}$ t_1 that [$_S$ Clifford played t_2]]]]]

The first movement of *which tune* from t_2 to t_1 is acceptable; it moves into specifier of C, crossing only S. The second movement from t_1 to specifier of C in the main sentence is unacceptable because it crosses three bounding nodes, S', NP, and S. It is not so much a matter of counting how many bounding nodes are crossed as knowing whether there is one or more than one, as Berwick and Weinberg (1984) point out. The **Principle of Subjacency** can now be stated as:

Movement may not cross more than one bounding node.

This applies to each cyclical case of movement – each hop – rather than to the total bounding nodes crossed in the complete sentence. Thus movement cannot stretch further than a certain distance, counted in the bounding nodes S', S, and NP. 'Move-α' is restricted in terms of how far α may move; far from having unlimited freedom of movement, human languages are highly restricted.

The Subjacency Principle has to incorporate some parametric variation between languages. In English for instance it is not possible to say:

*The task which I didn't know to whom they would entrust.

with the bracketted s-structure:

The task which [$_S$ I didn't know [$_{S'}$ t_1 to whom [$_S$ they would entrust t_2]]].

The movement from t_1 to specifier of C crosses both S and S' and therefore contravenes subjacency by involving two bounding nodes. However in Italian it is possible to say (Rizzi, 1982):

Il incarico che non sapevo a chi avrebbero affidato.
(the task which I didn't know to whom they would entrust)

with the s-structure:

Il incarico che [$_S$ non sapevo [$_{S'}$ t_1 a chi [$_S$ avrebbero affidato t_2]]]

The link (*che*, t_1) crosses two bounding nodes S and S', contravening subjacency to the same extent as in English. Yet the sentence is grammatical. Similarly, while French allows:

Combien as-tu de pommes?

in which *combien* crosses both S and NP, English does not permit:

*How many have you of apples?

in which *how many* apparently crosses the same bounding nodes.

What counts as a bounding node for the Subjacency Principle is then a parameter. It was asserted earlier that the English bounding nodes were S', S, and NP. The French and Italian examples do not breach subjacency if one or other of the two nodes S' and S is not a bounding node; these languages restrict movement slightly less than English. There are slightly differing accounts of this in the literature. Chomsky (1981b) claims that the bounding nodes for all languages are S' and NP; the parameter of variation is whether a language includes S as a bounding node, English choosing one setting, French and Italian another. Rizzi (1982) and Sportiche (1981) regard English as having S and NP as bounding nodes and Italian and French as having S' and NP: the variation is a choice between S and S'. *Barriers* (Chomsky, 1986b) extends the concept of bounding node to all phrasal categories apart from I''. While the Subjacency Principle includes a variable parameter concerning what counts as a bounding node, there is no consensus on what its settings consist of.

BOUNDING THEORY

'Bounding theory poses locality conditions on certain processes and related items.' (LGB, p. 5)

Subjacency Principle:
  Movement may not cross more than one bounding node

Bounding nodes: S, S', NP

Parameters: languages differ over whether S or S' is a bounding node

Examples:
  A   *Which tune did Clifford play t?*
  B   **Which tune did Harold accept Max's guess that Clifford played t?*
  C   **The task which I didn't know to whom they would entrust.*
  D   (Italian) *il incarico che non sapevo t_1 a chi avrebbero affidato*

Gloss: In A movement of *which tune* from t crosses only S; in B *which tune* crosses S', NP, and S and is ungrammatical. In C and D movement crosses S and S', ungrammatical in English but grammatical in Italian

Extensions: see the remarks on chains in the last section of this chapter

---

Case Theory

Within GB theory there is always a reason for movement. Passive movement for example is 'triggered' by the passive morphology of the past participle. But this looks like an *ad hoc* solution specific to passives, rather than the general principles the theory is always looking for. A better explanation is found in the module called Case Theory. Case Theory is related to the traditional syntactic idea of case, which saw the relationship between elements in a sentence as being shown by their morphology as well as by word order. Latin is a familiar example:

amor (love)

is the subject of the sentence in Nominative case:

amorem

is the object of the sentence in Accusative case:

amoris

is in a possessive relationship, shown by the Genitive case. In languages such as German and Finnish, case figures prominently. Case in English is confined to the Genitive *s* in NPs, *John's book*, and to the pronoun system, where there is a greater range, *she*, *her*, *hers*, and so on. Thus in the sentence:

She rides a bicycle.

she can be said to be in the Nominative; in:

She disliked him.

him is in the Accusative; and in:

Her piano-playing was amazing.

her is in the Genitive. These examples show that case is still necessary in English, even if it manifests itself in the surface of the sentence in a comparatively small number of instances.

But Case Theory in GB goes far beyond morphological endings of Nouns. It deals not just with the case forms visible in the surface sentence but with 'abstract' Case, by convention given a capital letter to show its technical use. Abstract Case is an important element in the syntax even when it does not appear in the surface; the fact that *Helen* is not overtly Nominative or

Accusative does not mean that it does not have abstract Case. 'In some languages, Case is morphologically realized, in others not, but we assume that it is assigned in a uniform way whether morphologically realized or not' (KOL, p. 74). Case Theory is the module that assigns abstract Case to NPs and, by so doing, provides a principled explanation for several aspects of movement. Let us start from the full s-structure:

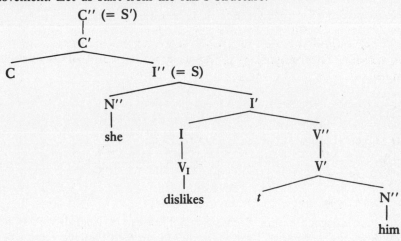

The first NP *she* is in the Grammatical Function of subject; it is assigned Nominative Case, *she*. The second NP *him* is in the Grammatical Function of object and is assigned Accusative Case, *him*. Thus the following sentence has the wrong case assignments:

*Her hit he.

Like θ-theory, Case Theory depends on the crucial GF configurations; Case is assigned according to the particular GF within which the NP is located (the definition of subject being slightly redefined from that in chapter 4 to take account of I').

Nominative and Accusative Cases are assigned in the s-structure; they are 'structural' cases since they are assigned according to the GF configurations of the sentence. In each of these GFs a particular element acts as the 'case assigner'. The assignment of Nominative to the subject NP depends on Tense as a feature of INFL; sentences without Tense do not have subjects in the Nominative Case. In:

For him to resign is silly.

and:

His resigning is silly.

neither *him* nor *his* are in the Nominative Case *he*, although they are subjects of their respective embedded sentences. The assignment of Accusative to the object NP depends on the Verb within the VP. Tense and V are the assigners of structural case, as seen in the tree:

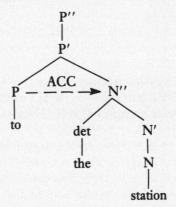

Case is also assigned within Prepositional Phrases. In English this is not distinct from the Accusative Case in form; it is termed Oblique Case when necessary to distinguish it from the Accusative. The preposition is the case assigner for the NP within the PP, the object of the PP, as in the following tree for the PP *to the station*:

A more complex instance is the Genitive Case seen in:

Her piano

So far Nouns and Adjectives have been excluded from the list of case assigners; what, however, assigns Genitive Case to *her* if not the Noun? Genitive assignment is treated as a property of the whole structure rather than one element; the context $_{NP}$ (NP __), i.e. NP followed by something within an NP, assigns Genitive (KOL, p. 195). This explanation covers not only:

Barry's book.

where the N *Barry* is followed by the N *book* but also:

Barry's reading the book aloud was distracting.

where the N *Barry* is followed by an apparent VP *reading the book aloud*. The assignment of the *s* depends upon the structural configuration within an NP. The Genitive Case is therefore assigned by the structure rather than by a specific case assigner. While Accusative and Nominative are assigned at s-structure, it is a moot point whether Genitive and Accusative of Preposition are assigned at s-structure or d-structure. Chomsky (KOL) treats them as 'inherent' Cases assigned at d-structure, in contrast to the s-structure 'structural' Cases.

As with θ-theory, the chief concern is the existence of Cases and their implications for the structure of the sentence rather than establishing which Case is which or which goes where. The main use of Case Theory within GB is to explain various restrictions that, on the face of it, have little to do with Case. The general principle involved is the **Case Filter**:

Every phonetically realized NP must be assigned (abstract) Case.
(KOL, p. 74)

That is to say, any NP in the surface of the sentence must be assigned Case by a case assigner; an NP to which Case cannot be assigned is ungrammatical. This filters out ungrammatical sentences in a similar fashion to the Doubly Filled COMP Filter. An alternative phrasing of the Case Filter is:

*NP if NP has phonetic content and has no Case. (LGB, p. 49)

This means it is ungrammatical (*) to have a surface structure NP that has not had Case assigned to it. The Case Filter interacts with other aspects of GB theory, in particular the θ-criterion: all θ-marked positions must have abstract Case because they must have NPs. Indeed the Case Filter may be replaced with a 'visibility' condition; 'a noun phrase can receive a θ-role only if it is in a position to which Case is assigned or is linked to such a position . . .' (KOL, p. 94). It is not so much that θ-marked positions have to receive Case as that θ-roles can only be assigned to NPs that already have Case.

The Case Filter is connected to the PF component; since it is couched in terms of 'visible' NPs that actually occur in the surface sentence, the PF component must be able to tell which these are. The Case Filter intervenes somewhere between the s-structure and the surface structure of the sentence, rejecting NPs that have phonetic form without a Case. The uses of the Case Filter can be seen in the passive. Let us take:

The lecturers will be dismissed.

derived from a d-structure:

e will be dismissed the lecturers.

The Case Filter requires the V in the VP to assign Accusative Case to the NP as in:

Bill dismissed them.

where *them* is assigned Accusative Case by virtue of its object position. Suppose the passive morphology prevents case assignment from taking place; *the lecturers* in

e will be dismissed the lecturers.

cannot be assigned Case, in breach of the Case Filter that all NPs must have Case. It must be moved to a position where it *can* be given Case, i.e. the empty NP position. NP-movement is compulsory in the passive in English. A more precise way of saying that passive morphology triggers movement is to see it as blocking case assignment: when case assignment is blocked, something has to give; the sentence can only be saved by movement. The movement of *the lecturers* into subject position is possible because its eventual resting place has Case, even if its original position *t* does not. Treating the passive in this way emphasizes general principles rather than the peculiarities of particular rules of English; the passive relates to NP-movement and the Case Filter, rather than being an idiosyncratic area of its own. Instead of triggering being an *ad hoc* explanation for the passive, it is a side-effect of the Case Filter with a parameter set a certain way. Movement must take place if the Case Filter is in danger of being breached.

The two filters seen so far (the Doubly Filled COMP Filter and the Case Filter) reflect a particular way of looking at syntax in the theory. Most of the discussion so far has concerned possible sentences; their grammaticality depends on their well-formedness at d- and s-structure. The use of filters in GB involves a different approach in which the syntactic levels represent structures that do not in fact relate to possible sentences; they are eliminated, not by constraints on the representation itself, but by a *post hoc* restriction. Thus:

*The man who that John saw *t* was Tim.

is a possible s-structure derived by wh-movement; it is ruled out by the Doubly Filled COMP Filter forbidding the simultaneous presence of *who* and *that*. Similarly the s-structure without movement seen in:

Was lost she.

is prevented by the blocking of case assignment by the passive morphology and the consequent breach of the Case Filter. Filters are a quality control on already existing structures. At the moment they provide a way of handling certain aspects of syntax but they are not so much principles of language as *ad hoc* ways of salvaging certain problems presented by the current syntactic analysis. Like rules, it is felt desirable to replace them with principles of UG whenever possible.

The same reasoning used for the passive can be applied to the NP-movement seen with verbs such as *seem*:

Sue may seem to be happy.

This is derived from a d-structure:

e may seem [Sue to be happy].

NP movement shifts *Sue* into the empty subject position. But why should it? The entry for *seem* reads:

seem [__ S'] <Proposition>

It has no external θ-role and must be followed by an S'. *Seem*, too, fails to assign Case to the elements that follow it. The solution is again NP-movement to the empty subject position, where the NP can receive Nominative Case. But this introduces the problem that the NP that is moved would have to cross not only an S but also an S', i.e.:

e may seem [$_{S'}$ [$_S$ Sue to be happy]].

in breach of subjacency. In the LGB account, but not in *Barriers*, this is handled by saying that verbs like *seem* are able to change S' into S through S' deletion, a marked peculiarity of English.

The Case Filter forces NP-movement; indeed it is now clear that the Case Filter is the reason for all movement of NPs; movement from an A-position to an empty subject A-position follows on the need for each NP to have Case. Certain Verbs such as *seem* and certain morphology such as the passive cannot act as case assigners, and so motivate NP-movement. Case Theory also prevents certain other ungrammatical sentences via the notion of 'adjacency'. It is possible to say in English:

I liked him very much.

but not:

*I liked very much him.

The case assigner, here the Verb, must be 'adjacent' to the item that receives Case, i.e. immediately beside it. The case assigner cannot be parted from the NP that receives Case by the insertion of *very much*. Other languages are not restricted in this way. In French for example it is possible to say:

J'aime beaucoup la France.

separating the case assigning V from the object NP, while English cannot say:

*I love very much France.

The adjacency parameter of Case Theory specifies whether case assigners must be adjacent to the NPs to which they assign Case.

In English the direction of case assignment is to the right; the assigner is on the left, the NP receiving Case on the right in the appropriate relationship. 'It is plausible to assume that the direction of Case-marking for lexical categories is uniform and, in the unmarked case, corresponds to the head parameter of X-bar theory' (KOL, p. 193). English is head-first for the head parameter so Case marking should be to the right – Verbs assign Case to the NP on their right, and Prepositions to the NP on their right. It is, however, possible for a language to assign Case in the opposite direction to the head parameter; for example, Chinese assigns Cases to the right although it assigns θ-roles to the left, i.e. is a head-last language (Koopman, 1983, pp. 122–6).

Finally we need to mention a parameter of Case Theory for which English has a marked setting. Take a sentence such as:

I believed him to be innocent.

Why does *him* have Accusative Case rather than the Nominative *he*? On the analysis used here, *him* is in the subject position of the embedded sentence, which would normally take the Nominative; Accusative is normally assigned to the object GF; yet *him* is not in an object relationship either to *believed* or to *be*. The solution with infinitival clauses with lexical subjects is **Exceptional Case Marking**. Verbs such as *ask* and *think* exceptionally assign Accusative Case to the subject of the S' that follows them; the mechanism for handling this, as with *seem*, is to allow such Verbs to delete the following S' brackets (this will be dealt with below under government). Exceptional Case Marking is then a marked peculiarity of English, not found for example in either French or German.

CASE THEORY

'Case theory deals with assignment of abstract Case and its morphological realization.' (LGB, p. 6)

Case is assigned to all NPs by case assigners:
- Nominative is assigned by the Tense part of INFL in s-structure to the GF subject
- Accusative is assigned by V in s-structure to the GF object
- Accusative (Oblique) is assigned by P to the GF object of Preposition
- Genitive is assigned by the structure $_{NP}$ (NP __)

Case Filter: 'Every phonetically realized NP must be assigned (abstract) Case.' (KOL, p. 74)

Parameters:
  (i) adjacency: some languages such as English require case assigners to be adjacent to the NP that receives Case
  (ii) direction: some languages such as English require case assigners to be to the left, others such as Chinese require them to be to the right
  (iii) Exceptional Case Marking: the lexical subject of infinitival clauses in English exceptionally has Accusative Case

Chains and LF Movement

Let us now put the modules that have been discussed in this chapter into the overall model. Movement relates the d- and s-structure of the sentence. This can be seen either as deriving s-structure from d-structure or as abstracting d-structure from s-structure. As both views capture the same relationship, 'for most purposes ... we may consider these as two equivalent formulations' (KOL, p. 156). Bounding Theory restricts movement by limiting the distance between related s- and d-structure positions to one bounding node; it applies to both the d- and s-structure. Case Theory assigns the appropriate Cases to d- and s-structures; the Case Filter applies to the s-structure and relates it to actual NPs realized by the PF Component. The sole purpose of d-structure is to show the original location of various elements in the sentence moved in s-structure, in particular to maintain the Projection Principle which 'expresses the idea that D-structure is a "pure" representation of thematically relevant GFs' (Chomsky, 1982a, p. 9).

An alternative way of expressing the relationship of d-structure to s-structure is through a 'chain' that records the successive steps of movement. Instead of relating the d-structure:

e were defeated the Saxons.

to the s-structure:

The Saxons were defeated *t*.

by movement, it is described as a chain:

(the Saxons, *t*)

This chain has a single link between 'the Saxons' and its trace *t* because movement has only occurred once. However the sentence:

The book was said t_1 to be lost t_2.

involves at least two movements, and hence a chain with two links. *The book* moves once to get *the book was lost*; twice to get *the book was said to be lost*.

The book was said t_1 to be lost t_2.

The first move is to the subject in the embedded S, an empty A-position; the second move is to the subject in the main sentence, again a vacant A-position. The chain linking the d-structure and the s-structure is:

(the book, t_1, t_2)

It has two links, one between *the book* and t_1, the other between t_1 and t_2. To sum up, 'a chain is the S-structure reflection of a "history of movement", consisting of the positions through which an element has moved from the A-position it occupied at D-structure' (KOL, p. 95). Some chains show NP-movement from an A-position in d-structure to an empty A-position that has neither contained an actual NP nor had a θ-role assigned to it. These are known as A-chains – movement from θ-marked A-positions in d-structure to non-θ-marked ones. Other chains show wh-movement from an A-position to specifier of C as in:

Who did he see?

which has the s-structure:

Who did he see *t*?

This is called a non-A-chain because it ends in a non-A-position, namely specifier of C. The use of chains to express movement has been growing in recent years, the most extensive discussion being Safir (1985). It is possible to convert the discussion of movement into equivalent statements about chains. Thus subjacency can be put as a restriction on chains: two links in a chain must be subjacent or:

If (α_i, α_{i+1}) is a link of a chain, then α_{i+1} is subjacent to α_i. (Chomsky, 1986b, p. 30)

(As noted, *Barriers* (Chomsky, 1986b) revises the concept of subjacency in ways not described here.) Case too can be seen as a property of chains; the Case Filter is another way of saying that all chains must contain an NP with Case: one of the elements in a chain such as:

(who, t)

must have Case. The θ-criterion can also be rephrased as a property of chains, as in Safir (1985):

a. every argument must be in a θ-chain
b. every θ-chain must have one and only one argument

where a 'θ-chain' is a chain that ends in a θ-position and each link binds the next. In general then a chain is like a single element. In Chomsky's words, 'a phrase can never move to a position that has a semantic role assigned to it or else the resulting chain will have two such positions: the position that the phrase initially occupied and the position to which it has now moved' (Chomsky, 1988, pp. 116–17). The requirement that a chain has Case means that a link in the chain must be in a position capable of receiving Case. The Projection Principle requirement that a category must be in its correct position is fulfilled by one part of the chain, but not the other, as Bouchard (1984) points out.

Finally let us raise the question of whether there are languages without syntactic movement of the kind described here, a possibility mentioned in chapter 1. English needs wh-movement to account for questions. In Japanese however the statement:

Restoran wa soko desu.
restaurant there is (The restaurant is there)

and the question:

Restoran wa doko desu ka.
restaurant where is (Where is the restaurant?)

have exactly the same word order; the questioned element *doko* (*where*) remains in its usual position in the sentence; the fact that it is a question is shown by the final question marker *ka*. For languages that do not have syntactic movement, the discussion of movement in this chapter is redundant; no distinction between s- and d-structure is necessary.

But another form of movement is also needed, namely **LF movement**. While the nature of LF representation is not well-established, it is commonly assumed to be in a form that requires questioned elements to be at the beginning of the sentence; the 'quantifiers' need to come before the 'variables'. If we take it that such an ordering is necessary, the LF representations for all languages must have wh-phrases in initial position. English s-structure is adequate for LF interpretation because wh-movement has moved the wh-phrase to the beginning. But Japanese s-structure does *not* suffice for LF interpretation as the wh-phrase is in its original position in mid-sentence. Since Japanese has no syntactic movement it needs to move the wh-phrase to the correct initial position at the level of LF. A further type of movement is needed called LF movement that does not relate d- and s-structure but reshuffles s-structure into LF. The s-structure of Japanese, and consequently the surface sentence, has wh-phrases in their original locations. In English they are moved by syntactic movement relating d- and s-structure. Or, to be more precise, *one* wh-phrase is moved: some questions have several wh-phrases, one of which is moved in syntax:

Who did what where?

not:

*Who what where did?

Only one wh-phrase is affected by syntactic movement. Hence English too requires LF movement to move multiple wh-phrases to the beginning in order to obtain the correct LF representation. The parameter is not whether a language has movement at all, but whether all movement is at LF or some takes place in syntax. A parameter of 'Move-α' is whether 'α may include wh-phrases in the syntax proper . . . or α may include wh-phrases only in the LF component . . .' (KOL, p. 155).

This chapter has spelled out the relationship of movement between the d- and s-structure. Movement, like the rest of the theory, is an interaction of UG principles and sub-theories with parameters of variation between languages. It draws on Bounding Theory to define its limits, on Case Theory to motivate it, and on the LF component; its parameters include the choice of what constitutes a bounding node and whether syntactic movement is used. Overall it depends on the theory of government, to be developed in the next chapter.

The logic of the chapter was to start from the broadest possibility for human language and then see how this could be narrowed down. The widest definition of movement is 'Move-α', which was seen to be limited in several ways. However Lasnik and Saito (1984) have argued that even this starting point is too specific. 'Move-α' implies the only relationship between d- and s-structure is movement. Some syntactic analysis may require deletion of items from the sentence; this cannot be accommodated within 'Move-α'. It may be better to use a formulation that does not prejudge the issue, say, 'Affect-α (do anything to anything: delete, insert, move)' (KOL, p. 74). As always, the theory is searching for the greatest generalization compatible with the facts of language.

6 Government

C-command and Government

Now that the overall framework has been assembled it is possible to look at government, which 'plays a central unifying role throughout the system' (Chomsky, 1982a, p. 7). This chapter gathers together areas that have already been introduced and puts them in a broader context. The source of the word 'government' can be found in the familiar terms of traditional grammar. A typical statement might be that made by William Cobbett in 1819: 'Nouns are *governed*, as it is called, by verbs and prepositions; that is to say, these latter sorts of words *cause nouns to be in such or such a case*; and there must be a *concord* or an *agreement* between the nouns and the other words, which along with the nouns, compose a sentence' (Cobbett, 1819, p. 67). The major differences in the theory are that government is defined configurationally and is a generalized relationship rather than one affecting only Nouns.

Much of the discussion so far has revolved around the set of Grammatical Functions (GFs) of subject, object, and object of Preposition. These were required as A-positions to which θ-roles could be assigned, NPs moved, and Cases assigned. Their definitions were in terms of syntactic configurations employing two syntactic notions: domination (what comes below a particular item on the tree) and sisterhood (what comes alongside it). Government, however, requires a more complex structural configuration. Let us take a sentence on which to hang the argument, namely:

Helen drove her to the station.

represented in the d-structure tree shown on p. 149. The GF configurations establish that the NP *Helen* is the subject, the NP *her* is the object, and the NP *the station* is the object of Preposition.

But several crucial relationships are not captured by the GF configurations. V must relate to *her*, otherwise it could not assign Accusative Case to it. P must relate to *station* to give it the right Case. Conversely elements must *not* relate to certain other elements; the object NP *her* is independent of the subject NP *Helen* for instance and is not assigned Case by it. The simplest way of defining the relevant relationship would be in terms of sisterhood; government relates all the elements immediately dominated by another element, in effect the head and its complements – V and its sister NP, P and

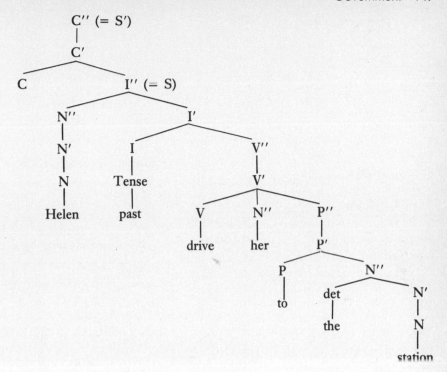

its sister NP; this definition excludes elements that are not sisters, such as the object NP and the subject NP. While adequate for most purposes, some important exceptions necessitate a more complex definition.

The first step is to define the **domain** of an element more precisely than in chapter 2 as the least maximal projection that contains it. The domain of a category is everything within the next category above it with two bars – N'' (NP), V'' (VP), P'' (PP), A'' (AP), I'' (IP i.e. S) and C'' (CP i.e. S'). The domain for the subject NP *Helen* in the above sentence includes everything within the maximal projection I'' (S); that for the V *drive* is everything within the VP; that for the P *to* is everything within the PP. The concept of domain is crucial to the configuration called **c-command** (constituent command): 'α *c-commands* every element of its domain that is not contained within α' (KOL, p. 162). Using the same sentence, the V *drive* c-commands everything that is within its domain (the VP) – its sisters and everything they dominate – but does not c-command anything above the VP, such as the S, or anything directly dominated by itself. Similarly P c-commands everything in the PP except *to*, which it dominates, but nothing above the PP; *det* c-commands the N *station* but not the VP. The object NP *her* does not c-command the subject NP *Helen*, because it is separated from it by a maximal projection (VP); nor does *to* c-command the V *drive* or the NP *her* because of the intervening PP. The c-command configuration extends upwards till it meets a maximal projection at the top of the domain and downwards as far as the tree goes

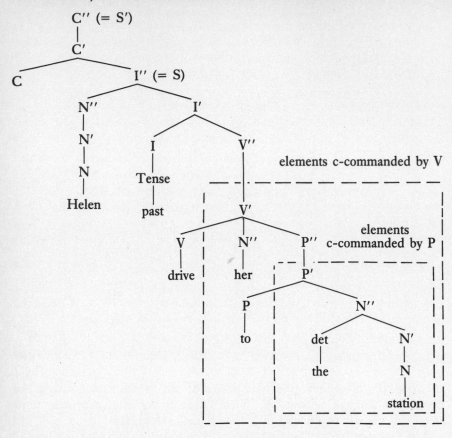

C-COMMAND

'α *c-commands* every element of its domain that is not contained within α' (KOL, p. 162)

'The domain of α is the least maximal projection containing α' (KOL, p. 162)

Gloss: c-command is the relationship between an element and those other elements it is 'superior to' but does not dominate. When it is defined in terms of maximal projections it is also termed 'm-command'.

Example: *The woman will arrest John*

The domain of the NP *the woman* is the C'' (S') and hence it c-commands all elements except for *the* and *woman* (which it dominates)

The domain of *arrest* is the VP and hence it c-commands *John* but not the subject NP (which is outside its domain).

without a bottom limit, excluding those parts of the tree that are not within its domain or that it itself dominates. The definition of c-command has been refined slightly over the years: the formulation used here is the one of Chomsky (KOL), derived from that in Reinhart (1983); in *Barriers* (Chomsky, 1986b, p. 8) this version is called 'm-command'.

Government employs c-command in a narrower form by restricting the elements that may govern and by setting a bottom limit as well as a top. Take the sentence:

Peter paid the dentist.

which can be represented as:

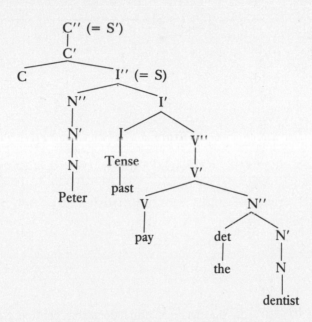

A category governs another category if three conditions are met.

1 *It c-commands the other category.* Thus the NP *Peter* is within a domain I″ (S) so it c-commands everything within S that is not part of the NP itself; V is within a domain VP and c-commands everything within its complement NP.

2 *It is a lexical category N, V, A, or P, or a projection of a lexical category, or INFL (I).* This narrows government further by eliminating elements such as COMP and *det*. These five **governors** form a vital group in the later discussion. The N *Peter* is a lexical category and may act as governor, as may the V *pay*, but not *det* or COMP.

3 *Every maximal projection dominating the other constituent also dominates the first.* The governed constituent must be in a 'reverse' or 'mutual' c-command relationship; no maximal projection can come between the governor and the

governed. The subject N *Peter* governs the VP because they are within the same maximal projection I'' (S); it does not govern the object NP *the dentist* because the maximal projection VP intervenes. While c-command is limited by maximal projections at the top, government is limited by them at both top and bottom. Just as bounding nodes restrict movement, so maximal projections restrict government. This results in a tight relationship, still confined in the examples here to complements, apart from INFL. The N *Peter* only governs between the ceiling of I'' and the floor of V'', a 'flatter' configuration than c-command.

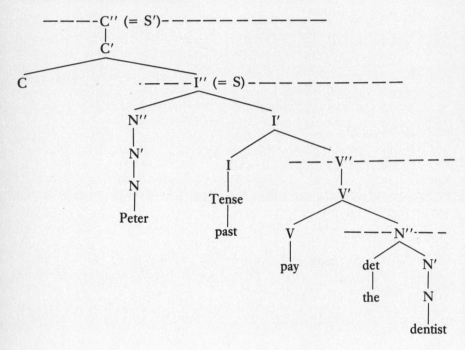

The lines of dashes show the maximal projections that confine government within top and bottom limits.

Government can now be extended to other parts of the theory. In Case Theory, Case is assigned by one of the three case assigners, INFL, V, or P, to an NP in a certain structural relationship to the assigner, as in:

He gave it to her.

The tree shown on p. 153 gives the limits of government and general configurations for GFs. The assignment of Nominative Case to the GF subject can be interpreted as government; INFL (Tense) (the case assigner) governs the subject NP *he* since INFL c-commands NP, INFL is a governor, and there is no intervening maximal projection. The assignment of Accusative to

```
———C'' (= S')—————
     |
     C'
 ┌────────┴──────────┐
 C        ———I'' (= S)—————— -
       ┌──────┴────────┐
      N''              I'
       |         ┌──────┴────────┐
      he         I      ——V''—————
                 |              |
               Tense           V'
                 |         ┌────┴────┐
               past        V    N''  ——P''——·
                           |    |        |
                         give   it       P'
                                        ┌─┴─┐
                                        P   N''
                                        |   |
                                        to  her
```

the GF object involves the case assigner V *give* governing the NP *it* since V c-commands NP, V is a governor, and there is no maximal projection between. Assignment of Accusative to the GF object of Preposition again depends on government since P c-commands NP, P is a governor, and no maximal projection comes between them. In each instance the case assigner governs the NP that receives Case. Case Theory therefore relies on government; 'If the category α has a Case to assign, then it may assign it to an element that it governs' (KOL, p. 187). Indeed one account of Exceptional Case Marking (though not the *Barriers* version) sees:

He believed him to be wrong.

in terms of government; if Verbs such as *believe* have S'-deletion, they may eliminate the maximal category following them and can therefore govern the subject of the infinitival clause and give it Accusative Case.

The projections from the lexical entry onto the syntax also depend on government. Turning first to c-selection, the lexical entry specifies the complements that must occur within its projection, i.e. the sisters of the lexical category. The entry:

give [__ NP, PP] <Agent, Patient, Goal>

specifies that the complements NP and PP are required within the projection of *give*. But V governs NP and PP since it c-commands them, it is a governor, and no maximal projections act as barriers. The same is true of s-selection. The entry for *give* specifies three θ-roles, Agent, Goal and Patient. The assignment of the two internal θ-roles depends on government in the same way as c-selection. Only the external θ-role is not governed by the Verb since it fails to meet requirement 3 of mutual c-command; V is dominated by a maximal projection VP that does not dominate the subject NP. Such apparently different aspects of the theory as Case, s-selection, c-selection and θ-theory are linked by the common factor of government.

A more particular use of government is to deal with the agreement between different elements in the sentence; in English the Verb agrees with the subject in number:

He smokes a cigar but they smoke pipes.

not:

*He smoke a cigar but they smokes pipes.

English does not use agreement as extensively as some languages; it is only visible in the surface sentence in the present tense *s* ending, with the exception of the past tense of *be*:

He was breathless but they weren't.

Other languages use it on a wider scale. In French number agreement is maintained throughout the verb tenses, for example, the difference in the written language between the singular imperfect:

Il marchait. (he walked)

and the plural:

Ils marchaient. (they walked)

Agreement of gender is also required in many languages; the adjective and the Noun must agree in French, e.g.:

le beau vin (the good wine)

and:

la belle chambre (the beautiful room)

Agreement is a pervasive aspect of syntax even if it is comparatively unimportant in the surface structure of English.

The theory accommodates some aspects of agreement through INFL and government. For ease of exposition INFL has up to now been seen as consisting chiefly of the feature Tense, with the auxiliary and agreement (AGR) being mentioned when necessary. In a sense all the features are simultaneous; when V-movement applies, they are gathered together into the morphology of the Verb; *present* and *singular* are simultaneously shown in English by the *s* ending allocated by the PF component. Let us take an example sentence:

The drummer hits the cymbal.

with the tree:

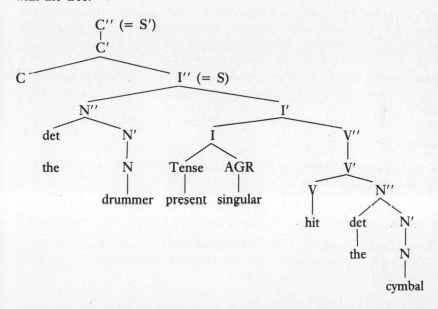

The choice of *singular* or *plural* for INFL (AGR) influences the number of the Verb. The relationship of I to VP is government since I c-commands VP, I is a governor, and they are within the same maximal projection I''. Agreement therefore depends on government; INFL – or to be precise INFL (AGR) – governs the VP and assigns number to it. While this is a typical GB analysis, in *Barriers* (Chomsky, 1986b) V moves into INFL to pick up features such as AGR and becomes V_I; it is not directly relevant that INFL (AGR) governs V.

In both analyses it is still necessary to describe how the subject has the same number as the Verb. The AGR feature of I is assigned the same number as the subject NP. 'AGR is automatically co-indexed with the subject to express the agreement relation' (KOL, p. 162). Agreement brings us back to the pro-drop parameter, outlined in chapter 2, which reflected the difference between null subject languages and those that require a lexical subject. In a non-pro-drop language, INFL (AGR) assigns number to the subject so there must be an actual subject to which the number can be assigned; INFL (AGR) is behaving like a kind of noun in governing the subject position. In English it is possible to say:

He likes tennis.

but not:

*Likes tennis.

because INFL (AGR) needs something in subject position to govern. In a pro-drop language such as Italian however INFL (AGR) does not assign number to the subject so there need be no overt subject. Because of the Extended Projection Principle even pro-drop languages need a subject in d- and s-structure, namely *pro*. In these languages INFL (AGR) does not need a subject to govern; the feature of number need not be assigned to the subject – perhaps partly because in most pro-drop languages it is shown more fully elsewhere in the morphology of the sentence than in non-pro-drop languages.

GOVERNMENT

'A category α *governs* a maximal projection X'' if α and X'' c-command each other' (KOL, p. 162)

'only lexical categories and their projections can be governors' (KOL, p. 162)

Gloss: government is the relationship between two elements defined by mutual c-commands within a ceiling and floor of maximal projections, provided one element is a governor

Example: *They will give it to him.*
the V *give* governs *it* because it is a governor within the same maximal projection VP, and c-commands it.
Hence:
(i) Case is subject to government.
The NP *him* is governed by the case assigner *to*.
(ii) c-selection is subject to government.
The NP *it* and the PP *to him* are governed by the Verb *give* and so are projected from the entry.
(iii) s-selection is subject to government.
The θ-roles Goal and Patient are assigned to A-positions governed by *give*.
(iv) The agreement in number of the Verb is due to it being governed by the AGR feature of INFL
(v) a parameter of variation is whether INFL (AGR) governs the subject (pro-drop languages) or does not (non-pro-drop languages)

The other major characteristic of pro-drop languages is that they may have Verb/subject order, as in the Italian:

telefona Sophia. (telephones Sophia)

In s-structure the subject position is filled by *pro*. The NP *Sophia* occurs within the VP, apparently having moved there. The novelty of this type of movement is that it creates a position out of nowhere into which the NP can be moved, rather than moving it into an existing A-position, as is normal in NP-movement. In principle 'Adjunction is possible only to a maximal projection (hence X″) that is a nonargument' (Chomsky, 1986b, p. 6). NPs are arguments but VP is not. The major form of adjunction adjoins NPs to VPs, seen in the Verb/subject order possible in pro-drop languages.

Binding Theory Revised

Let us now return to the relations within the sentence dealt with in Binding Theory. The main concern of Binding Theory is how different categories of NP are distributed in the sentence, in particular anaphors such as *himself* or *each other*, pronominals such as *him*, and referring expressions such as Nouns. At d-structure all A-positions receive an arbitrary index. Coindexing indicates which ones may corefer by assigning them the same index. An element is said to bind another element if it c-commands it and has the same index; 'α *binds* β if α c-commands β and is coindexed with β' (KOL, p. 164). The version of Binding Theory introduced in chapter 2 restricted binding through three principles:

A: An anaphor is bound in a local domain.
B: A pronominal is free in a local domain.
C: A referring expression is free.

These are illustrated in the sentences:

Simon deceived himself.

and:

Simon deceived him.

Since *himself* is an anaphor, by Principle A it must be bound by an antecedent in the local domain of the S' (i.e. C″) and must be coindexed with something within it, namely the NP *Simon*. *Him* is a pronominal free in the domain of the S' by Principle B and refers to something outside the S'. *Simon* in both sentences is a referring expression and so, according to Principle C, refers out of the sentence to someone called Simon.

In the context of chapter 2 the sentence was cited as an example of a local domain without further amplification. The reason for this lack was that local domain needs to be defined in terms of **governing category**; the local domain of α is 'the minimal *governing category* of α, where a governing category is a maximal projection containing both a subject and a lexical category governing α . . .' (KOL, p. 169). The additional qualifications to make a domain into a governing category are that it contains a c-commanding subject and a governor, which may be the same. To see what this involves let us take the sentence:

Shirley distrusted her.

seen in the tree:

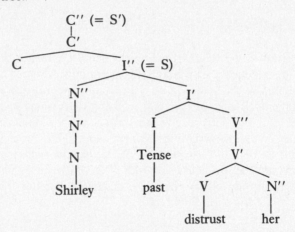

S (I'') is now the relevant local domain rather than S' (C''), because it is the phrase within which the GF subject is defined. Is S (I'') here a governing category for *her*?

S is a category above the NP that contains *her*

S is one of the pair NP or S that can contain a subject; the subject NP *Shirley* c-commands *her*

S contains a governor V that governs *her*

Therefore S is a governing category for *her*. Having established a local domain for binding, the appropriate principle can now be invoked. Since *her* is a pronominal, Principle B applies, preventing *her* from having an antecedent within the local domain S; it is possible to say:

Shirley$_i$ distrusted her$_j$.

in which *her* refers to someone other than *Shirley* but not to say:

*Shirley$_i$ distrusted her$_i$.

in which *Shirley* and *her* refer to the same person. An equivalent sentence with an anaphor is:

Shirley distrusted herself.

The governing category for *herself* is again S. *Herself* must corefer within this local domain, by Principle A:

Shirley$_i$ distrusted herself$_i$.

not:

Shirley$_i$ distrusted herself$_j$.

In all of these *Shirley* corefers outside its governing category S, by Principle C. Let us take another sentence:

*Herself$_i$ was distrusted by Shirley$_i$.

For *herself* to be bound to *Shirley* it needs not only to be within an S containing a subject, but also to have a lexical governor. The subject is present but INFL is not a lexical category. One of the two requirements for a governing category is not met: anaphors broadly speaking cannot occur in subject position in main sentences, though there are various exceptions to this in English such as the possibility in my own speech of saying

John and myself went out.

As so often, the discussion has come back to the anomalies of government of the subject. It should be pointed out, however, that the definition of governing category may be a parameter that varies slightly from one language to another, as suggested by Wexler and Manzini (1987) on the basis of evidence from Icelandic.

Infinitival Clauses and Control Theory

Let us now look at embedded sentences with infinitives. Their main interest is the nature of their subjects. In English it is possible to have an actual lexical subject as in:

I wanted Sally to go.

and an empty subject, as in:

I wanted to go.

In other languages, such as French, lexical subjects cannot be used with infinitival clauses, i.e.:

*Je voulais Sally partir.

The Projection Principle requires the properties of the Verb to project onto the syntactic levels: the entry:

go <Agent>

entails projecting Agent onto an NP argument. The Extended Projection Principle requires the embedded S to have a subject. The empty subject *e* meets these requirements. So the d-structure for the sentence:

I asked to go.

must be:

I asked [*e* to go].

What could this *e* be? It might be the empty category *pro* that occurs in subject position. However *pro* does not exist in all languages, English being one example: this *e* exists in all languages. Let us call it PRO ('big' PRO) to distinguish it from *pro* ('little' *pro*).

The interesting question is what PRO refers to. In:

I asked [PRO to go].

PRO must be coindexed with the subject of the main sentence; it is the speaker *I* who is going, not anyone else:

I_i asked [PRO_i to go].

Assuming the main S to be the governing category, PRO must have an antecedent within its local domain; hence it is covered by Binding Principle A and is behaving like an anaphor. However, take the sentence:

It is time to go.

with the d-structure:

It is time [PRO to go].

It is clear that PRO is not bound to anything within its domain but refers to *someone* or *people in general* not explicitly mentioned. In this sentence PRO is free; according to Principle B, it is behaving like a pronominal. Paradoxically PRO sometimes behaves like a pronominal under Principle B, sometimes like an anaphor under Principle A. For this reason it is given the hybrid name of 'pronominal anaphor'. Indeed Chomsky quotes an ambiguous sentence where PRO could have either interpretation (KOL, p. 127):

They asked me [how PRO to rig the boat].

This can variously imply *they* are going to rig the boat or *people in general* are going to rig the boat. The Binding Principles are then being used in reverse; having been set up to distinguish the behaviour of overt NP categories of anaphor, pronominal, and r-expression, they are now being used to discover which of these classes each empty category belongs to.

The characteristic of the initial subject position in infinitival clauses is that there is nothing to govern it; the I does not have the AGR feature and INFL without AGR is not a governor. The curious properties of PRO can be explained by saying that it must *only* occur when it is not governed:

PRO is ungoverned. (KOL, p. 183)

Consequently PRO can never receive Case (since it has no governor); the Case Filter, which forbids overt NPs without Case, ensures an overt NP *never* appears in this type of sentence. The paradox of a pronominal anaphor implied an impossible situation in which PRO was simultaneously subject to two Binding Principles. But, if PRO is ungoverned, the concept of governing category no longer applies; as there is *no* governor for PRO, it could never have a governing category. It is not so much an exception to the Binding Principles as outside their scope altogether; its reference is determined not by Binding Theory but by Control Theory, which 'determines the potential for reference of the abstract pronominal element PRO' (LGB, p. 6). One type of reference is with the subject as in:

John$_i$ expected PRO$_i$ to pass.

This is **obligatory control**. The other type is indefinite reference to people in general as in:

It is time PRO to go.

This is **arbitrary control**. Two varieties of obligatory control can be distinguished – whether PRO is controlled by the subject as in:

John$_i$ asked [PRO$_i$ to go].

or controlled by the object as in:

John told Peter$_i$ [PRO$_i$ to go].

To sum up, the peculiarities of PRO mean that it is not subject to Binding Theory but to a theory of its own. Control Theory, however, is slightly anomalous as it concerns a single empty category rather than applying to non-empty categories or even to other empty categories. Bouchard (1984) argues that PRO can be seen as either an anaphor or a pronominal, depending on context, rather than as both; in which case PRO fits into Binding Theory without the need for a separate Control Theory.

CONTROL THEORY

'Control theory determines the potential for reference of the abstract pronominal element PRO.' (LGB, p. 6)

Principle: 'PRO is ungoverned.' (KOL, p. 183)

Obligatory control: PRO has the main sentence subject as antecedent as in *John asked PRO to go* or the object as antecedent as in *John asked Peter PRO to go.*

Arbitrary control: PRO refers indefinitely to people in general as in *It is time PRO to go.*

Gloss: the empty subject position of infinitival clauses either takes as antecedent an NP that may be subject or object in the main clause, or has indefinite 'arbitrary' reference.

Types of Noun Phrases

The earlier discussion implicitly divided overt NPs into three distinct types, anaphors, pronominals, and r-expressions:

1 *Anaphors* such as *himself* must be bound within their governing category. One way of describing such NPs is to say that they have a feature (+anaphor) or (+a) for short.
2 *Pronominals* such as *him* must be free outside their governing category; these have the feature (+pronominal), or (+p).
3 *Referring expressions* such as *John* must refer outside the sentence; they have the properties neither of anaphors nor of pronominals and hence are (−a, −p).

The same analysis may be extended to the four empty categories, NP trace, wh-trace, *pro*, and PRO:

1 **NP-trace**. In:

John seems *t* to be nice.

NP-movement takes the NP from an A-position, leaving an NP trace behind. The chain:

(John, NP-trace)

coindexes the NP and the trace within the same governing category; reference is not changed by movement. Similarly in the passive:

John$_i$ was killed t_i.

and:

They said John$_i$ was killed t_i.

the antecedent is within the governing category. Hence Binding Principle A suggests that the empty category NP-trace behaves exactly like the overt NP category of anaphor; it is (+a).

2 **pro**. A second empty category is the null subject found in pro-drop language but not in non-pro-drop languages. In terms of binding *pro* is subject to Principle B; it has to be free in its governing category because there is nothing inside for it to be coindexed with; in:

pro telefona Sophia. (telephones Sophia)

it cannot refer to the same person as *Sophia* because this NP is in the VP and hence cannot c-command the Subject position. 'The element *pro* is a pure pronominal element with the sense of *he*, *they*, and so forth, or an expletive, an element not instantiated in English but only in the null subject languages' (KOL, p. 164). Hence *pro* is the empty category counterpart to the pronominal NP and is (+p).

3 **wh-trace**. In wh-movement a wh-phrase is moved to specifier of C, a non-A-position leaving a wh-trace behind; the d-structure:

e you like what books.

becomes the s-structure:

what books do you like *t*?

t must refer outside the sentence; by Principle B it is an r-expression like a full Noun and has the features $(-a, -p)$.

4   **PRO.** The last type of empty category is PRO. With obligatory control seen in:

John wants PRO to go.

PRO must be bound within its governing category, i.e. be an anaphor. PRO with arbitrary control as in:

It is time PRO to go.

must refer outside its governing category, i.e. be a pronominal. This paradox can be resolved by giving it both features $(+a, +p)$; it is indeed a pronominal anaphor. While this combination is missing from the overt NPs, it is present among the empty categories.

The similarities between overt and empty categories of NP can be summarized in the following chart:

Types of Noun Phrase

	overt	anaphor	pronominal
anaphor	+	+	−
NP-trace	−	+	−
r-expression	+	−	−
wh-trace	−	−	−
pronominal	+	−	+
pro	−	−	+
PRO	−	+	+

While this analysis postulates four distinct empty categories, these can also be seen as varieties of the same category determined by their function in the sentence, as suggested in Chomsky (LGB, pp. 321–3), the so-called functional definition of empty categories, though this is rejected in *Barriers* (Chomsky, 1986b, p. 57).

Binding Theory can now be redefined to include not just overt NPs, but also the empty categories by making the principles refer to the features $(+a)$ and $(+p)$ rather than to actual categories as in:

A: **An anaphor $(+a)$ is bound within its local domain.**

B: A pronominal (+p) is free outside its local domain.
C: An r-expression (−a, −p) is free.

The three categories NP-trace, wh-trace, and *pro* now come within Binding Theory. The properties of PRO are explained by it being subject to both Principles A and B.

Let us acknowledge the curious properties of INFL through the concept of **proper government**. The list of governors was given as lexical categories and their projections, and INFL. INFL without AGR is not a governor; it is also the odd man out in not being a lexical category. Governors can now be divided into 'proper governors', which are lexical categories, and those that are not proper governors, namely INFL. The **Principle of Proper Government** is therefore:

α **properly governs** β **if and only if** α **governs** β **and** α **is lexical.**
(LGB, p. 73)

Only government by lexical category is proper. INFL is an odd governor; the earlier discussion used it as governor for the subject so far as Case Theory and assignment of AGR were concerned, but tried to exclude it from the list of governors so far as Binding was concerned. One possibility is indeed that the different sub-theories require slightly different governors.

Let us combine proper government with the idea of trace. Traces were left primarily by NP- and wh-movement. They were consequently left in A-positions, which were properly governed because GFs are assigned by lexical categories. Traces do not occur randomly in the sentence, but only in certain circumscribed situations; otherwise the syntax of the sentence would become impossible. To prevent their random occurrence, there must be a way of linking them to the elements that have been moved. To start with NP-movement, the sentence:

John was killed.

has a chain:

(John, *t*)

NP-movement is always movement out of an A-position; hence the trace *t* is always properly governed by V, N, A, or P. This can be put as the **Empty Category Principle** (ECP):

A **nonpronominal empty category must be** *properly governed.*
(Chomsky, 1986b, p. 17)

Since the only two (−p) categories are NP-trace and wh-trace, the ECP is confined to traces of movement. It must be possible to recover the position of the trace from the configuration of the sentence. Given the chain:

(John, *t*)

the position of *t* can only be in a properly governed position. The same applies to wh-movement as in:

Which did you prefer?

with the chain:

(which, *t*)

t must be in an A-position that is properly governed, though *which* is not. The ECP and proper government tidy up some loose ends by making certain that a trace is always in a predictable place in the sentence. It is probable that the ECP in fact 'reduces to a chain property' (Chomsky, 1986b, p. 88).

This section brings to a close the technical presentation of the sub-theories of Government/Binding Theory. The intention has been to provide an overall framework to demonstrate the workings of the whole model rather than to develop each area in depth or to evaluate the competing alternatives for each area. For a more detailed treatment of versions of GB substantially in line with the one presented here the reader is recommended to van Riemsdijk and Williams (1986), Sells (1985), and Radford (1988). While the broad concept is Chomsky's and most of the above is based on his writings, his own work builds on and synthesizes the work of many researchers. The version of X-bar syntax given here for example comes out of a rich tradition of work by Jackendoff (1977), Huang (1982) and Stowell (1981).

We are left with a highly complex I-language model that applies the principles and parameters concept across the board; all languages and all rules are brought within its compass. The proposal for a Universal Grammar is not an empty boast; each sub-theory of the grammar tries to achieve universality while allowing parametric variation between languages. Each of these proposals is also a claim for learnability. The past three chapters have refrained from using acquisition examples to avoid further complicating the exposition. The touchstone of learnability can be applied throughout. The discussion of Control Theory for instance introduced a parameter of whether a language has lexical subjects in infinitival clauses. Which is the unmarked setting? If children start from the no-lexical subjects setting, they need positive evidence of actually occurring lexical subjects to set it the other way; if they start from the lexical subjects setting, they need indirect negative evidence of the non-occurrence of lexical subjects to set it the other way. Since it is preferable to see the child as learning from positive evidence, the no-lexical subjects setting is unmarked; English children have to set the parameter to a marked setting, French children don't. Each aspect of syntax is susceptible to analysis in terms of learnability.

It is not within the scope of this book to evaluate whether the whole enterprise succeeds better than its rival linguistic theories. As a theory of Universal Grammar it has made astonishing progress in a relatively short period. It suggests principles and variable parameters that cover a wide range of language phenomena. A few years ago generative grammar was often attacked for being overly concerned with English. Nowadays it deals with language at a universal level and bases itself on a range of languages; to take a selection, Italian (Rizzi, 1982), Catalan (Picallo, 1984), Arabic and Hebrew (Borer, 1983), Vata and Gbadi (Koopman, 1983), Chinese (Huang, 1982; 1984). In many cases English turns out to make a marked choice of values for parameters, for example Exceptional Case Marking and adjacency. To devise principles and parameters that stand up across such a range of evidence is no mean achievement.

I will nevertheless mention some personal reservations as a non-syntactician. One is the jump from the Universal Grammar concept to the Government/Binding framework. While the claim that UG is a theory of principles and parameters is powerful and attractive, these are not necessarily coterminous with the actual constructs used in the Government/Binding framework. Much of the current framework seems highly relevant to UG, for instance X-bar syntax and the head parameter; some parts deal with small areas, such as Control Theory. I have sometimes felt a mismatch between the broad exciting aims of UG and the triviality of some of the details. Even compared to the generative grammar of twenty years ago, the syntax covered is narrow and specialized; one finds little discussion of the imperative, of negation, of tag questions, for example, all of which used to figure prominently. While it is true that these are separate topics or 'rules' rather than principles and so do not directly concern the theory, many involve connections with the principles that need at least explicit dismissal if not discussion; the nature of the subject of imperatives, the binding of the pronominal in tag questions, the location of negatives in X-bar syntax, and many more. The theory is not just about syntax as such; it is obsessively concerned with certain areas of it, such as the subject. Other areas may be important to UG that are not as yet dealt with. The narrow concern with certain topics means that often the examples used savour of special pleading. One sometimes feels the same sentences and constructions self-perpetuate themselves in the literature, and are potentially misleading because they take a single point without fitting it into a larger picture. Structure-dependency, say, is illustrated by variations on the sentence:

*Is the man who here is tall?

such as:

*¿está el hombre, que contento, está en la casa? (Chomsky, 1988, p. 42)

This stands for a large number of possible sentences and of possible constructions to which structure-dependency applies; it is a perfectly legitimate example. However, take the recurring example of the reduction of *want to* to *wanna* that betrays the effects of the invisible *t* on the phonology. Not all speakers of English observe this distinction; it does not apply to all verb and *to* combinations; it is not set in a background of how the other weak and strong forms in English are affected by *t*; it is not related to a broader account of contraction in English or other languages; in short it appears to be an isolated example chosen because it happens to support the point in question. The counterargument would be that most of these objections are essentially about E-language; the fact that *wanna* reduction occurs somewhere needs to be explained. Yet while such examples can be used occasionally as apt illustrations, it seems suspect to repeat such one-off examples to prove the same point time and again when UG aims to go beyond the idiosyncracies of particular constructions.

One difficulty with presenting the material in the past three chapters has been the diversity of views on particular issues and the rapid rate of change. Although the overall framework is agreed by many researchers, as soon as any particular issue is examined a multiplicity of interpretations come to light. On the first page of *Barriers* Chomsky talks of 'some murky questions' many of which are 'still poorly understood' and says he is going to consider 'several paths through the maze of possibilities that come to mind' (Chomsky, 1986b, p. 4). In part this difficulty is a consequence of the parameters and principles approach; a small change in one aspect has multiple consequences throughout the whole theory. A slight change in the definition of government, for example, has repercussions everywhere. However, take the pro-drop parameter: the evidence seems relatively straightforward and uncontroversial; some languages have null subject sentences and this is usually coupled with Verb/subject order. But there are several interpretations of pro-drop within Government/Binding Theory; it has something to do with agreement, something to do with government, but precisely what depends on whether you consult Chomsky (1981a), Rizzi (1982), Chomsky (1982a), Hyams (1986), Huang (1984), Bouchard (1984), van Riemsdijk and Williams (1986), or any of half a dozen others. The same is true of other syntactic areas – overall agreement but passionate local disagreements. If the theory is scientific and testable, it is dangerous that multiple interpretations of a single phenomenon should be possible; given its claims to universality, one may question whether the same theory should be capable of accommodating such diverse and conflicting explanations as there are for pro-drop, to take one instance. It is one thing when an aspect of a theory is challenged and overthrown by a new explanation, another thing when the theory apparently permits competing explanations for the same phenomenon. Such varieties of explanation may reflect either that the theory is still in its infancy or may be an inherent danger in any theory that is such a tightly constrained network of principles and parameters. Learnability, as always, provides a possible way out, either through the logical argument of acquisition about the types of evidence available to the child, or through theoretically relevant empirical studies such as Hyams (1986).

These personal quibbles have dealt with some of the execution rather than with the theory itself. I nevertheless find the model both stimulating and fascinating. Compared to other theories it encompasses a wide variety of phenomena, bringing phrase structure, Case, θ-roles, and the lexicon within a unified structure. It simplifies syntax to a few broad principles with certain parametric variation. It appeals because of its broad sweep; any aspect of human language somehow is covered by it; everything seems to fit into place. Because of this, it goes some way to being a description of Universal Grammar. Even if the details change or disappear, an answer of some kind is being proposed to the question of what human beings know about language and consequently what they have to learn. Few other theories until now have even set themselves these goals, let alone gone anywhere near achieving them.

7 Uses of the Theory: Second Language Learning

Uses of the Theory

Does the theory presented here have relevance for other fields? As yet neither Universal Grammar nor Government/Binding Theory are widely known outside linguistics. This chapter cannot provide a summary of the ways in which they have been used since such uses have not had time or opportunity to materialize. Instead we shall look at some general issues, review some of the connections with language teaching, psychology, and computing, and finish with a detailed account of the sole area that has made extensive use of UG theory, namely second language learning research. To give some idea of what is involved in making use of the theory, let us represent it with some sample quotations, starting from the general level where it is least susceptible to change and going to the most particular where it changes almost from minute to minute.

1 'The statements of a grammar are statements of the theory of mind about the I-language ...' (KOL, p. 23). At the most general level the theory represents language as knowledge rather than as social behaviour. The overall commitment to I-language has been essentially unchanged throughout the history of generative grammar and is crucial to any use outside linguistic theory proper. It is compatible only with approaches in other areas that are also basically I-language in orientation.

2 'The property of mind described by UG is a species characteristic, common to all humans' (KOL, p. 18). The mental reality of language is shared by all human beings; variation between languages is limited by the properties of the mind. Universal Grammar studies what human minds, and hence human languages, have in common. Again this element of the theory is stable; any use must recognize the common aspects of language rather than individual or situational differences.

3 'UG is taken to be a characterization of the child's pre-linguistic initial state. Experience ... serves to fix the parameters of UG, providing a core grammar ...' (LGB, p. 7). Universal Grammar is not learnt but already

present in the mind; language input fixes the mental grammar into one of the few permissible forms. The overall 'innatist' position has been associated with generative grammar almost from the start, its explicit formulation in terms of UG has been current since the 1970s. Any use in other fields must allow an essential component of language knowledge to be built in to the mind.

4   'The language that we then know is a system of principles with parameters fixed, along with a periphery of marked exceptions' (KOL, pp. 150–1). This represents a specific commitment to a 'principles and parameters' model and to a core/periphery distinction: knowing a language means knowing a core grammar where the principles are instantiated and the values of parameters fixed and a peripheral grammar of other elements. Any relationship to other areas must be based on principles if it is to take into account progress in the theory during the 1980s.

5   'UG consists of various subsystems of principles ...' (KOL, p. 146). In one sense this asserts the modularity of the theory; it is a complex inter-relationship of sub-theories. In another sense it leads to the more specific content of such sub-theories as X-bar syntax or Case. The implication is that valid uses must exploit the whole system rather than any individual component. While individual aspects of the theory may be potentially useful – X-bar theory might appeal to child language researchers independently of UG theory – such uses will be despite their role in the theory rather than because of it.

A full use means adapting these five statements, or their equivalent, something which has not yet been attempted. The practitioners in other fields must decide for themselves what use they may make, in the light of their own needs. To quote Chomsky's own cautious words, 'People who are involved in some practical activity such as teaching languages, translation or building bridges should probably keep an eye on what's happening in the sciences. But they probably shouldn't take it too seriously, because the capacity to carry out practical activities without much conscious awareness of what you're doing is usually far more advanced than scientific knowledge' (Chomsky, 1988, p. 180). Let us tentatively look at some areas that have been influenced by Chomsky in the past. First, foreign language teaching, which has historically found the main use of Chomsky to be as a weapon against behaviourist views of language learning. In particular his arguments in favour of creativity and against stimulus/response learning, first outlined in his review of B. F. Skinner's *Verbal Behavior* (Chomsky, 1959), have been used to justify rejecting the habit-formation theories associated with the audiolingual methodology popular in the early 1960s; 'these principles are not merely inadequate but probably misconceived ...' (Chomsky, 1966). The negative use of Chomsky's creativity argument is widespread among language teachers up to the present day and is still cited in Stern (1983), Harmer (1983), Howatt (1984) and

Richards and Rodgers (1986), to take a small sample of methodology texts, none of which cite any work by Chomsky later than 1968.

Chomsky's positive influence on language teaching, on the other hand, has been comparatively weak. A minor theme for a few years was 'cognitive code learning' (Carroll, 1966) which extrapolated the idea of language as knowledge to teaching students conscious awareness of linguistic structure; 'provided the student has a proper degree of cognitive control over the structures of the language, facility will develop automatically with use of the language in meaningful situations' (Carroll, 1966). A more persistent theme concerned the built-in language faculty. If the students' minds were equipped with an ability to acquire language, a LAD, the best course of action for the teacher is the *laissez-faire* approach of supplying sufficient samples of language for LAD to make use of; students would acquire language much better without teacher interference. 'The main control the teacher needs to exert over the materials to be studied is that they be graspable as usable items by the learner. The language learning capabilities of the student will gradually take care of the rest' (Newmark and Reibel, 1968, p. 161). Allied with this was a hypothesis-testing theory of learning: the student was supposed to hypothesize a rule and then to test out whether it succeeded or failed in actual use, an important theme in the communicative language teaching approach (Allwright, 1977) and indeed in second language learning research (Ellis, 1985). The other typical reference to Chomsky by methodologists is when they reject his definition of linguistic competence in favour of Hymes' (1972) communicative competence, on the grounds that students need to communicate. 'This theory of what knowing a language entails offers a much more comprehensive view than Chomsky's view of competence, which deals primarily with abstract grammatical knowledge' (Richards and Rodgers, 1986, p. 70).

Apart from the general disapproval of behaviourist methods, little of this bears any relationship to current Chomskyan thinking. The argument that we are so ignorant of the nature of UG that the students should be left to apply their own talents no longer has the same force, since UG theory claims to know what the mysterious contents of LAD are; hypothesis-testing in the sense of learning by feedback from the environment is unacceptable as a method of learning for the reasons detailed in chapter 3; linguistic competence now contrasts with pragmatic competence, a broader concept than communicative competence. Much language teaching today is incompatible with a Chomskyan approach because of its E-language emphasis on communication and social interaction. A full use of the theory in language teaching would stress the goal of language teaching as the acquisition of knowledge of language; it would see language acquisition as the interaction between specific features of the UG in the learner's mind and triggering experience from the environment. Its teaching methods would emphasize the provision of appropriate evidence rather than communicative interaction or grammatical explanation. Since current syntactic description is directly related to learning, the description of what the students have to learn – the syllabus – could make use of concepts such as the pro-drop parameter or the head parameter, and the core/periphery distinction. As a teacher of English as a Foreign Language for example I was unaware of the markedness of English in having lexical subjects for infinitival clauses, and in being non-pro-drop, both of which would have influenced the content of what I was teaching. A teaching method would take into account the differences between competence of whatever kind and performance, and between acquisition and development. Further implications may be drawn from the work on second language learning to be described below.

The historical connections with psychology have followed a not dissimilar course. Chomsky's early stance on language learning was as influential in countering behaviourist accounts of language in psychology as in language teaching; it is still perhaps the major point of contact, as evidenced by its mention in introductory textbooks such as Garnham (1985) and Harris and Coltheart (1986). The major positive theme was the attempt to show that grammatical competence had 'psychological reality'; the consequence was experiments to show the effects of syntax on processing or recall of language, using whatever form of syntactic description that was then current, starting with the kernels and transformations of the *Syntactic Structures* model, as in Miller (1962), going on to the deep and surface structure of *Aspects*, for example Blumenthal and Boakes (1967), and reaching its height in the Derivational Theory of Complexity, analysed in Fodor, Bever and Garrett (1974). The overall aim has been described by Berwick and Weinberg (1984, p. 39) as 'type transparency': 'the condition that the logical organization of rules and structures incorporated in a grammar be mirrored rather exactly in the organization of the parsing mechanism.' Such an approach was difficult to reconcile with the competence/performance distinction; chapter 1 also pointed out the dangers in restricting 'psychological reality' to only one kind of evidence. When the search for the psychological reality of competence became exhausted, psychologists lost interest in the Chomskyan approach. Outside the circle of linguists, general discussions usually pay tribute to 'still arguably the most important figure in linguistics' (Garnham, 1985, p. 16) or show how research was given a 'new impetus by Chomsky's writings' (Harris and Coltheart, 1986, p. 4), but he appears a shadowy Wundt-like founding father, remote from present day issues. In Judith Greene's words, 'Chomsky's later reformulations of transformational grammar are of great interest to linguists but have had little impact on psychological theories of language' (Greene, 1986, p. 75).

As with language teaching, there seems comparatively little recognition by psychologists that in many respects Chomsky's most fruitful period has been the 1980s, leading to what he sometimes refers to as 'the second major conceptual shift' (Chomsky, 1987). A psychological approach that took his current ideas seriously would have to regard language as knowledge, but more specifically treat it as a system of principles and parameters rather than 'rules'.

It would see this knowledge as derived from fixing the grammar into one of its possible forms. The new inter-relationships of the theory may have more detailed consequences; the inter-linking of vocabulary and syntax via the Projection Principle, or the semantic roles of θ-theory suggest implications for models of performance and memory.

The theory might also be presumed to have close relationships with those areas of computing concerned with Natural Language Processing (NLP), in particular with 'parsing' – the assignment of grammatical structure to sentences. At one level, aspects of Chomsky's thinking on mathematics have informed part of the work in this field. At another level the framework of the *Aspects* model (Chomsky, 1965), in particular the notion of transformation, has had an impact, as described in Winograd (1983). The current GB framework has attracted few disciples among those working on parsing. In *Knowledge of Language* (KOL, p. 151) Chomsky points out that GB parsers should consist of principles and parameters rather than the rules that parsers have typically employed; 'Rule based parsers are in some respects implausible.' Barton (1984) produces general arguments in favour of principles rather than rules; Berwick and Weinberg (1984) show the feasibility of adapting the type of parser associated with Marcus (1980) as a form of GB parser; the French parser of Wehrli (1984) shows that a parser can cope with central GB issues such as Binding Principles, Control Theory, and movement. But so far, the bulk of work in parsing has pursued other lines such as Augmented Transition Networks and GPSG. As Chomsky (1987) points out, 'With regard to the "parsing problem", considerable rethinking seems to be in order, at least if this problem is understood to relate to issues of so-called "psychological reality".' To suit the requirements outlined above, a parser would have to be essentially 'declarative' in representing language as a network of interlocking principles rather than 'procedural' in seeing parsing as linear steps. A parser would supply yes/no answers to the question 'Is this sentence grammatical?' rather than being a model of psychological processing or data querying.

The Relationship between First and Second Language Learning

The rest of this chapter deals with the only area that has so far tried to cope with the principles and parameters model of UG, namely second language learning research. Compared with the paucity of relevant L1 acquisition research, the L2 area boasts almost an embarrassment of riches; general overviews of UG and L2 learning have been written by Ellis (1985, chapter 8), Flynn (1988), Lightbown and White (1988) and Cook (1985), among others. It should perhaps be pointed out that Chomsky himself has published few observations in L2 learning.

A starting point is to rephrase the relationship between L2 learning and L1 learning in terms of UG. For this to be valid, L2 learning needs to be stated in equivalent terms to L1 learning. L1 children start with the zero state, S_0, and go on to steady state, S_S; they progress from an initial state of knowing nothing but their innate endowment to a final state of knowing everything about a particular language. L2 learners already know a first language; they possess one instantiation of the UG principles in the form of their first language. Some L2 learners, however, are not in full possession of S_S in the first language but are at intermediate points between S_0 and S_S; adults learning an L2 possess competence in their L1, children are far from it. The extent of the knowledge of the first language incorporated in the S_0 therefore varies. L2 learners also speak any L1; the S_S that forms part of the initial L2 state may be any instantiation of UG ranging from Chinese to English to Yoruba. The starting point for L2 learning is thus not only far from absolute zero but also varies from one learner to another. The initial state of the L2 learner I will call S_i to distinguish it from S_0; S_i includes knowledge of one of the possible human languages to a varying degree, while S_0 does not.

In L1 acquisition the final S_S is adult competence, which is by definition complete: a native speaker's competence is whatever a native speaker knows, neither more nor less. But the final state in L2 learning is hard to define. One possibility is to regard it as the equivalent to the L1 S_S; the task of L2 learners is complete when they speak the L2 as well as they speak the L1. Chomsky appears to deny that it is meaningful to talk of second language learners having systematic languages of their own, 'interlanguages'. Instead he argues for the 'commonsense' view that only the complete knowledge of language counts, rather than intermediate states:

> We do not, for example, say that the person has a perfect knowledge of some language L, similar to English but still different from it. What we say is that the child or foreigner has a 'partial knowledge of English' or is 'on his or her way' toward acquiring knowledge of English, and if they reach this goal, they will then know English (KOL, p. 16).

But most people are substantially less efficient in their L2 than in their L1; many succeed in learning little of the L2, sometimes despite their best efforts. If the adult S_S is the final state in L2 learning, paradoxically it is reached by hardly anyone. L1 competence is whatever it is; L2 competence is defined as what it is typically *not*, in short as if it were L1 competence. The steady state that many L2 learners achieve differs from an L1 S_S and varies from one learner to another. I will refer to this as the terminal state S_t, to distinguish it from S_S in L1 learning. The differences between L1 and L2 learning are then:

L1 learning $S_0 \dots\dots\dots\dots\dots S_S$
L2 learning $S_i \dots\dots\dots S_t$

Children acquire S_S in the L1 regardless of individual or situational differences. Only a small proportion of L2 learners become balanced bilinguals and attain S_t equivalent to their S_S in the L1; successful progress to S_t depends on being the right type of person in the right situation. A theory of L2 acquisition must explain why some L2 learners succeed, some do not; in other words why S_t varies and S_S does not.

One possibility is that second languages can be learnt by other means than the language faculty. I learnt Latin by translating Virgil and memorizing the grammatical explanations in *Kennedy's Latin Primer* (Kennedy, 1948); such teaching methods employ what Palmer (1926) called the 'studial capacity', Krashen (1981) the Monitor, both of which are outside the language faculty. 'Natural' L2 acquisition, which employs the language faculty, must be distinguished from 'non-natural' L2 learning, which uses other faculties; the resulting S_ts may also differ. To some extent this corresponds to the difference between taught and untaught L2 learning. The teacher may employ a variety of teaching techniques that have no correspondence in the L1 child's situation: much classroom L2 learning is non-natural. Conversely, classrooms can involve natural learning and real-life situations can involve non-natural learning: learners outside classrooms may still employ non-natural means such as grammar books and dictionaries. The initial and final states, S_i and S_t, are different from S_0 and S_S, and also the possible routes in between are more diverse for L2 learners. Not only may S_S differ from one learner to another in terms of coverage or of adequacy, but also competence acquired by non-natural means may be different from competence acquired by natural means, if we indeed want to call the former grammatical competence at all.

L2 Learning and the Poverty of the Stimulus Argument

If L2 learners possess knowledge they could not have acquired from the evidence they have encountered, its source must be within their own minds: the poverty of the stimulus argument applies equally to L2 learning. Take the classic pair of sentences used in the *Aspects* model (Chomsky, 1965):

John is easy to please.

and:

John is eager to please.

The difference between them is that in the former *John* is interpreted as the object of the Verb *please*, in the latter as its subject, although the two sentences have the same surface structure. Since no actually occurring sentences would ever signal the difference, this distinction could not be derived from positive evidence; the knowledge must come from within the mind. L1 learners were shown to acquire this difference around the age of seven (Chomsky, 1969; Cromer, 1970; 1987). If L2 learners also acquire it from positive evidence, its origin must still be within the mind. Several experiments confirmed that L2 learners consistently acquire it after a certain period of time (d'Anglejan and Tucker, 1975; Cook, 1973). One logical cause might be the availability of other forms of evidence such as grammatical explanation; most teachers and textbooks do not teach this syntactic difference however. Another logical cause might be transfer from an equivalent construction in the first language; this fails to explain why it takes L2 learners so long to acquire it, and why they do so at about the same moment.

Let us now go through the methods of learning that were rejected for L1 acquisition to see whether they could be more successful at explaining L2 learning. The occurrence and uniformity requirements proposed in chapter 3 function slightly differently in L2 learning theory; since S_t is itself variable, explaining how a learner acquired something means showing that the postulated situational effect actually occurs for that learner, but does not necessitate showing it occurs for all learners.

1 Imitation

As in L1 acquisition, sheer imitation only provides positive evidence; repeating sentences does not in itself allow the learner to know what cannot be said. Indeed a similar argument was responsible for the decline of language teaching methods that rely on imitation, in particular audiolingualism, since they did not appear to help students to go beyond the information given. Repeating:

John fancies himself.

ten times does not confer knowledge of Binding Principle A.

2 Grammatical explanation

Though grammatical explanation does not figure prominently in the experience of the L1 child, some L2 learners encounter it constantly, others not at all. Whatever explanations of syntactic points L2 learners receive only concern those points that are consciously accessible to the speaker; Binding, or *easy/eager to please*, or perhaps any of the principles of UG, are unlikely to be part of the teacher's conscious grammatical knowledge. Teachers or native speakers can only explain what they are consciously aware of. 'It must be recognized that one does not learn the grammatical structure of a second language through "explanation and instruction" beyond the most rudimentary level for the simple reason that no one has enough explicit knowledge about this structure to provide explanation and instruction' (Chomsky, 1969). Even if grammatical explanation works for some aspects of L2 learning, it cannot account for how people learn what they are not taught. The explanations of 'reflexives' in pedagogical grammar books for instance do not go very far towards explaining the Binding Principles the L2 learner knows.

3   Correction and approval

Children rarely receive correction or approval of syntactic forms in the L1; chapter 3 used the occurrence requirement to rule this out as a method of first language acquisition. Such feedback is provided in many L2 learning situations, most conspicuously in the classroom, but also in natural situations. For correction to be successful, the L2 learner must produce sentences that deviate in the appropriate way. To learn Binding, the learners must produce sentences such as:

The Joneses asked the Smiths to help themselves.

meaning that the Joneses wanted help, i.e.:

The Joneses$_i$ asked the Smiths to help themselves$_i$.

and the correctors must point out:

No in that case you mean 'The Joneses asked the Smiths to help them'.

Though the language of L2 learners exhibits a variety of peculiarities, such mistakes are not numbered among them. Turning to other areas, there are no reports that L2 learners breach principles such as structure dependency. Furthermore the corrector has to be able to identify the problem to correct it. Many of the possible deviations from UG are unlikely to be spotted by the ordinary native speaker. Correction cannot be ruled out as a source of evidence in the classroom; traditionally minded teachers use it frequently; conventional students often request it. But correction of the type of mistakes needed to acquire UG principles seems unlikely. Correction is no more liable to lead to L2 knowledge in non-classroom settings than in L1 acquisition. As L2 learners manager to learn UG principles without such correction, it cannot be the most important element. While correction potentially meets the occurrence requirement for some areas of language for some learners, it is an ineffective way of learning the central areas of UG.

4   Social interaction

In considering social interaction it is necessary to separate those exchanges that are 'natural' exchanges from that that are 'non-natural'; though L2 learners may engage in the same routines of social interaction as L1 children, in addition they may have controlled 'artificial' exchanges, for instance those found in such teaching techniques as the structure drill. Natural social exchanges seem a clear route to pragmatic competence in the L2 but they are no more able to help the acquisition of UG principles in the L2 than in the L1. Non-natural exchanges have been used by teachers in many ways ranging from grammatical correction to asking the students to talk about the differences between two pictures to the classic three-fold exchange Teacher's question/Pupil's answer/Teacher's evaluation. These exchanges could aim at teaching principles such as Binding, say through a carefully constructed Socratic dialogue in which the student is led to see the binding possibilities in the sentence. But this approach has not been attempted to my knowledge, and would indeed necessitate the provision of negative evidence or grammatical explanation if it were to succeed. Vital as social interaction may be to the communication needs of foreign language students, it is an unlikely vehicle for the acquisition of core UG grammar.

5 Dependence on other faculties

The use of other mental faculties was ruled out in L1 acquisition, primarily because of the uniqueness of the language principles. The same argument applies to L2 learning; there is no compelling reason why it should be derived from other mental facilities, certainly so far as S_ts that resemble ordinary S_Ss are concerned. However, as we shall see, the argument is more complex in L2 learning because the learner is usually at a later stage of cognitive development and hence the relationship between language and cognition differs from that in the native child.

All in all, the poverty of the stimulus argument still applies to L2 acquisition, provided various provisos are borne in mind about the alternative starting and finishing points and intervening routes. If some L2 learners who have used natural means know UG principles, the source must be in their own minds. The difficulty is that their minds include an S_S which may be the source rather than the UG itself.

The Universality of UG

If UG is truly universal, no language that breaches its principles should be learnable by a human being through natural means. Thus L2 learners at any stage of development between S_i and S_t would have competences that conform to UG; there would be no 'wild' grammars. L2 learning is an interesting test case. Lydia White's study of pro-drop showed French-speaking learners of English found null subject sentences such as:

*In winter snows a lot in Canada.

much less acceptable than did Spanish learners of English (White, 1986).

However both groups of learners rejected sentences with Verb subject order such as:

*Slept the baby for three hours.

If the pro-drop parameter affects both null subject sentences and inversion, something is different in L2 learning.

The head parameter has also been studied in L2 learning; do L2 learners consistently place heads first or last in phrases? Alison Henry (1986) found that English speaking learners of Chinese did indeed generalize the head-last setting for the head parameter from main sentences to the relative clause and produced sentences such as:

Wo renshi xuexi Zhongwen de xuesheng.
(I know study Chinese students.)
I know students who are studying Chinese.

Taking Principal Branching Direction as a form of the head parameter, Flynn (1984) tested foreign learners of English on sentences such as:

The boss informed the owner when the worker entered the office.

which is a Right Branching sentence with the *when* clause coming last, and:

When the man dropped the television, the woman hugged the child.

which is Left Branching with the *when* clause coming on the left. Her results were that speakers of Spanish, a right branching (RB) language, were better, level for level, than speakers of Japanese, a left branching (LB) language; Spanish speakers in addition found RB sentences easier than LB sentences though they were equally difficult for the Japanese. Since Japanese has more than one form of *when* (Netsu, 1984), the cause might be something other than PBD. However Flynn (forthcoming) subsequently found that speakers of Chinese, also an LB language, displayed the same pattern as Japanese. Nevertheless, to show that the head parameter is concerned rather than a rule about *when* clauses, its influence on other constructions has to be demonstrated.

A further demonstration of universality was Schmidt (1980) who showed that L2 learners of English produced only natural surface orders such as:

John sang a song and played the guitar.

rather than unnatural orders such as:

*Sang a song and John played guitar.

Ritchie (1978) also found that adult learners of English correctly judged sentences such as:

*That a boat had sunk was obvious that John had built.

ungrammatical and sentences such as:

That a boat had sunk that John had built was obvious.

grammatical; they still had access to a principle of UG that elements may not be moved across certain kinds of boundary, then known as the Right Roof Constraint and now subsumed under subjacency.

To sum up, there is no evidence of violation of UG in L2 learning – no wild grammars. But what would such a violation show if it were found? The strongest consequence would be that some postulated aspect of UG is incorrect; if a language learnt by a human mind through natural means appeared to contravene UG, then our concept of UG needs changing. Thus White's account of pro-drop suggested that the two aspects of null subject sentences and Verb subject inversion do not go together in L2 learning; consequently it could be wrong to combine them into the same parameter of pro-drop. The importance of L2 learning to some researchers is that it supports linguistic theory by showing whether a principle is present or absent from an area where it might well be expected to occur. Such a strong conclusion could seldom be drawn, since it must be qualified by the stipulation 'by natural means'; L2 learning can proceed in non-natural ways. On my desk is a textbook for Japanese (Kershul, 1982) that requires the reader to go round the room sticking labels on the furniture, and to read sentences such as:

While in *Nihon, anata wa* will probably use a *chizu* to find your way around.

by no stretch of the imagination natural language learning. Evidence that L2 learners apparently breach UG is open to other interpretations; they may have been influenced by a teaching method, have used other faculties of the mind, have transferred something from their first language, and so on. A counter-example to a universal found in L2 development could indeed require UG to be reformulated, but such examples are seldom unambiguous and could often be dismissed as nothing to do with UG. Interesting as L2 learning may be in its own right, its connection with UG theory is fraught with problems of interpretation.

The Availability of UG

The poverty of the stimulus argument led to the conclusion that at least some L2 learners know things they could not have acquired from the environment. In L1 learning such knowledge was attributed to the inherent properties of the mind, UG; in L2 learning this has to be qualified because of the differences in both S_i and S_t. What could be the role of UG in L2 learning? L2 learners might start from scratch; they have direct access to UG and are uninfluenced by the L1; learning a second language is potentially exactly the same as acquiring a first. Or they might start from their knowledge of their first language; they have indirect access to UG only through the L1. Or they might not treat the L2 as a language at all; they make no use of UG and learn it without reference to it. The choice can be spelled out in three alternative models.

1   *Direct access to UG*

L2 learners may use the principles of UG and set the parameters without any reference to their L1 values, as in figure 7.1. They have parallel competences in L1 and L2, two instantiations of UG.

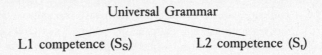

Universal Grammar

L1 competence (S_S)　　　　　L2 competence (S_t)

Figure 7.1

The L2 parameters are not presumed to be initially set one way or another, apart from the usual claims about markedness. A Japanese learner of English, who has no syntactic movement in the L1, is no different from a French learner of English, who does.

2   *Indirect access to UG*

L2 learning might also take the L1 instantiation of UG as a springboard and utilize the principles and parameters in the same way in the new language, as in figure 7.2.

Universal Grammar
|
L1 competence (S_S)
|
L2 competence (S_t)

Figure 7.2

In this case L2 knowledge is tied in to L1 knowledge. For instance, L1 speakers of Japanese might assume that syntactic movement is not necessary and have to learn over time that English is different; L2 learners would consistently start from the L1 settings for the parameters.

3 No access to UG

Second languages might also be acquired through non-natural means. In the 'no-access' model, L2 competence is distinct from L1 competence and indeed from the language faculty, as shown in figure 7.3.

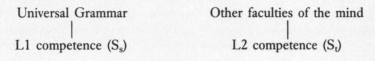

Universal Grammar	Other faculties of the mind
L1 competence (S_s)	L2 competence (S_t)

Figure 7.3

L2 learning might be entirely distinct from L1 learning in making no use of UG; a second language can be learnt from a grammar book or by sheer imitation.

The problem in choosing between the three models is that they might be true for different learners, or for different aspects of language for the same learner; L2 learning depends on an interaction between learner and situation. Versions of all three models have been advocated in language teaching: a translation method implies indirect access in that the learner creates S_t by relating the L2 constantly to the L1; the communicative approach and the direct method imply direct access since they rely on the target language; techniques of grammatical explanation imply no-access and exploit other faculties of the mind. The problem for language teachers is that undoubtedly all of these have produced some successful L2 learners; the dispute is over the proportion of successes to failures. Hence in a sense all models are possible. Let us, however, set aside the no-access model as being the concern of a general learning theory rather than of a theory of language acquisition, with the caveat that an S_t that fully instantiates UG principles is unlikely to be arrived at by this means because of the intrinsic differences of the language faculty from the others.

The evidence for universality is mostly neutral between the two remaining models; the accounts of the Right Roof Constraint (Ritchie, 1978) or Principal Direction (Flynn, 1984) show that L2 learners are employing UG principles but do not indicate whether their source is UG itself or the L1 which incorporates them. What is required is an aspect of UG which is *not* present in the L1. Some principles for example are absent from some languages; if syntactic movement is not used, structure dependency is not needed for movement. Such evidence is not as yet available. Mostly the argument has focused on seeing whether the form of the L1 influences the learning of the L2 through parameter setting. Suppose the L1 sets the parameter one way, the L2 another. The indirect access model predicts differences between learners according to the L1 setting; with direct access, all learners start equal. According to the principle of subjacency, the elements that are moved must not cross more than one 'bounding node', with the definition of bounding node varying from one language to another, as was seen in chapter 5; English can be considered to have S', S, and NP as bounding nodes; Spanish and French to have S' and NP, but not S (Chomsky, 1981b, p. 55). L1 learners set the parameter to reflect the bounding nodes used in the language they are learning. If L2 learners have direct access to UG, all of them should use the same bounding nodes for subjacency, say S', S, and NP; if they have only indirect access, speakers of Spanish or French should treat S' and NP but not S as bounding nodes in English. Lydia White (1985) asked groups of Spanish and French learners of English to judge whether sentences such as:

*This is a book of which I hate the title.

were grammatical. If they were influenced by their L1 setting, they should accept it since only one boundary node, NP, is crossed; if they were uninfluenced by the L1 setting, they should reject it since the number of bounding nodes now amounts to two, NP and S. The learners indeed accepted it, providing evidence for the transfer of L1 settings, and hence for the indirect access model. However, this behaviour has to be demonstrated to be different from other L2 learners whose L1 are like English in having S as a bounding node; the French setting without S might be the unmarked setting used first by all learners, not just by those whose L1 is different from English.

Such a contrast was incorporated in White's work on the pro-drop parameter mentioned earlier (White, 1986). Spanish learners of English were contrasted with French learners of English; the Spanish learners accepted null subject sentences more readily than the French. Sharon Hilles (1986) also studied a twelve-year-old Spanish-speaking child learning English and found over 80 per cent pro-drop sentences such as:

Is the pelo black.

at the early stages, falling to about 10 per cent over time. While such research supports indirect access, Hyams (1986) claimed pro-drop as unmarked, non-pro-drop as marked; it could be that what needs explaining is why French learners still have direct access to the unmarked forms, but Spanish do not.

Without going in detail into the mushrooming L2 learning literature, much research suggests that the indirect access model is correct: L2 learners use their L1 instantiations of UG as a stepping stone to S_t. This is not to say that they no longer have UG itself, that they have thrown away the ladder through which they achieved L1 competence. The poverty of the stimulus argument showed that S_t includes knowledge of UG principles in some form; the problem is still discovering where they come from. The learners' possession of an L1 is no guide in itself to languages that have other settings, unless UG is still present in their minds to prescribe the limits within which languages may vary. The more that research shows the initial effects of the L1 setting of parameters, the more it raises the problem of how they are reset from insufficient evidence. The indirect access model should not then be confused with a 'transfer' model of L2 learning in which characteristics of the L1 are projected onto the L2; indirect access sees the L1 as an instantiation of a human language within a still-existing UG framework; the learners have access to non-L1 values for the parameters even if they initially prefer the values set in the first language.

The discussion so far has implied a clearcut choice between the models without paying heed to variation between learners. But a particular model may be only available to a certain type of learner. For example, the grammar-translation method of language teaching has claimed success with students of high academic calibre; perhaps the no-access model is related to academic ability. Let us take the often-discussed question of age slightly further. A second language can be learnt at any age: usually L2 learners are older than L1 children at similar stages of language development. In other spheres adults might be expected to learn faster than children; it is popularly believed that adults are worse than children at learning a second language; we all know children who appear to learn a second language with ease and adults who never lose their foreign accent. The usual explanations for such age differences are variants of the **'Critical Period Hypothesis' (CPH)**, chiefly associated with Lenneberg (1967), which claims that the ability to learn language disappears after a particular point in the early teens. Interpreted in terms of the present theory, UG is no longer available after a particular point of maturation; just as the milk teeth drop out, so UG becomes defunct. The reason is variously held to be physical developments such as loss of brain plasticity (Penfield and Roberts, 1959) and the specialization of brain functions to one hemisphere (Lenneberg, 1967), or cognitive development such as the transition to the Piagetan stage of formal operational thinking (Tremaine, 1975; Felix, 1978). The formulation of UG as a system of principles and parameters permits the CPH to be restated in more precise terms, as Ritchie (1983) points out. Clear evidence for the Critical Period Hypothesis is hard to come by in first language acquisition since L1 acquisition after the early teens typically concerns the regaining of competence destroyed by some physical or mental trauma rather than 'normal' acquisition. Gleitman (1984, p. 578) has nevertheless observed that in deaf people learning American Sign Language 'the character of final knowledge of the manual language is predictable from the age of the learner at first exposure, independent of the number of years the individual subsequently used it.'

So the CPH often falls back on L2 learning to bolster its arguments.

Lenneberg insisted that L2 learning was via the L1; the fact that a person over forty can learn to communicate in a foreign language 'does not trouble our basic assumption that the cerebral organization for language learning as such has taken place during childhood and since natural languages tend to resemble each other in many fundamental aspects ... the matrix for language skills is present' (Lenneberg, 1967, p. 176). The CPH asserts that the availability of UG depends on the age of the learner; direct access is possible till the early teens, indirect access is possible after this. Krashen's Monitor Model suggests almost the opposite in that direct access is always possible, but the no-access model cannot be used until the late teens (Krashen, 1981). Felix (1985) proposes a Competition Model in which the adult L2 learner is held back by competition between the linguistic faculty and other mental faculties. The existing research does not support the popular idea of adult deficiency in L2 learning with any great authority; Cook (1986) claimed it mostly concerns the accent of immigrants rather than wider aspects of language or broader types of learner. Nor does the CPH succeed in evading the poverty of the stimulus argument. As Chomsky has pointed out, 'while it may be true that "once some language is available, acquisition of others is relatively easy", it nevertheless remains a very serious problem – not significantly different from the problem of explaining first-language acquisition – to account for this fact' (Chomsky, 1972a, p. 175). The mere possession of an L1 cannot explain the acquisition of new settings for UG parameters; UG is not extinct in older learners but has had one set of values assigned to its parameters.

Acquisition and Development in L2 Learning

The distinction between acquisition and development is as important to L2 learning as to L1 acquisition, though with a slightly different import. As always, acquisition is the instantaneous transition from S_i to S_t; from the presence of 'unlearnable' L2 knowledge in the S_t we can work back to S_i, the contribution of the mind. Data from the sequence of learner's development is irrelevant to the logical argument. L1 development was seen to be involved with channel capacity; the ability to use language depends on a variety of faculties other than language, each with its own developmental schedule. Studies of L2 learners' development are open to the same qualification; the results reflect not just the language faculty itself but its interaction with other factors. As with L1 learning, the learner's performance is constrained; there are limits on the amount that the L2 learner can deal with, perhaps a by-product of the short-term memory system. Evidence from developmental studies has to be interpreted with caution as evidence for language acquisition.

As a consequence of the greater age of the L2 learner the contribution of other psychological processes to speech may be different. An L1 learner aged three has the language development of a three-year-old and the information processing capacity of a three-year-old. A person who has been learning a foreign language for three years may perhaps be at a language stage equivalent to a native three-year-old but have the mental capacity of his or her true age, thirteen, thirty or seventy. In L1 development language is in step with the development of channel capacity; in L2 development it is not. Gass and Ard (1980) suggested that L2 learning is closer to acquisition than L1 development. In a mature L2 learner the channel capacity is already established; data from the learner's development are unsullied by the effects of the maturation of non-language faculties. Hence L2 research can have a unique role in testing out UG theories. In particular it might be possible to test the no-growth model of UG; if adult L2 learners go through the same stages in introducing the principles into their grammars and setting the parameters as native children, they must be developmental rather than maturational.

However true in principle, in practice this position is difficult to accept *in toto*. One reason is its vagueness; precise accounts of the interaction between language and other processes are needed before their importance in L1 and L2 learning can be evaluated. Part of the rationale for the logical argument of language acquisition is that it concentrates on 'pure' acquisition rather than the uncertain connections to other cognitive processes. Furthermore research does not confirm the straightforward transfer of existing cognitive capacity to a second language. Ability to carry out mental arithmetic depends on the language (Marsh and Maki, 1976); STM is reduced in an L2 (Cook, 1977; Lado, 1966); the ability to extract information from discourse is reduced (Long and Harding-Esch, 1977); even speed of reaction is reduced (Lambert, 1955). Cognitive processes of whatever kind cannot be assumed to transfer to a new language. The difficulty of studying L2 development is that the contribution of non-language faculties is not developing in step with the language knowledge; far from transferring automatically, they operate in a restricted fashion unlike either the native child or the L1 adult.

Let us now try to put the use of UG theory in L2 learning into perspective. Most of the broad demands established at the beginning of this chapter are met: it is an I-language account that sees language as built-in principles and variable parameters, which it has studied in some depth. Much of it implicitly investigates whether particular syntactic notions actually apply to L2 learning. From the research discussed here, it is evident that the UG/GB framework indeed sheds new light on numerous points in L2 learning. It is still necessary to show that it is the most appropriate way of studying L2 acquisition and that the methodological problems it poses are solvable. To tackle central issues of Chomskyan Universal Grammar, it must remain within the broad framework outlined here. The relevant research concerns the central core principles and parameters – the head parameter, the θ-criterion, the Projection Principle, to take examples; to date only a small fragment of such core grammar has been investigated, notably by Lydia White.

One tendency is to widen the scope of the universals concept beyond the Chomskyan framework. Nothing forces L2 learning research to confine itself to Chomskyan type universals; implicational universals such as the Accessibility Hierarchy are for example a fascinating area of study explored by *inter alia* Susan Gass (1979) and Roger Hawkins (1987). But such universals are not as yet incorporated in the theory, even if eventually it may accommodate them. The relevance of Universal Grammar itself to second language learning can be neither established nor refuted from evidence unconnected to its major substantive claims.

Even within the current framework, as UG consists of interacting subsystems, L2 research has to deal with broad issues that traverse the grammar. Much of it has narrowly concentrated on a few small syntactic issues rather than a broad sweep, resembling a 'rules' rather than a 'principles and parameters' approach. Let us take a much-cited paper by Clahsen and Muysken (1986) as an example. They argue elegantly from extensive data that L1 learners of German start from the correct assumption that German is a Verb final language; L2 learners, however, start from the assumption that it is a Verb medial language and learn the correct order only with time. This account depends on an analysis of German which derives the SVO order of main sentences by V-movement of the Verb from the final position in which it appears in other constructions in German. At best this research is about one subtype of one type of movement in one language; the details of V-movement are not yet well established in Chomsky's writings, apart from *Barriers* (Chomsky, 1986b). Whether L1 learners differ from L2 learners in their sequence of acquisition of V-movement is an interesting question, but it forms a small part of movement and indeed of the grammar itself; the question of whether UG as a whole is available to L2 learners is barely touched on. Clahsen and Muysken argue that the children's sequence of acquisition shows they have access to Universal Grammar and the L2 learners' sequence shows they do not. But there seems no intrinsic reason within the theory why the children's position is closer to UG. In terms of acquisition a quick appeal to the positive evidence argument suggests that learners might well prefer the verb medial constructions they hear in the main sentences they are often exposed to in German; the children may be peculiar, not the L2 adults. The Subset Principle also means considering whether a language with V-movement is a subset of one without, or vice versa; the language without V-movement looks like the one that is a subset, again the opposite of the argument here. But in fact the claim from sequence is based on development rather than acquisition, and is clouded by all the factors of channel capacity and so on discussed earlier. For example Cook (1973) found that, while both adult L2 learners and young L1 learners showed a 'primacy' effect in which they repeated the first words of a sentence, only L1 children showed a 'recency' effect in which they repeated the last words of the sentence. The differences between L1 learners and L2 learners in processing the last few words of the sentence may well interact with development of word order in all sorts of ways that bias the study of development, for example facilitating V-movement from end position for children compared to adults.

As with L1 acquisition, it is important to stress that UG research into L2 learning is concerned with core grammar rather than other issues. UG theory at some point will have to explain how two languages reflecting principles and parameters are simultaneously known by the same mind; the implications for the logical argument of language acquisition of L2 resetting of parameters also need to be considered. But the research methodology in this area is still fraught with difficulty. In addition to the problems involved in investigating L1 acquisition, such as competence/performance and acquisition/development, the difficulty of L2 learning research is compounded by the variations in S_i and S_t, and the apparent effects of differing learner personality and experience. As with L1 acquisition, the UG approach may indeed tackle the most profound aspects of L2 learning; but it does not deal with anything else. UG plays a central and vital part in L2 learning, but there are many other parts.

References

Allwright, R. 1977: Language learning through communication practice. *ELT Documents*, 77/1.

Anderson, J. 1983: *The Architecture of Cognition*. Cambridge, Mass.: Harvard University Press.

d'Anglejan, A., and Tucker, G. R. 1975: The acquisition of complex English structures by adult learners. *Language Learning*, XV/2.

Baker, C. L. 1979: Syntactic theory and the projection problem. *Linguistic Inquiry*, 10/4, 533–81.

Barton, G. E. 1984: Toward A Principle-Based Parser. MIT Artificial Intelligence Lab Report, A.I. no. 788.

Berwick, R. C., and Weinberg, A. S. 1984: *The Grammatical Basis of Linguistic Performance*. Cambridge, Mass.: MIT Press.

Blumenthal, A. L., and Boakes, R. 1967: Prompted recall of sentences. *JVLVB*, 6, 674–6.

Borer, H. 1983: *Parametric Syntax*. Dordrecht: Foris.

Bouchard, D. 1984: *On the Content of Empty Categories*. Dordrecht: Foris.

Brown, R. 1973: *A First Language: The Early Stages*. London: Allen & Unwin.

Brown, R., and Hanlon, C. 1970: Derivational complexity and the order of acquisition in child speech. In J. R. Hayes (ed.), *Cognition and the Development of Language*. New York: John Wiley.

Bruner, J. 1983: *Child's Talk*. Oxford: Oxford University Press.

Carroll, J. B. 1966: The contribution of psychological theory and educational research to the teaching of foreign languages. In A. Valdman (ed.), *Trends in Language Teaching*. New York: McGraw-Hill, 93–106.

Chomsky, C. 1969: *The Acquisition of Syntax in Children from 5 to 10*. Cambridge, Mass.: MIT Press.

Chomsky, N. 1957: *Syntactic Structures*. Mouton: The Hague.

Chomsky, N. 1959: Review of B. F. Skinner *Verbal Behavior. Language*, 35, 26–58.

Chomsky, N. 1964: *Current Issues in Linguistic Theory*. Mouton: The Hague.

Chomsky, N. 1965: *Aspects of the Theory of Syntax*. Cambridge, Mass.: MIT Press.

Chomsky, N. 1966: Linguistic theory. In *North-East Conference on the Teaching of Foreign Languages*, ed. R. Mead. Reprinted in J. P. B. Allen and P. van Buren, *Chomsky: Selected Readings*. Oxford: Oxford University Press (1971).

Chomsky, N. 1969: Linguistics and philosophy. In S. Hook (ed.), *Language and Philosophy*. New York: New York University Press.

Chomsky, N. 1970: Remarks on nominalisation. In R. Jacobs and E. Rosenbaum (eds), *Readings in English Transformational Grammar*. Waltham, Mass.: Ginn & Co.

Chomsky, N. 1972a: *Language and Mind*, enlarged edition. New York: Harcourt Brace Jovanovitch.
Chomsky, N. 1972b: Some empirical issues in the theory of transformational grammar. In S. Peters (ed.), *Goals of Linguistic Theory*. New Jersey: Prentice-Hall.
Chomsky, N. 1972c: *Problems of Knowledge and Freedom*. London: Fontana.
Chomsky, N. 1976: *Reflections on Language*. London: Temple Smith.
Chomsky, N. 1979: *Language and Responsibility*. Brighton: Harvester Press.
Chomsky, N. 1980a: *Rules and Representations*. Oxford: Basil Blackwell.
Chomsky, N. 1980b: On cognitive structures and their development. In M. Piattelli-Palmarini (ed.), *Language and Learning: the Debate between Jean Piaget and Noam Chomsky*. London: Routledge and Kegan Paul.
Chomsky, N. 1981a: *Lectures on Government and Binding*. Dordrecht: Foris.
Chomsky, N. 1981b: Principles and parameters in syntactic theory. In N. Hornstein and D. Lightfoot (eds), *Explanations in Linguistics*. London: Longman.
Chomsky, N. 1982a: *Some Concepts and Consequences of the Theory of Government and Binding*. Cambridge, Mass.: MIT Press.
Chomsky, N. 1982b: On the representation of form and function. In J. Mehler, E. C. T. Walker, and M. F. Garrett (eds), *Perspectives on Mental Representation: Experimental and Theoretical Studies of Cognitive Processes and Capacities*. Hillsdale: Erlbaum.
Chomsky, N. 1982c: *The Generative Enterprise: A Discussion with Riny Huybregts and Henk van Riemsdijk*. Dordrecht: Foris.
Chomsky, N. 1986a: *Knowledge of Language: Its Nature, Origin and Use*. New York: Praeger.
Chomsky, N. 1986b: *Barriers*. Cambridge, Mass.: MIT Press.
Chomsky, N. 1987: Kyoto Lectures. unpublished MS.
Chomsky, N. 1988: *Language and Problems of Knowledge: The Nicaraguan Lectures*. Cambridge, Mass.: MIT Press.
Clahsen, H., and Muysken, P. 1986: The availability of universal grammar to adult and child learners – a study of the acquisition of German word order. *Second Language Research*, 2, 2, 93–119.
Clark, H. H., and Clark, E. V. 1977: *Psychology and Language*. New York: Harcourt Brace Jovanovich.
Cobbett, W. 1819: *A Grammar of the English Language*. Reprinted by Oxford University Press, 1984.
Cook, V. J. 1973: The analogy between first and second language learning. *IRAL*, VII/3.
Cook, V. J. 1977: Cognitive processes in second language learning. *IRAL*, XV/1, 1–20.
Cook, V. J. 1985: Chomsky's universal grammar and second language learning. *Applied Linguistics*, 6, 1, 2–18.
Cook, V. J. 1986: Experimental approaches to two areas of second language learning research. In V. J. Cook (ed.), *Experimental Approaches to Second Language Learning*. Oxford: Pergamon Press.
Cromer, R. 1970: 'Children are nice to understand': surface structure clues to the recovery of a deep structure. *British Journal of Psychology*, 61.
Cromer, R. F. 1987: Language growth with experience without feedback. *Journal of Psycholinguistic Research*, 16/3, 223–31.
Ellis, R. 1985: *Understanding Second Language Acquisition*. Oxford: Oxford University Press.

Felix, S. W. 1978: Some differences between first and second language acquisition. In N. Waterson and C. Snow (eds), *The Development of Communication*. New York: Wiley.

Felix, S. W. 1985: More evidence on competing cognitive systems. *Second Language Research*, 1/1, 47–72.

Flynn, S. 1984: A universal in L2 acquisition based on a PBD typology. In F. R. Eckman, L. N. Bell, and D. Nelson, *Universals of Second Language Acquisition*. Rowley, Mass.: Newbury House.

Flynn, S. 1988: Second language acquisition and grammatical theory. In F. Newmeyer (ed.), *Linguistics: The Cambridge Survey*. Cambridge: Cambridge University Press.

Flynn, S. (forthcoming): Head-initial/head-final parameter in adult Chinese L2 acquisition of English. *Second Language Research*.

Fodor, J. A. 1981: Some notes on what linguistics is about. In N. Block (ed.), *Readings in the Philosophy of Psychology*. London: Methuen, 197–207.

Fodor, J. A. 1983: *The Modularity of Mind*. Cambridge, Mass.: MIT Press.

Fodor, J. A., Bever, T., and Garrett, M. 1974: *The Psychology of Language*. New York: McGraw-Hill.

Gardner, B. T., and Gardner, D. A. 1971: Two way communication with an infant chimpanzee. In A. Schrier and F. Stollwitz (eds), *Behavior of Non-Human Primates, Vol. 4*. New York: Academic Press.

Garnham, A. 1985: *Psycholinguistics: Central Topics*. London: Methuen.

Gass, S. 1979: Language transfer and universal grammatical relations. *Language Learning*, 29/2, 327–44.

Gass, S., and Ard, J. 1980: L2 data: their relevance for language universals. *TESOL Quarterly*, XIV/443–52.

Gazdar, G. 1987: Generative grammar. In J. Lyons, R. Coates, M. Deuchar and G. Gazdar (eds), *New Horizons in Linguistics 2*. Harmondsworth: Penguin.

Gazdar, G., Klein, E., Pullum, G., and Sag, I. 1985: *Generalised Phrase Structure Grammar*. Oxford: Basil Blackwell.

Gleitman, L. 1982: Maturational determinants of language growth. *Cognition*, 10, 103–14.

Gleitman, L. 1984: Biological predispositions to learn language. In P. Marler and H. Terrace (eds), *The Biology of Learning*. New York: Springer.

Gold, E. M. 1967: Language identification in the limit. *Information and Control*, 10, 447–74.

Goodluck, H. 1986: Language acquisition and linguistic theory. In P. Fletcher and M. Garman (eds), *Language Acquisition*, second edition. Cambridge: Cambridge University Press.

Goodluck, H. and Solan, L. (eds) 1978: *Papers in the Structure and Development of Child Language*. University of Massachusetts Occasional Papers in Linguistics, 4.

Greene, J. 1986: *Language Understanding: A Cognitive Approach*. Milton Keynes: Open University Press.

Harmer, J. 1983: *The Practice of English Language Teaching*. London: Longman.

Harris, M., and Coltheart, M. 1986: *Language Processing in Children and Adults*. London: Routledge and Kegan Paul.

Hawkins, J. 1982: Cross-category harmony, X-bar syntax, and the predictions of markedness. *Journal of Linguistics*, 18, 1–35.

Hawkins, R. 1987: The notion of 'typological markedness' as a predictor of order of difficulty in the L2 acquisition of relative clauses. Paper presented to the BAAL seminar on The Place of Linguistics in Applied Linguistics, University of Essex.

Henry, A. 1986: Linguistic theory and second language teaching. Paper presented to CILT workshop on Acquiring Language and Learning Languages, Windsor.

Hilles, S. 1986: Interlanguage and the pro-drop parameter. *Second Language Research*, 2/1, 33–52.

Hirsh-Pasek, K., Treiman, R., and Schneiderman, M. 1984: Brown and Hanlon revisited: mothers' sensitivity to ungrammatical forms. *Journal of Child Language*, 11/1, 81–8.

Horrocks, G. 1987: *Generative Grammar*. Harlow: Longman.

Howatt, A. 1984: *A History of English Language Teaching*. Oxford: Oxford University Press.

Huang, C.-T. J. 1982: *Logical Relations in Chinese and the Theory of Grammar*. Unpublished Ph.D thesis, MIT.

Huang, C.-T. J. 1984: On the distribution and reference of empty pronouns. *Linguistic Inquiry*, 15.

Hyams, N. 1986: *Language Acquisition and the Theory of Parameters*. Dordrecht: Reidel.

Hymes, D. 1972: Competence and performance in linguistic theory. In R. Huxley and E. Ingram (eds), *Language Acquisition: Models and Methods*. New York: Academic Press.

Jackendoff, R. 1977: *X'-Syntax: A Study of Phrase Structure*. Cambridge, Mass.: MIT Press.

Keenan, E., and Comrie, B. 1977: Noun phrase accessibility and universal grammar. *Linguistic Inquiry*, 8, 63–100.

Kennedy, B. H. 1948: *The Shorter Latin Primer*. London: Longman

Kershul, K. 1982: *Japanese in Ten Minutes a Day*. Washington: Bilingual Books.

King, E. S. 1980: *Speak Malay!* Kuala Lumpur: Eastern Universities Press Sdn. Bhd.

KOL: see Chomsky, 1986a.

Koopman, H. 1983: *The Syntax of Verbs*. Dordrecht: Foris.

Krashen, S. 1981: *Second Language Acquisition and Second Language Learning*. Oxford: Pergamon Press.

Lado, R. 1966: Memory span as a factor in second language learning. *International Review of Applied Linguistics*, 3, 123–9.

Lambert, W. E. 1955: Measurements of the linguistic dominance of bilinguals. *Journal of Abnormal and Social Psychology*, 50, 197–200.

Lasnik, H., and Saito, M. 1984: On the nature of Proper Government. *Linguistic Inquiry*, 15, 235–89.

Lenneberg, E. 1967: *Biological Foundations of Language*. New York: John Wiley.

LGB: see Chomsky, 1981a.

Lightbown, P. M., and White, L. 1988: The influence of linguistic theories on language acquisition: description versus explanation. *Language Learning*, 37/4.

Lightfoot, D. 1982: *The Language Lottery: Toward a Biology of Grammars*. Cambridge, Mass.: MIT Press.

Long, J., and Harding-Esch, E. 1977: Summary and recall of text in first and second languages: some factors contributing to performance difficulties. In H. Sinmaiko and D. Gerver (eds), *Proceedings of the NATO Symposium on Language Interpretation and Communication*. New York: Plenum Press.

Lovelace, E. 1985: *The Dragon Can't Dance*. London: Longman.

Lust, B. 1983: On the notion 'Principal Branching Direction': a parameter in

Universal Grammar. In Otsu et al (1983), op. cit.

Marcus, M. P. 1980: *Theory of Syntactic Recognition for Natural Languages*. Cambridge, Mass.: MIT Press.

Marsh, L. G., and Maki, R. H. 1976: Efficiency of arithmetic operations in bilinguals as a function of language. *Memory and Cognition*, 4/4, 459–64.

Matthei, E. 1981: Children's interpretation of sentences containing reciprocals. In Tavakolian (ed.), 58–101.

Miller, G. A. 1962: Some psychological studies of grammar. *American Psychologist*, 17, 748–62.

Netsu, M. 1984: The role of Error Analysis in classifying linguistic distinctions between English 'when' and its Japanese equivalents. *International Review of Applied Linguistics*, 22, 193–202.

Newmark, L., and Reibel, D. A. 1968: Necessity and sufficiency in language learning. *International Review of Applied Linguistics*, VI/3.

Newport, E. L. 1977: Motherese: the speech of mothers to young children. In N. Castellan, D. Pisoni, and G. Potts (eds), *Cognitive Theory, Vol. 2*. Hillsdale: Erlbaum.

Ochs, E., and Schieffelin, B. 1984: Language acquisition and socialisation: three developmental stories and their implications. In R. Shweder and R. Levine (eds), *Culture and its Acquisition*. New York: Cambridge University Press.

Otsu, Y., van Riemsdijk, H., Inoue, K., Kasimo, A., and Kawasaki, N. (eds) 1983: *Studies in Generative Grammar and Language Acquisition*. Tokyo: International Christian University.

Palmer, H. E. 1926: *The Principles of Language Study*. London: George G. Harrap.

Patterson, F. G. 1981: Innovative uses of language by a gorilla: a case study. In K. Nelson (ed.), *Children's Language, Vol. 2*. New York: Gardner.

Penfield, W. G., and Roberts, L. 1959: *Speech and Brain Mechanisms*. New Jersey: Princeton University Press.

Piaget, J. 1980: The psychogenesis of knowledge and its epistemological significance. In Piattelli-Palmarini (1980) op. cit.

Piattelli-Palmarini, M. (ed.) 1980: *Language and Learning: the Debate between Jean Piaget and Noam Chomsky*. London: Routledge and Kegan Paul.

Picallo, M. C. 1984: The INFL node and the null subject parameter. *Linguistic Inquiry*, 15.

Platt, C. B., and McWhinney, B. 1983: Error assimilation as a mechanism in language learning. *Journal of Child Language*, 10, 104–14.

Radford, A. (1988): *Transformational Syntax*, second edition. Cambridge: Cambridge University Press.

Reinhart, T. 1983: *Anaphora and Semantic Interpretation*. London: Croom Helm.

Richards, J. C., and Rodgers, T. S. 1986: *Approaches and Methods in Language Teaching*. Cambridge: Cambridge University Press.

Ritchie, W. 1978: The right roof constraint in an adult acquired language. In W. Ritchie (ed.), *Second Language Acquisition: Issues and Implications*. New York: Academic Press.

Ritchie, W. C. 1983: Universal Grammar and second language acquisition. In D. Rogers and J. A. Sloboda (eds), *The Acquisition of Symbolic Skills*. New York: Plenum Press.

Rizzi, L. 1982: *Issues in Italian Syntax*. Dordrecht: Foris.

Safir, K. J. 1985: *Syntactic Chains*. Cambridge, Mass.: MIT Press.

Schmidt, M. 1980: Coordinate structure and language universals in interlanguage. *Language Learning*, 30/2, 397–416.

Seidenberg, M. S. 1986: Evidence from great apes concerning the biological basis of language. In W. Demopoulos and A. Marras (eds), *Language Learning and Concept Acquisition*. New Jersey: Ablex.

Sells, P. 1985: *Lectures on Contemporary Syntactic Theories*. Stanford: CSLI.

Sharpe, T. 1982: *Vintage Stuff*, Secker and Warburg.

Sportiche, D. 1981: Bounding Nodes in French. *The Linguistic Review*, 1, 219–46.

Stern, H. H. 1983: *Fundamental Concepts of Language Teaching*. Oxford: Oxford University Press.

Stowell, T. 1981: *Origins of Phrase Structure*. Unpublished Ph.D. Thesis, MIT.

Tavakolian, S. L. (ed.) 1981: *Language Acquisition and Linguistic Theory*. Cambridge, Mass.: MIT Press.

Tremaine, R. V. 1975: Piagetan equilibration processes in syntax learning. In D. P. Dato (ed.), *Psycholinguistics: Theory and Applications*. Georgetown University Round Table.

van Riemsdijk, H., and Williams, E. 1986: *Introduction to the Theory of Grammar*. Cambridge, Mass.: MIT Press.

Wehrli, E. 1984: A Government-Binding Parser for French. Institut pour les études semantiques et cognitives, Université de Genève: Working Papers no. 48.

Wells, C. G. 1985: *Language Development in the Preschool Years*. Cambridge: Cambridge University Press.

Wexler, K., and Manzini, M. R. 1987: Parameters and learnability. In T. Roeper and E. Williams (eds), *Parameter Setting*. Dordrecht: Reidel.

White, L. 1985: The acquisition of parameterized grammar: subjacency in second language acquisition. *Second Language Research*, 1, 1, 1–17.

White, L. 1986: Implications of parametric variation for adult second language acquisition: an investigation of the pro-drop parameter. In V. J. Cook (ed.), *Experimental Approaches to Second Language Acquisition*. Oxford: Pergamon Press.

Winograd, T. 1983: *Language as a Cognitive Process, Vol. 1: Syntax*. Reading, Mass.: Addison-Wesley.

Index

The addition of (b) to a page number indicates that the reference is to a box on the page concerned.

Accessibility Hierarchy, 18, 188
Accusative Case, 136–40, 142–143(b), 148, 153
acquisition of language, 1, 2–6, 9, 11, 20–1, 27, 30, 39, 51, 54–85, 89, 107, 129, 166, 170–1, 172, 174–6, 186–9
ACT* model, 21
adjacency parameter, 133, 141–143(b)
Adjective Phrase (AP/A''), 8, 95, 98
adjunction, 92, 157
affect-α, 147
age in second language learning, 185–7
Agent θ-role, 112–117(b), 153–4
AGR (agreement), 36–7, 89, 118, 130, 154–6; see also plural, singular
anaphors, 43–9, 52–3, 157–60, 162–5
Anderson, J., 21, 71
animal language, 22, 73–4
ape language, 73–4
A-positions, 113–17, 124, 132, 148
Arabic, 48, 51, 167
arbitrary control, 161–2, 164; see also Control Theory
arguments, 111–16
Aspects model (Chomsky, 1965), 13–14, 28, 176
auxiliaries, 3–5, 89, 130–2
availability of UG, 182–6

Bahasa Malaysia, 17–18
bar ('), 31, 95–7, 100–1
Barriers (Chomsky, 1986b), 1, 28, 86, 117–20, 129–32, 135, 153, 155, 164, 168, 188

Barton, J., 174
Basque, 19
believe, 10, 48, 112
Berwick, R., and Weinberg, A., 65, 134, 173–4
Binding Principles, 46–50, 52–3, 58, 63, 65, 157, 178; see also Binding Theory
Binding Theory, 28, 33–4, 43–49(b), 157–9, 160–5; see also anaphors, pronominals
biology and language, 21–2, 38, 51, 55
Borer, H., 167
Bouchard, D., 145, 162
bounding nodes, 133–5, 152, 184
Bounding Theory, 33–4, 121, 133–135(b); see also subjacency principle
bracketting, 45, 87–9
brain, 21, 25
Brown, R., 64, 66
Bruner, J., 67–9

C'', 119–20, 126–9; see also COMP
c-command (constituent command), 149–150(b), 151–2, 155–6
c-selection (category selection), 102–106(b), 111–14, 116, 122, 153, 156; see also Projection Principle
Carroll, J., 172
case assigner, 137–9, 141–143(b), 152–3
Case Filter, 139–41, 143(b), 161
Case Theory, 33–4, 58, 121, 136–143(b), 148, 152–6, 161
category selection, see c-selection

chains 143–5, 163, 165–6
Chinese, 39–40, 42, 48, 53, 100, 142–3, 167, 180
Chomsky, C., 176–7
Chomsky, N., influence of, 172–4; for particular theories *see Aspects* Model, *Barriers*, Government/Binding Theory, *Syntactic Structures* Model; for particular concepts *see* biology and language, competence, evidence for language acquisition, evidence for linguistic theory, generative grammar, Language Acquisition Device, language faculty, performance, Plato's problem, psychological reality, stimulus argument, Universal Grammar
Clahsen, H., and Muysken, P., 188–9
Cobbett, W., 35, 43, 148
cognitive code learning, 172
cognitive development and language, 21, 69–70, 179, 187–8
communication, 13, 15, 20, 179
communicative competence, 14, 17, 172
COMP, 89–90, 92, 101, 117–20, 126–9
competence, 13–14, 56, 173, 175, 182–3
Competition Model (Felix, 1985), 186
complementizers, 89–90, 128
complements, 97–100, 102–3, 117–20, 149
computational linguistics, 13, 174
configurational languages, 59
conscious knowledge of language, 63, 176
constituent command, *see* c-command
constituent structure, 7, 86
Control Theory, 33–4, 159–162(b), 166; *see also* arbitrary control, infinitival clauses, obligatory control, PRO
Cook, V., 174, 177, 187, 188
core grammar, 50, 52–4, 56, 60, 171, 187–9
correction of learner, 60, 63–7, 178
creativity, 15, 51–2, 62, 68, 171
Critical Period Hypothesis (CPH), 185
Cromer, R., 72, 176–7

d-structure, 30–4, 91–2, 104–5, 109, 122–5, 132
declarative knowledge, 26, 174

deep structure, 28, 30
Derivational Theory of Complexity, 173
descriptive adequacy, 56
determiner (*det*), 87, 99
development of language, 56, 81–4, 173, 186–9
direct access to UG, 182–4
direct negative evidence, 60–1, 63–4
direction of case assignment, 142–143(b)
do support, 131, 133
domain, 46–49, 149–51
dominates, 88, 148–51
Doubly Filled COMP Filter, 128–9, 140–1
Dutch, 128–9

e (empty category), 40–1, 92, 122–5, 160–1, 163–6, 166(b); *see also* NP-trace, PRO, *pro*, *t*, wh-trace
E-language, *see* Externalized language
easy/eager to please, 72, 176–7
empty category, *see e*
Empty Category Principle (ECP), 39, 42, 165–6
English, particular features of, *see* adjacency parameter, bounding nodes, Exceptional Case Marking, PRO, subjacency principle
environment and language acquisition, 27, 55, 59–68, 72, 74–7
EPP, *see* Extended Projection Principle
evidence for language acquisition, 55, 59–72, 74–7, 177–9
evidence for linguistic theory, 2, 12–13, 19–20, 25–7, 53
Exceptional Case Marking, 142–143(b), 153
explanation of rules to learners, 61, 63, 172, 177
explanatory adequacy, 56
expletive subjects, 115, 124
Extended Projection Principle (EPP), 115–16, 122, 160
Extended Standard Model, 28
external θ-role, 115–17, 141, 153–4
Externalized (E-) language, 12–17, 55, 172

Felix, S., 185, 186

filters, 128–9, 139–41, 143, 161; *see also* Case Filter, Doubly Filled COMP Filter
final state of the mind, *see* S$_t$, S$_S$
Finnish, 136
first and second language acquisition, 174–6, 188–9
Flynn, S., 174, 180, 183
Fodor, J., 21, 25, 51
foreign language teaching, 63, 171–3, 176, 178–9
formats, 67–8
French, 4, 5, 12, 40, 42, 134–5, 142, 154, 160, 182, 184

Gardner, B., and Gardner, D., 73
Garnham, A., 173
Gass, S., 187
Gazdar, G., 25, 94, 124
gender, 154
General Learning Theory, 69
Generalized Phrase Structure Grammar (GPSG), 25, 94, 107, 174
generative grammar, 24–5, 28, 167
Genitive Case, 136, 138–9, 143(b)
German, 40, 134, 136, 188–9
give, 32, 57, 105–6, 153
Gleitman, L., 61–2, 83–4, 185
Goal θ-role, 112, 115, 117(b), 153–4
Goodluck, H., 82
governing category, 158–9, 161–4
government, 28, 35–7, 40, 148–69
Government/Binding Theory, 1, 7, 11, 25, 28, 34(b), 40, 57, 166–7; *see also* Bounding Theory, Case Theory, Control Theory, movement, Projection Principle, θ-theory, T-model, X-bar theory
Government Theory, 35, 43, 58, 148–69, 156(b)
governors, 35, 151–3, 155–156(b), 158, 161
grammar, 12–13, 54; *see also* core grammar, generative grammar, periphery/peripheral grammar
grammatical competence, 14, 17, 52, 56–7
grammatical functions (GFs), 106–110(b), 124, 137, 148

Greene, J., 173

Harris, M., and Coltheart, M., 173
head-first, 7, 8, 98–9
head-last, 7, 8, 98–9
head parameter, 7–9(b), 12, 20, 22–4, 31, 34, 38, 53, 58, 98–100, 102, 142
head requirement, 94–7
Henry, A., 180
Hilles, S., 184
Hirsh-Pasek, K., 66–7
Huang, C., 100–1, 166–7
Hyams, N., 75–7, 80, 169, 184
Hymes, D., 14, 172

I′′, 117–19, 129–32, 151–3; *see also* INFL
I-language, *see* Internalized language
Icelandic, 159
imitation as a method of language acquisition, 62–3, 177
immediate domination, 88
implicational universal, 18–19, 188
independence of language, 20, 69
indexing (*i*), 44
indirect access to UG, 182–4
indirect negative evidence, 60–1, 166
infinitival clauses, 33–4, 143–4, 153, 159–62, 166, 173; *see also* Control Theory
INFL (inflection), 36–7, 40–2, 89–90, 117–19, 129, 151–5, 159
inherent case, 139
initial state in second language learning, *see* S$_i$
initial state of the mind, *see* S$_0$
innate aspects of language, 27, 54–8, 69–71, 84, 182
interlanguage, 175
internal θ-roles, 115–17, 141, 153–4
Internalized (I-) language, 12–17, 56, 170, 187
Italian, 38–42, 134–5, 156, 167

Jackendoff, R., 101, 166
Japanese, 7–9, 17–18, 22, 28, 57–8, 60, 73, 98–9, 180–3

Kahuli, 62

knowledge of language, 1, 12–14
Koopman, H., 142, 167
Krashen, S., 176, 186

LAD, *see* Language Acquisition Device
language, 12–17, 54
language acquisition, *see* acquisition of language
Language Acquisition Device (LAD), 56, 172
language faculty, 19–23, 38, 50–1, 57, 63, 69, 73–4, 81–2, 84, 172, 176
language use, 13–15
Lasnik, H., and Saito, M., 147
Latin, 41–2, 136, 176
Lenneberg, E., 73, 185–6
lexical categories, 94–8, 100–3, 106, 151, 159; *see also* X-bar theory
lexical entry, 9–12, 23, 35, 48, 103–8, 111–12, 114, 117, 120, 153; *see also* Projection Principle
lexicon, 11–12, 31–3, 94
LF (Logical Form) component, 29–34, 104–5
LF (Logical Form) movement, 17, 145–7
like, 10–12, 113–15, 117, 129–130, 133, 142, 163–4
linguistic competence, 13–14
local domain, 46–9, 157–60
Logical Form, *see under* LF
L2 acquisition, *see* second language acquisition
Lust, B., 77–9

Malagasy, 18
Marcus, M., 174
markedness, 53–4, 129, 142
Matthei, E., 83, 85
maximal projections, 103, 121, 149–50, 152–3, 155–6, 158
mental organ, 21, 72–4
modules of mind, *see* language faculty
Move-α, 127, 132(b), 134
movement, 2–6, 17, 22, 30–4, 38, 91, 108, 109, 121–35, 140; *see also* LF movement, Move-α, NP-movement, V-movement, wh-movement

N'', *see* Noun Phrase

negative evidence in language acquisition, 59–61, 63–8, 70, 75, 80, 84, 178–9
Newmark, L., and Reibel, D., 172
Newport, E., 68
no access to UG, 183–4
Nominative Case, 136–143(b)
non-A-positions (Ā-positions), 114, 126–7, 129, 132, 163
non-obligatory control, *see* arbitrary control
Noun Phrase (NP/N''), 7, 9, 24, 33, 95–6, 98–101, 118; *see also* NP-movement
NP-movement, 121–7, 132(b), 140, 163
NP-trace, 163–6
null subject, *see* pro-drop parameter
number, 36, 154

object, 107, 108, 110(b), 113, 121
object of preposition, 107, 110(b), 117, 137, 148
obligatory control, 161–2; *see also* Control Theory
Oblique Case, 138; *see also* object of preposition
occurrence requirement, 61–4, 177

Palmer, H., 176
parameter-setting, 54, 57–8, 71–2, 74–80, 170–1, 183–6, 189
parameters, 1–2, 8, 13, 18, 37–8, 54, 120, 135, 167, 169; *see also* adjacency parameter, head parameter, markedness, parameter-setting, pro-drop parameter
parsing, 65, 174
passive, 4, 17, 24, 34, 121–5, 132, 140–1, 163
passive morphology, 123–4, 136, 140–1
past, 36, 89–90
Patient θ-role, 112–13, 117(b), 153–4
Patterson, F., 74
performance, 13–14, 16, 26, 38, 53, 61, 186–7
periphery/peripheral grammar, 50–4, 56, 60, 171, 173
Phonetic Form (PF) component, 29–34, 89–90, 93, 110, 129, 139, 155
phonetic representation, 29–30, 34, 89, 93–4, 139–40

phrase structure, 86–94, 103
Piaget, J., 21–2, 69, 185
Plato's problem, 55, 70
Platt, C., and McWhinney, B., 65
plural, 36–7
positive evidence in language acquisition, 59, 62–3, 89, 166, 177, 188
pragmatic competence, 14, 17
Prepositional Phrase (PP/P''), 7–8, 95–6, 98, 100, 108, 138
present, 36, 89, 129
Principal Branching Direction (PBD), 77–9, 180, 183
principles, 1–2, 5–7, 13, 20, 23–7, 34, 37, 48, 64, 97, 120, 166–7, 169, 179; *see also* Binding Principles, Empty Category Principle, Extended Projection Principle, movement, Projection Principle, Proper Government Principle, structure-dependency, Subjacency Principle, Subset Principle
PRO (big PRO), 160–1, 163–6; *see also* Control Theory
pro (little *pro*), 40–2, 156, 160–6; *see also* pro-drop parameter
pro-drop parameter, 37–42(b), 52–4, 58, 60–1, 155–7, 163, 168, 179–81, 184
procedural knowledge, 26, 174
Projection Principle, 9–12(b), 23, 31, 34, 103–106(b), 109–10, 122–3, 153, 156, 160, 174, 187; *see also* c-selection, θ-theory
pronominal anaphors, 160–1, 164
pronominals, 43–49, 157–9, 161, 164–5
Proper Government Principle, 41–2, 165–6
psychological processes of speech, 16, 80–2, 186–8; *see also* performance
psychological reality, 25–6, 174
psychology and linguistics, 20–7, 173–4

question-words, 4–5, 91; *see also* wh-movement, wh-phrase
questions, 2–6, 17, 26, 67, 91, 108, 109, 125–8, 132

r-expressions, *see* referring expressions
Radford, A., 101, 131

raising, 125
reciprocals, *see* anaphors
referring expressions (r-expressions), 44–9, 157–9, 162, 164–5
reflexives, *see* anaphors
Reinhart, T., 151
relative clauses, 3, 18–19, 127–9, 132, 180
rewrite rules, 10, 24, 87
Richards, J., and Rodgers, T., 172
Right Roof Constraint, 181, 183
Ritchie, W., 181–3, 185
Rizzi, L., 134–5, 167
rule R, 129–30
rules, 10–12, 15, 23–6, 48, 94, 125, 141, 167, 173–4

S (sentence), 24, 26, 45, 87, 89–90, 101–2, 117–20
S' (S-bar), 89–90, 101–2, 117–20
S' deletion, 141–2, 153
s-selection (semantic selection), 110–17, 122; *see also* θ-theory
s-structure, 30–4, 89, 91–3, 104–5, 109, 122–5
S_0 (initial state of the mind), 55–8, 175–6
Sapir, E., 51
Schmidt, M., 180–1
scientific theory, 25, 53
second language (L2) acquisition, 62, 174–89
seem, 115, 125, 141–2
semantic representation, 29–30, 34, 110–17, 145–7
semantic selection, *see* s-selection
sentence, *see* S
S_i (initial state in second language learning), 175–6, 179, 189
singular, 36–7, 129, 154–5
sisterhood, 148–9
situation, 13–14
Skinner, B., 171
social interaction, 13–16, 67–8, 179
Spanish, 54, 123, 168, 180, 184
species-specific nature of language, 22–3, 70, 72–4, 84, 170
specifier/head order, 100; *see also* head parameter
specifiers, 99–103, 118–20, 126–8

Sportiche, D., 135

S$_S$ (steady state of the mind), 55, 175–6, 179

S$_t$ (final state of the mind), 175–6, 179,189

Standard Model, 28

steady state of the mind, *see* S$_S$

stimulus argument, poverty of, 55, 59–61, 67, 176, 184–5

Stowell, T., 166

structural case, 137–9

structure-dependency, 2–7, 9, 12, 18–20, 22, 26, 33, 35, 48, 50, 52, 56, 64–5, 121, 167–8, 178

Subjacency Principle, 133–135(b), 141, 181, 184; *see also* Bounding Theory

subject/object asymmetry, 89, 115, 118

subject of sentence, 10, 33, 36, 38–42, 94, 107, 110(b), 113–15, 119, 121, 137, 155, 158–62; *see also* Extended Projection Principle, external θ-role

subject-Verb inversion, 2–3, 39–40, 42, 52–3, 60, 130, 132, 157, 180–1

Subset Principle, 86

surface structure, 28, 30–1, 139

syntactic movement, 17–18; *see also* movement

syntactic representation, 30–1, 34, 126

Syntactic Structures Model (Chomsky, 1957), 10, 28, 173

t (trace), 30–1, 34, 40, 92–94, 109–110, 122–125

T-model, 31

Tense, 36, 89, 118, 137–8

θ-criterion, 32–3, 115–117(b), 124, 139

θ-marking, 115, 124, 128, 132

θ-roles, 31–2, 34, 111–13, 115, 117(b), 124, 139, 153–4

θ-theory, 32–4, 111–117(b), 154, 174; *see also* Projection Principle, θ-criterion, θ-roles

traditional grammar, 24, 35

type transparency, 173

uniformity requirement, 61, 63, 177

Universal Grammar (UG), 1, 2, 5, 8, 18, 37, 49, 52, 56–7, 97, 120–1, 166, 169–71, 179–84, 187–9; *see also* acquisition of language, Language Acquisition Device, language faculty, parameters, principles

Urdu, 5, 12

V″, *see* Verb Phrase

V-movement, 129–132(b), 133, 155, 188–9

van Riemsdijk, H., and Williams, E., 39, 57, 128–9

Verb Phrase (VP/V″), 7, 9, 10, 23, 26, 88, 95, 96, 98, 100, 118

Verb/subject order, *see* subject/Verb inversion

V$_I$, 129–32, 155

visibility condition, 139

vocabulary acquisition, 57

wanna, 92–4, 168

Wehrli, E., 174

Wells, G., 56, 67

Welsh, 19

Wexler, K., and Manzini, R., 80, 159

wh-movement, 4–5, 91, 125–132(b), 133–5

wh-phrase, 91, 125, 163

wh-trace (variable), 126, 132, 163–6

White, L., 179–80, 184, 187

wild grammars, 82–4, 179

X-bar (X′-bar) Theory, 7, 31–34, 86, 94–103(b), 117–20, 167, 171; *see also* head parameter, head requirement